THE TANK FACTORY

THE TANK FACTORY

WILLIAM SUTTIE

BRITISH MILITARY VEHICLE DEVELOPMENT AND THE CHOBHAM ESTABLISHMENT

The
History
Press

Cover images
Front: Challenger 1 trials vehicle fitted with prototype visual and infra-red screening smoke-grenade launchers. (Crown Copyright). *Back*: Three generations of Main Battle Tank developed at Chertsey.

First published 2015
The History Press
The Mill, Brimscombe Port
Stroud, Gloucestershire, GL5 2QG
www.thehistorypress.co.uk

British Library Cataloguing in Publication Data.
A catalogue record for this book is available from the British Library.

ISBN 978 0 7509 6122 6

Typesetting and origination by The History Press
Printed and bound in Great Britain by TJ International Ltd, Padstow

CONTENTS

AUTHOR'S NOTE

This book has been compiled using information from a significant number of documents and resources; the key open-source documents are listed in the bibliography. Most importantly, I have been able to have access to a significant number of MOD reports, and hence I include much information that has never been published before and ensure that, as far as possible, all the information within this book is correct. A large number of MOD reports used are still classified and, therefore, are not listed in this book. Where open-source literature and Internet sources have been used, information has been checked for coherence with information from official reports. An interesting aspect of compiling this document is to see how in these days of the World Wide Web incorrect 'facts' become widely repeated and quoted on different websites until they are assumed to be right.

Some of the best, and most interesting, inputs have been provided by ex-members of staff who have sent me stories, facts and pictures. It was the staff who made the Chertsey establishment the successful place it was, and so these personal inputs are valued.

This book contains a large number of pictures never before published. Many come from MOD reports and are used with permission, but others have been sent by ex-members of staff, or are pictures from my own collection. Some of the pictures are of poor quality, having been taken from electronic scanned copies of old documents, but these have been included because they are of specific interest.

The resulting document is likely to have many omissions and despite the checks may have some errors. Any additional information or corrections are always welcome.

I am grateful to the Ministry of Defence, and the Defence Science and Technology Laboratory in particular, for permission to publish this document and to use information and pictures from MOD sources.

ACKNOWLEDGEMENTS

This book was compiled with inputs, encouragement and support from many people who worked at or had associations with the establishment. Particular mention is made of the following people for their contributions:

Ian Burch
Brian Clark
Alan Cooper
Simon Davis
Paul Fenne
Thomas Forbes
Dave King
Colin Newell
Richard Rawlins
Neil Service
Neil Sparshott
Derek Talbot
Julian Walker

ABBREVIATIONS

ACAVP	Advanced Composite Armoured Vehicle Programme
AD	Assistant Director
AEV	Armoured Engineer Vehicle
ALPS	Advanced Land Platform System
APC	Armoured Personnel Carrier
APDS	Armour Piercing Discarding Sabot
APFSDS	Armour Piercing Fin Stabilised Discarding Sabot
ARRV	Armoured Repair and Recovery Vehicle
ARV	Armoured Recovery Vehicle
ASC	Army Service Corps
ASPAT	Air-portable Self Propelled Anti-Tank
AT	Anti-Tank
ATDT	Automatic Target Detection and Tracking
ATSA	Army Technical Support Agency
AVLB	Armoured Vehicle Launched Bridge
AVR	Armoured Vehicle Reconnaissance
AVRE	Armoured Vehicle Royal Engineers
BAC	British Aircraft Corporation
BAOR	British Army Of the Rhine
BARV	Beach Armoured Recovery Vehicle
BTID	Battlefield Target Identification Device
BEF	British Expeditionary Force
CAC	Climatic and Altitude Chamber
CER	Controller Establishments and Research
CET	Combat Engineer Tractor
CHIP	Chieftain/Challenger Improvement Programme
CIA	Chief Inspector of Artillery
CR1	Challenger 1
CRARRV	Challenger Armoured Repair and Recovery Vehicle
CTDP	Component Technology Demonstrator Programme

CVCC	Complete Vehicle Climatic Chamber
CVR(T)	Combat Vehicle Reconnaissance (Tracked)
CVR(W)	Combat Vehicle Reconnaissance (Wheeled)
DD	Duplex Drive (Swimming Tank system)
DD	Deputy Director
DD(M)	Design Department (Mechanical)
DD(V)	Design Department (Vehicles)
DERA	Defence Evaluation and Research Agency
DFWES	Direct Fire Weapon Effects Simulator
DIT	Driver In Turret
DLO	Defence Logistics Organisation
DO	Drawing Office
DOE	Department Of the Environment
DRA	Defence Research Agency
DRIFT	Driving Remotely In Following Truck
DSEi	Defence Systems and Equipment International
Dstl	Defence Science and Technology Laboratory
DTD	Department of Tank Design
DTD&E	Department of Tank Design and Experimentation
ECU	Engine Control Unit
EMC	Electromagnetic Compatibility
EM gun	Electromagnetic gun
EOD	Explosive Ordnance Disposal
ETL	Engineering Test Laboratories
FCR	Fire Control Rig
FCTP	Fire Control Technical Programme
FLAV	Future Light Armoured Vehicle
FMBT	Future Main Battle Tank
FRES	Future Rapid Effects System
FV	Fighting Vehicle
FVDD	Fighting Vehicles Design Department
FVPE	Fighting Vehicles Proving Establishment
FVRDE	Fighting Vehicles Research and Development Establishment
GS	General Service
HE	High Explosive
HEAT	High Explosive Anti-Tank
HESH	High Explosive Squash Head
hp	Horsepower
HQ	Headquarters
IDCE	Integrated Driving Control Experiment
IED	Improvised Explosive Device

IFCS	Improved Fire Control System
IFV	Infantry Fighting Vehicle
KE	Kinetic Energy
kW	Kilowatt
LCS	Landing Craft Ship
LCT	Landing Craft Tank
LP	Liquid Propellant
MAID	Mobile Autonomous Intelligent Device
MARDI	Mobile Advanced Robotics Defence Initiative
MBT	Main Battle Tank
MEE	Mechanical Experimental Establishment
MEXE	Military Engineering Experimental Establishment
MCV80	Mechanised Combat Vehicle 80
MGB	Medium Girder Bridge
MGO	Master General of the Ordnance
MICV	Mechanised Infantry Combat Vehicle
MLRS	Multi-Launch Rocket System
MMP	Mean Maximum Pressure
MOD	Ministry of Defence
MT	Motor Transport
MVEE	Military Vehicles and Engineering Establishment
MWEE	Mechanised Warfare Experimental Establishment
MWSD	Mechanical Warfare Supply Department
NBC	Nuclear Biological Chemical
NEC	Network Enabled Capability
NGP	Nominal Ground Pressure
ODP	Operational Demonstrator Programme
OF	Ordnance Factory
PANTILI	Panoramic Thermal Imager Laser Integrated
PE	Procurement Executive
PERME	Propellants Explosives and Rocket Motors Establishment
POL	Petrol Oils and Lubricants
PPP	Public Private Partnership
PSA	Property Services Agency
R&D	Research and Development
RA	Royal Artillery
RAC	Royal Armoured Corps
RAF	Royal Air Force
RARDE	Royal Armaments Research and Development Establishment
RASC	Royal Army Service Corps
RE	Royal Engineers

REME	Royal Electrical and Mechanical Engineers
RMG	Ranging Machine Gun
RNAS	Royal Naval Air Service
ROF	Royal Ordnance Factory
ROVA	Road Vehicle Autonomous
RSRE	Royal Signals and Radar Establishment
RTC	Royal Transport Corps
RUDA	Reduced Update Driving Aid
SAE	Special Armour Establishment
SC	Shaped Charge
SCAR	Signature Classification And Reduction
SID	Signature Integration Demonstrator
SITV	Sprung Idler Test Vehicle
SP	Self Propelled
SP70	Self Propelled Gun 70 – Joint UK-German project
SPAT	Self Propelled Anti-Tank
SRV	Suspension Research Vehicle
STAMPLAR	Sight, Thermal, Armoured, Periscope, Laser Ranging
STT	School of Tank Technology
SVDC	Special Vehicle Development Committee
TD&E	Trials Design and Experimentation
TDU	Trials and Development Unit
TED	Tom Elliott Detector
TICM	Thermal Imager Common Module
TOG	'The Old Gang'
TOGS	Thermal Observation and Gunnery Sight
TS Dept	Tank Supply Department
TVA	Test Vehicle Aluminium
URV	Unmanned Research Vehicle
VE	Vehicle Engineering
VSI	Vehicle Systems Integration
WASAD	Wide Area Surveillance and Aided Detection
WSD	Weapon System Demonstrator
WVEE	Wheeled Vehicles Experimental Establishment

INTRODUCTION

There is currently a triangle of land on the north-east corner of Chobham Common in Surrey enclosed by a security fence. It is bounded on one side by the M3 between junctions 2 and 3 and on another by the Reading-to-Waterloo railway line at Longcross station. On the site can be seen a mixture of buildings including modern brick-built offices, corrugated iron hangars and, by the station, a large industrial-looking concrete-built building. The site is currently used by film and television crews as a set, but it has been sold for redevelopment and so soon all traces of the current buildings are likely to disappear. Once that happens there will be nothing left to indicate the significant activity that went on there for over fifty years when it was the centre for British military vehicle Research and Development (R&D).

A government research and development establishment for military vehicles existed on this site at Chobham Common from 1942 through to 2004, when the last government employees were relocated. Although on Chobham Common it was always referred to officially, and by staff, as the 'Chertsey' site due to its postal address. The establishment went through various name changes, but for most of its life it was known as the Fighting Vehicles Research and Development Establishment (FVRDE) and then the Military Vehicles and Engineering Establishment (MVEE). The locals simply called it the 'Tank Factory'. To the wider world it is known as 'Chobham', the name given to the game-changing armour technology developed there.

Through the time it existed the Chertsey establishment became world leading in the field of military vehicle research and design, and could claim many 'firsts' in military vehicle technology. This document attempts to capture some of the history of UK Government involvement in tank design and testing, the factors that led up to the formation of the Chertsey establishment and its subsequent roles and activities. Above all it is intended as a tribute to those who worked there and their world-leading achievements.

The first part of the book provides an overview of tank development in the United Kingdom up until the end of the Second World War, with a focus on the role of government and the various bodies and establishments that form the lineage of Chertsey. The rest of the book focuses on Chertsey itself, describing how the structures and roles changed, the development of the site and the facilities, and finally the vehicles and technologies studied and developed there.

1

THE BIRTH OF THE TANK

The first attempt at setting up a government organisation in Britain for the procurement of military transport was in 1645 when Oliver Cromwell appointed a comissionary to hire or requisition coaches, wagons and carts for the troops in the New Model Army. Then in 1664 the Royal Carriage Works was set up at Woolwich to build wagons and gun carriages for the army, the design and build of gun carriages being a skilled activity if a robust and stable firing platform was to be provided. The comissionary was answerable to the Treasury, not the army, and this remained the situation until 24 January 1855 when a warrant was signed for the formation of the Land Transport Corps. This was set up primarily to support the Crimean campaign and had its headquarters at Horfield Barracks in Bristol.

Mechanisation in the British Army came slowly. In 1769 a French military engineer, N.J. Cugnot, built a steam-powered wheeled vehicle for towing guns, but it was much later in Britain, in 1845, that the Inspector General of Fortifications suggested that steam-powered engines could be used for military purposes. Therefore in 1855 trials of a Boydell traction engine were undertaken at Woolwich Arsenal where it towed a 68pdr gun weighing 8 tons. There are some suggestions that Boydell traction engines were deployed during the Crimean War (1853–56) to haul heavy guns into position. In 1855 James Govan suggested that a Boydell Tractor could be fitted with a cannon and an armoured cover. This was one of the first practical proposals for an armoured fighting vehicle, but the idea was rejected by Lord Palmerston as being 'uncivilised', particularly as the design included rotating scythes fitted to the wheels. In 1857 the Superintendent of Machinery at Woolwich Royal Carriage Department undertook a trial in which a Boydell Traction Engine was driven from Thetford to Woolwich. The 15-ton traction engine towed a load of 29 tons, the 99½-mile journey taking thirty-two hours and consuming 91cwt of coal. Having demonstrated their utility, military traction engines, including armoured Fowler engines, were deployed by the British Army in South Africa in 1885 where their uses included towing road trains.

In 1900, following some trials of petrol-driven cars and lorries for the army, a 'Mechanical Transport Committee' was set up. This consisted of interested branches, the Royal Artillery (RA), Royal Engineers (RE) and the Army

Fowler Armoured Traction engine, as used in the Boer War around 1900. (Crown Copyright-MOD)

Service Corps (ASC), who co-ordinated requirements and conducted trials. Requirements included vehicles for mobile searchlights and to tow guns.

Key to the ultimate success of tanks was the development of tracks. The first known patent of a track-like system dates from 1713. It was filed by a Mr d'Herman at the Royal Academy of Sciences and had a system of interconnected rollers. British Patent 953/1770 of 15 February 1770, which was filed by Richard Lovell Edgeworth, proposed the use of 'portable railways' in which 'several pieces of wood are connected to the carriage which moves on in regular succession in such a manner that a sufficient length of railway is constantly at rest for the wheels to roll on'. In 1826 Sir George Cayley patented a scheme for a continuous track. An 'endless railway wheel' was patented by a British Engineer James Boydell in 1846 and this was used on the traction engine that took part in the Woolwich trials. An Australian, Mr J.B. Hughs, reported back to his government some observations of those trials, noting that when working in the rain the wheels of the engine, which weighed 12 tons, did not sink into the ground, but those of wagons weighing 2 tons did sink.[*] The Boydell system, sometimes called 'Boydell's Girdle', consisted of a number of plates attached to the wheels. Similar schemes of plates or feet attached to wheels included the 'Tippings Plates' system used for launching lifeboats across soft beaches and the Diplock Pedrail system. A Pedrail traction engine was tested at Aldershot in 1905 and the 'Boydell's Girdle' system was used on some heavy First World War artillery pieces to improve mobility when being towed. In the USA, Alvin Lombard was granted a patent for a tracked log hauler and in 1901 built the first of eighty-three machines. In 1903 Benjamin Holt bought the patent rights from Lombard and in 1906 started to build the world's first commercially successful vehicle to use tracks – the Holt Tractor.

---

[*] *South Australian Advertiser*, 11 August 1859.

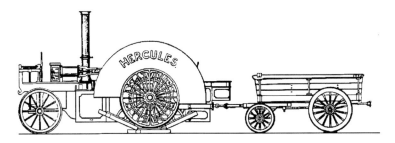

Boydell Traction Engine. From a 1944 School of Tank Technology document on the history of Tracks by E. Micklethwaite. (Crown Copyright-MOD)

Meanwhile, in Britain in 1899 F.R. Simms fitted a Maxim machine gun with armoured shield to the handle bars of a Beeston Quadricycle powered by a 1.5hp de Dion engine. This he called a 'Motor Scout' and he demonstrated it at Richmond in Surrey. He went on to develop concepts for armoured cars and was asked by Vickers to design a 'war car', which they then built. Although such armoured cars had also been proposed by others, for example by the American E.J. Pennington in 1896, Simms was the first to turn his ideas into a fully functional prototype vehicle. It had a 16hp engine giving a speed of 9mph, was armed with two machine guns and a 1pdr gun, and had 6mm armour. It was displayed at Crystal Palace in April 1902 and offered for sale to the British and European governments without success.

In 1903 *The Strand Magazine* published a story by H.G. Wells, called 'The Land Ironclads', in which he described the battlefield of the future dominated by steam-propelled, iron-clad vehicles running on large Pedrails. During the war he was taken to visit a factory in Birmingham where tanks were being built to see how his vision of future warfare was becoming reality.

In 1907 the War Office offered a prize for a cross-country vehicle that could tow a howitzer for 40 miles without refuelling. The prize was won by a tracked

The Hornsby Tractor. From a 1944 School of Tank Technology document on the history of Tracks by E. Micklethwaite. (Crown Copyright-MOD)

petrol-driven tractor designed by David Roberts and built by R. Hornsby and Sons, who had been working on tracked tractor designs since 1905. Although it had fragile tracks with wooden shoes, a Major Donoghue suggested that it could mount a gun surrounded by an armoured shield. Another suggestion submitted to the War Office came from Australian engineer L. de Mole in 1912, who proposed an advanced tracked, armoured machine with suspension and steering through the use of bowed tracks.

Although these ideas for armoured vehicles were not taken forward, mechanisation (or Mechanicalisation as it was then called) was underway in the British Army. In 1903 it had been agreed that the Army Service Corps would take over responsibility of mechanical transport from the Royal Engineers. In 1905 the ASC set up a Motor Transport Repair Depot at Hurley, near Henley-on-Thames, to support manoeuvres to test the suitability of mechanical motor transport and by 1906 a training establishment had been set up in Aldershot.

In 1914 the Admiralty purchased 100 Rolls-Royce cars for use by the Royal Naval Air Service (RNAS) for base protection. Some of these were subsequently provided with armour protection. The RNAS also carried out trials of the Killen-Strait tractor. This had tracked running gear in a tricycle arrangement and after successful trials and a demonstration on 30 June 1915 a contract was placed the following month for an armoured version with a Delaunay-Belleville armoured body. This is claimed to be the world's first tracked, armoured vehicle that was actually built and tested.

In September 1914 Lieutenant Colonel E.D. Swinton RE (Assistant Secretary of the Committee of Imperial Defence) suggested that the US Holt Agricultural tracked tractor, then in use to tow 8in guns, could be used as the basis for an armoured vehicle. This suggestion was turned down as it was assumed that such a vehicle would be too vulnerable to artillery fire. Swinton did, however, discuss his ideas with Lieutenant Colonel M. Hankey, who was the secretary of the Committee

Rolls-Royce Armoured Car.
(Copyright W. Suttie)

of Imperial Defence. As a result, in February 1915, a demonstration was made to that committee of a Holt tractor towing an armoured trailer. The demonstration was considered unconvincing by the army, but Winston Churchill, as First Lord of the Admiralty, passed Swinton's ideas on to the Admiralty Landships Committee. When Swinton met with Albert Stern, the secretary of the Landships Committee, he was said to remark, 'Lieut. Stern, this is the most extraordinary thing that I have ever seen. The Director of Naval Construction appears to be making land battleships for the army who have never asked for them, and are doing nothing to help. You have nothing but naval ratings doing all your work.' Swinton went on to play a key role in generating interest in tanks in the army.

The Landships Committee had only just been formed, with support from Winston Churchill, and on 24 February 1915 Mr Eustace Tennyson d'Eyncourt, a naval architect, had been appointed as Chairman. Winston Churchill had already written to Mr Herbert Asquith, the Prime Minister, complaining about the lack of efforts on behalf of the army to address the problems associated with trench warfare and modern firepower. He suggested:

> It would be quite easy in a short time to fit up a number of steam tractors with small armoured shelters, in which men and machine guns could be placed, which would be bullet-proof. Used at night, they would not be affected by artillery fire to any extent. The caterpillar system would enable trenches to be crossed quite easily, and the weight of the machine would destroy all wire entanglements.

Originally the Landships Committee was housed in offices over Admiralty Arch. It is interesting to note that some members of that team had a long association with tank development. Mr N.C. Tervet worked as a draughtsman on early tank designs and at the time of his death in 1952 was working in the running-gear branch at Chertsey. The Landships Committee looked at a range of ideas for armoured vehicles suitable for crossing rough terrain. One was the Bramah Diplock 'Pedrail', which had evolved from a system of large pads around a wheel into a continuous track solution. In 1913 Pedrail Transport Ltd of Fulham had displayed a 10-ton petrol-driven truck that demonstrated the principle of the 'Diplock Patent Anti-friction Self-contained Railway'. This was used as the basis for an articulated vehicle with two pairs of tracks on each side, which was assessed by the Landships Committee. The design was driven by a requirement to carry a trench-storming party of forty men stood side by side in two rows, but it was soon realised that the long length of the vehicle would cause problems.

Another vehicle was the Tritton Trencher. This had wheels on a long chassis extension to reach across a gap so that planks could then be emplaced for the rest of the vehicle to cross; this design was dropped after trials in June 1915 as it proved too cumbersome.

Even less practical were concepts that used very large wheels to cross rough terrain. A concept for a device with 40ft wheels and powered by an 800hp submarine engine was developed and a design contract placed with Messrs Foster and Company of Lincoln. The contract was soon stopped when full-size mock-ups were being built as it was realised that such a large vehicle would provide an easy target for enemy artillery.

By 23 June 1915 the Landships Committee was in possession of a Killen-Strait tractor, two Diplock experimental 1-ton wagons and two Giant Creeper Grip tractors purchased from the USA. A test site had been acquired at Burton-upon-Trent and the Ministry of Munitions Experimental Ground at Wembley was also used for trials. Appointed to provide support to the committee was 20 Squadron of the Royal Naval Armoured Car Division because at that time the army was unable, or unwilling, to provide support. Two 'Land Battleships' were under construction, one based on the Pedrail solution and the other using the 'creeper grip' tracks from the USA. A more practical solution was based on armouring a US Bullock-tracked tractor and an RNAS team commanded by Lt Walter G. Wilson conducted trials of this machine at Burton-upon-Trent. The development work on the Bullock tractor had been carried out by Fosters of Lincoln who made wheeled tractors for the artillery and had already been involved in the big-wheel concepts.

D'Eyncourt asked Fosters to design a machine that had 'strong armour, powerful guns and the ability to cross trenches and other obstacles'. On 15 June 1915 Swinton issued a specification for such a machine, which included the ability to climb a 5ft bank, cross a 5ft gap, be proof against armour-piercing bullets, carry a quick-firing gun and machine guns, and have a speed of around 4mph. A number of complex and ingenious solutions were considered, but in the end it was recognised that a simple robust solution was needed. Finally in response to the requirement they built Lincoln No. 1 – the world's first true tank. Designed by William Tritton, and so also called the 'Tritton Machine', it used a pair of 9ft Bullock tracks. The actual contract for the vehicle was placed on 29 July 1915 and it ran on 6 September 1915 with trench crossing trials first carried out on 19 September. The vehicle was constructed using available parts including the Bullock tracks and the engine and transmission used in heavy howitzer tractors. It was built of boiler plate of the correct weight and had a dummy turret also of the correct weight. Although it demonstrated the ability to cross a small trench, the tracks were inadequate.

Design of a second vehicle had started before the first was completed, and a wooden mock-up was viewed by members of the Landships Committee on 26 August. Key to improvements with the second vehicle was the development of a new track based on pressed-steel plates designed by Tritton and Lt W.G. Wilson. This vehicle, called Little Willie, retained the same hull but had longer tracks of the new design and was completed in December 1915. The September trials had highlighted mobility limitations and so, with the input of Swinton's ideas, Fosters had immediately started work on concepts that evolved into a new design. This was variously called the Wilson Machine, Centipede, Big Willie and finally Mother. The term 'Tank' was used for the vehicles at this time as part of secrecy measures. The requirement for a suitable name had been recognised as the term 'Landship' was thought to be too descriptive. Mr d'Eyncourt suggested the term 'Water Carrier' as the cover name, but as government departments tended to be referred to by their initials this idea was rejected and the name 'Tank' adopted; hence the Landships Committee became the Tank Supply, or TS, Committee.

Although the design of Little Willie was obsolete before the vehicle was completed it actually formed part of the UK defences in the Second World War, initially as a static strongpoint north of Bovington camp before moving to enhance the defences of a Gloucestershire airfield. Such uses of this and other vehicles in the Bovington museum collection prevented them from being melted down for much needed scrap metal.

'Mother' introduced the classic rhomboid shape of First World War heavy tanks, which was driven by the requirement to climb over high walls and parapets. A full-size mock-up was quickly completed and displayed at Wembley on 29 September, and despite reservations from some army officers instructions were given to Tritton to build a prototype as soon as possible. 'Mother' was ready for its first run at Lincoln on 3 December 1915. There was concern about the impact of firing the main weapon on the sponsons in which they were mounted, and on the crew, and therefore soon after it was ready Mother was taken to a nearby field for a test firing of one of the QF 6pdr guns. The first shot was a misfire and when the crew were still examining the breach the round went off. As the direction the shot went in was not known there was initial concern for the safety of Lincoln Cathedral, which was only a mile away, but after searching for two hours the shot was eventually found and no damage had been done. Mother left Lincoln on 26 January and was taken by train to Hatfield Station where it was unloaded at night and driven to Hatfield Park.

Instructions had been given by Lord Kitchener on 29 December 1915 for a trial of the sample machine being built, stating that, 'the first thing … would be to test its practical utility under field conditions; without such a test we may be wasting material and men uselessly.' Hatfield Park had been lent by Lord Salisbury for the trials following an arrangement made with Mr d'Eyncourt in the previous October as Wembley was considered inadequate for full testing and demonstration. A working party consisting of men of the 3rd (Mid Herts) Battalion Herts Volunteer Regiment and a company of engineers, lent by the War Office, began to construct trenches and obstacles early in January 1916. The machine successfully negotiated the resulting course on 29 January and the following day Mr d'Eyncourt informed Lord Kitchener that the 'Centipede' could be demonstrated on 2 February.

The official demonstration took place in the presence of Lord Kitchener and officers of the General Staff, War Office, Officers of the Staff of the Commander-in-Chief, the First Lord and other members of the Admiralty and the Minister of Munitions. Soon afterwards, on 8 February, the machine was demonstrated to the King. The demonstrations were in three parts, negotiating obstacles that reflected the official performance requirements, a test course representative of assumed combat use and finally negotiating obstacles that demonstrated the full capabilities of the vehicle. The official test obstacles included a parapet 4ft 6in high followed by a gap 5ft wide. The representative test course included gaps and parapets, wire entanglements, two shell craters, water-logged ground and typical German defences. The demonstration of actual capability included a 5ft 6in parapet and a 9ft-wide gap, which were successfully navigated. On 14 February Mr d'Eyncourt wrote to Mr Churchill describing the success of the vehicle stating:

> Wire entanglements it goes through like a rhinoceros through a field of corn. It carries two 6-pdr. guns in sponsons (a naval touch) which can fire right ahead and enfilade the trenches on the broadside. It is proof against machine-gun fire. It can be conveyed by rail (the sponsons and guns take off, making it lighter), and can be put together ready for action and proceed independently at short notice … The wheels behind form a rudder for steering a course and also absorb the shock over banks, but are not absolutely necessary.

Following the successful demonstrations on 12 February, Lloyd George, Minister for Munitions, signed a Charter for the TS Committee to deliver 100 tanks, with a request that they be available within six months. This was followed on 3 April by orders for a further fifty tanks. Orders for fifty Mark IIs and fifty Mark IIIs followed. Of the first 100 tanks twenty-five were built by Fosters and the rest by the Metropolitan Carriage, Wagon and Finance Company at Wednesbury. Armour plate was ordered from Cammell Laird, Vickers-Armstrong and Beardmore. The Mark II and Mark III versions had a number of minor improvements over the Mark Is and the Mark IIIs had improved-quality armour to defeat the German anti-tank rifle. There had been ongoing work to improve the quality of armour since it had been discovered that some German bullets could easily penetrate the plates used on armoured cars. Further improved armour materials to defeat the German armour-piercing bullet were developed with help from the 'Armour-Plate Design Department' of Messrs Beardmore.

In March 1916 the forerunner of the Tank Corps was formed under Colonel Swinton as the Heavy Section of the Machine Gun Corps, initially based at Bisley. The Machine Gun Corps had itself been formed in October 1915 with

Mark IV Tank. (Copyright W. Suttie)

Infantry, Cavalry and Motor branches. The Motor Branch brought together the Motor Machine Gun Service, which had been administered by the Royal Artillery and equipped with motor cycle mounted machine guns, and the armoured car squadrons from the Royal Naval Armoured Car Service. Therefore when the Heavy Section was formed there was a mix of officers and men from the Royal Navy and the motor trade as well as from the army. In addition to initial training at Bisley, the Naval Gunnery School at Whale Island provided training in the use of the 6pdr guns. The Heavy Machine Gun Corps with forty-nine vehicles took part in the first operational use of tanks at Flers-Courcelette on 15 September 1916.

By August 1916 a training camp for the Heavy Section had been set up at Elveden Camp in Norfolk. The training area there was well guarded to keep people away and the presence of Royal Engineers, to build trenches and earth works for realistic training, led to a rumour among the local populous that it was the site of a tunnel being built to Germany. In October 1916 the Heavy Section was relocated to Bovington Camp near Wool where the 'Tank Centre' was set up under the command of Brigadier Anley. This had been used as an Infantry Training Area since 1899 but had expanded significantly at the start of the war in order to train the many new recruits who had responded to Lord Kitchener's call for volunteers. Thus began the association of Bovington with armoured vehicles, which still continues today. In November 1916 the Heavy Section became the Heavy Branch.

Even after the success of the first tanks work continued on the Pedrail concept. A Major A.R. Glasford made some proposals in a paper on the 'neutralisation of the trench as an obstacle', forwarded through G.H.Q. France on 3 September 1915. The paper suggested that it would be possible to 'carry the attack with lethal gases right into the enemy hues by means of a Pedrail caterpillar, of which the main armament would be a liquid, such as hydrocyanic acid, deadly in effect but not so persistent as to hamper the attacking infantry'. The design and manufacture of a Pedrail machine carrying a flame-projector was then already in progress, in line with requirements agreed at a conference held on 28 August 1915. Construction of the parts of this machine was largely completed by 17 February 1916 but it lacked a solution for armour, which would have been too heavy due to its size. The machine, which was commonly called the 'Trench Warfare Caterpillar', was finally ready to leave the works on 22 July 1916. As completed it ran on two Pedrail units arranged in tandem and driven by Aster engines. The frame was 33ft 4in long by 9ft 4in wide. It was sent to Porton for trials early in August 1916, but development stopped due to problems with the Pedrail feet when running on roads.

In order to streamline processes with the focus now on production, the TS Committee became the Tank Supply Department. The TS Department had offices at 17 Cockspur Street, London and trial grounds at Dollis Hill in North London and Oldbury in Worcestershire. The Department continued design work and, seeing the need to maintain design and manufacturing capabilities pending new orders for tanks, started work on designing a gun carrier for 5in howitzers. Design work started in April 1916 and the design modified following review in June 1916. An order was placed for fifty, the last two of which were completed as 'Salvage Tanks' to aid the retrieval and dismantling of damaged or destroyed tanks.

The initial successes of the first tanks led to an order for a further 1,000 placed on 19 September 1916, just a few days after the first operational use. However, this order was cancelled by the Army Council just twenty-one days later on 10 October. Only the direct intervention of Lloyd George, then Secretary for War, enabled the order to be reinstated the very next day. The order resulted in the delivery of 1,015 of the Mark IV version, which had a number of improvements, particularly to crew conditions, and included thicker armour, an exhaust silencer (to give the enemy less notice of approach) and provision for an un-ditching beam. In February 1917 an additional 205 Mark IV tender tanks were ordered for carrying supplies to the fighting tanks. The Mark IV was adopted as the standard heavy tank at that time with earlier Marks being returned to the UK to be used for training.

In order to manage the task of building 1,000 new tanks, acceptance testing and delivery along with the supply of spares, the TS Department became the Mechanical Warfare Supply Department (MWSD) reporting to the Ministry of Munitions. Key staff from the TS Department continued to work in the MWSD with Sir Albert Stern as Director and Sir Eustace d'Eyncourt as the Chief Designer.

Building 1,000 tanks was challenging not least because the Ministry of Supply had stated that Tanks were the fifth priority after aeroplanes, guns and ammunition, mechanical transport and locomotives. This meant that the supply of men and materials for construction was constrained and a request to the Ministry of Labour for 2,000 men to be engaged in building tanks resulted in just 275 being provided. Initially there were even problems getting men working on tanks issued with 'War Lapel Badges' – these indicated that they were undertaking critical work in support of the war effort thus preventing criticism that they were avoiding active duty. Despite the problems, by May 1917 tanks were being produced at a rate of sixty a month.

The demand for tanks meant that as the war progressed the number of companies involved in manufacture increased and included the Metropolitan Carriage, Wagon and Finance Company in Birmingham, the Coventry Ordnance Works and three factories in Glasgow: Mirlees, Watson Co. Ltd and William Beardmore Co. Ltd. The MWSD set up the 'Tank Testing Section' based at Newbury Racecourse and all vehicles were sent there for testing before being shipped to France.

The need to train crews for the large number of new tanks had prompted the move of training to Bovington. It was stated that, 'The wooded country around Bovington is particularly adapted to the training of tank battalions, the rolling downs, the woods and the small streets being very similar to and as equally deserted as the battlefields of France.'[*] A range of training courses was developed for the new crew members including driving, maintenance, gunnery, signalling, reconnaissance and the care of pigeons. Carrier pigeons were carried by each tank for passing messages, but it is said the birds were often groggy due to the fumes in the vehicle and sometimes became emergency rations. To enhance driver training a range of courses and obstacles were built including trenches, bogs and areas of 'no man's land' created with explosives. Initially the desire to keep the new 'secret weapon' under wraps had an impact on local residents, especially when the vehicles were driven from Wool station to the camp. People who lived on the route were required by the Military Police to close their blinds and pedestrians were told to stand in a field with their backs to the road while tanks passed. How effective these precautions were is open to question; Mr James Spicer who owned Bovington Farm told the military authorities that he had no objections to trying to help keep tanks secret but requested the removal of one that had broken down and had been towed into his farmyard and left there for forty-eight hours.

On 3 March 1917 an exhibition of vehicles was held at the Oldbury test area. In addition to British military and civilian VIPs there was a delegation from France, where they were developing their own tanks. The vehicles demonstrated included a Mark IV Heavy tank, Tritton Chaser (Prototype Medium A), the gun-carrying tank and a number of Mark IVs with alternative transmissions. These were:

1. Williams-Janney Hydraulic transmission
2. Wilson Epicyclic transmission
3. Daimler Petrol-Electric transmission
4. Westinghouse Petrol-Electric transmission
5. Wilson Multiple Clutch transmission

---

[*] 'The History of 'E' (5th) Battalion' in Tank Corps Journal, Vol. 2, No. 14 (June 1920), p. 48.

In July 1917, based on experience from the Battle of Arras, it was agreed that the Heavy Branch should be expanded and become the Tank Corps, but in September 1917 the expansion was cancelled only to be revived again the next month. The Mark IV was the tank used at the Battle of Cambrai on 20 November 1917 when they were deployed as originally envisaged by Colonel Swinton – in large numbers across a wide front in a surprise attack across suitable ground. In comparison with previous offensive operations, spectacular advances were made but were not exploited due to lack of sufficient infantry reinforcements to secure the ground. Even after the success at Cambrai the Tank Corps still faced difficulties with ongoing debates on how best to organise the Corps. In April 1918 expansion of the Tank Corps was again suspended, but following the victory at Hamel in July 1918 General Headquarters requested more tanks. On 31 July 1918 a branch called SD7 was created under the Director of Staff Duties in the War Office to carry out the expansion. SD7 addressed manpower and training issues along with the need to improve facilities at Wool; however the expansion was still being implemented when the Armistice came.

In addition to serving in Western Europe, eight Mark I and II tanks were sent to Egypt in January 1917 and were used against the Turks at Gaza. Mark IV tanks were also sent to Egypt in November 1917.

Development of the heavy tanks continued with the Mark V, Mark VI and Mark VII. The Mark V was the first tank that could be driven by one man; previous versions required the co-ordinated efforts of the driver, commander and two gearsmen to change direction. Over 1,000 Mark Vs of different variants were manufactured including 'stretched' versions, which were 4ft longer to increase trench-crossing capability. The Mark VI was designed by Major Wilson and a wooden mock-up was built by Fosters. It was to have a lower ground pressure and be faster than existing tanks, but it did not go into production due to the urgent need to mass produce existing designs. The Mark VII was longer and had an improved transmission but only three were built. Improving the mobility,

'Indiana Jones' Tank
based on the Mark VIII.
(Copyright W. Suttie)

protection and fightability of tanks, as reflected in the early development work, remained an ongoing theme and was the subject of extensive research many years later at the Chertsey site. The Mark VIII was a completely new design and was intended as an Anglo-American vehicle although only three prototypes of the UK version were built. The US version was powered by a derivative of the Liberty aero engine and the same engine formed the basis of that used in a number of Second World War cruiser tanks, including the Crusader. The overall design did find fame as the basis of the tank in the Indiana Jones film *The Last Crusade*, although the producers requested that a turret be added! When it was being designed the builder of this vehicle sought advice on tracked vehicle steering from a member of Chertsey staff.

The final model in the family of heavy tanks was the Mark IX, which was not a tank but a purpose-designed stores or infantry carrier. Only thirty-five were built by the end of the war and they did not see action.

Even before the first tanks were fielded there was ongoing research to improve capabilities. The question of protecting tanks against shell fire was taken up after the first order was placed, and a double-skin solution was tried. It was discovered that a 1in plate with half the metal stamped out, thus halving the weight, and placed 1ft in front of the base armour, would detonate a German high-explosive shell and prevent any damage. The idea was not taken forward at that time, but more than eighty years later the Defence Science and Technology Laboratory (Dstl) demonstrated a cost-effective method for manufacturing perforated high-hardness armour steel to provide weight-efficient protection solutions.

Research was also undertaken into different solutions for roof protection. Other experiments assessed different means of communications including signal lamps, wireless and semaphore. An experimental plough was developed for laying telephone cables as the tanks advanced.

An important area of research and development was transmissions. It was realised that the initial system was inadequate and a number of alternatives were tested including a Daimler Company petrol-electric transmission, a British Westinghouse electrical tramway transmission, a Williams-Janney hydraulic transmission and the Ilcle-Shaw Company hydraulic transmission. In addition the Metropolitan Company built epicyclic and multiple-clutch transmissions designed by Major Wilson, and the St Diamond Company in France arranged to have their petrol-electric transmission installed in a hull, which was sent to them.

The original 105hp Daimler engine was known to be underpowered and so a contract was placed with Ricardo for the development of a 150hp engine. A requirement of this engine was that it should not use any aluminium or high-tensile steel parts to avoid diverting these materials from aero-engine manufacture.

Despite the success of the first tanks and great support for them from the front line, including from Sir Douglas Haig, the TS Department and MWSD that

followed tended to be subject to ongoing attack and interference from the War
Office and Army Council. Part of the criticism was due to the department having
its origins in the Admiralty and not in the army. In addition, in order to get things
done, the TS Department had often bypassed normal channels. Many in the War
Office had not seen tanks in action and had not grasped the full potential of
what they saw as 'pretty mechanical toys'. The tanks were also criticised for their
limitations, many of which were due to the fact they were new and were not used
to their best advantage on operations.

In May 1917 Sir Douglas Haig had suggested that, in view of their importance, a
Tank Committee should be set up to ensure good links between the army and the
MWSD. In practice the MWSD found the Tank Committee to be an unnecessary
layer of bureaucracy between them and front-line practitioners and soon stopped
attending committee meetings. Albert Stern tried to reduce the status of the Tank
Committee to that of an advisory panel, complaining that future tank supply had
been put at risk by a refusal to authorise the procurement of engines prior to a
confirmed order for vehicles. He also noted that where the TS Department had
started to manufacture heavy tanks with an equal number of Male (6pdr gun
armed) and Female (Machine Gun armed) variants the War Office had changed
that to a ratio of two females to one male and then to three males for every two
females – even though there were insufficient 6pdr guns available.

Despite the arguments of the MWSD, the War Office prevailed and Sir Albert
Stern, then Director of the MWSD, was moved out of the way to a job supporting
links with the US. He was replaced by Vice Admiral Sir Gordon Moore who had
never even seen a tank before taking up the appointment.

In addition to the heavy tanks, three medium tanks were designed. The Medium
Mark A, or Whippet, was designed in November 1916 and the prototype, the
Tritton Chaser, completed in February 1917. Approval for production was given
at an MWSD conference held on 4 March 1917. Two hundred were built and first
saw action in March 1918. The vehicle had two 45hp Tyler engines, one for each
track, and was steered by controlling the throttle of each – requiring much skill on
the part of the driver. The Tank Corp Central Workshops modified one by fitting
suspension and a 360hp Rolls-Royce aero engine. That vehicle was reported as
being capable of 30mph compared with 8.3mph for the standard vehicle. This
activity influenced the design of the later Medium Mark D. The other medium
tanks, Medium Mark B and Mark C were built in smaller numbers, less than fifty
of each, and they were not used in action. The Medium B was the first British
tank to have the engine in a separate compartment from the crew.

2

BRITISH TANK DEVELOPMENT FOLLOWING THE FIRST WORLD WAR

On 27 July 1917 the Royal Tank Corps (RTC) was formed by Royal Warrant and came to be commanded by Brigadier Elles and Colonel J.F.C. Fuller as his General Staff Officer (Grade 1). It was Fuller who put together what was called Plan 1919. This was a blueprint for tank warfare if the war had continued and focused on heavy tanks to break through enemy defences and lighter, faster tanks to exploit the breach. The strategy was to quickly advance and overrun enemy artillery positions and headquarters – something that had not been achieved to date due to the inability of horse-mounted cavalry to follow through after enemy lines had been breached. The plan required a fast tank with a long range.

In 1918 Major Philip Johnson (RTC) was based at the Tank Corps central workshops in Teneur, France, and he had been involved in the work to modify a Medium Mark A to have a higher power-to-weight ratio and suspension. He discussed his ideas with Colonel Fuller who recognised that a 'high speed destroyer tank' based on Johnson's ideas would have the range and speed required for Plan 1919. Johnson was promoted to Colonel and asked to form a Department of Tank Design and Experiment (DTD&E), which reported directly to the War Office. The first vehicle from this department was the Medium Tank Mark D, a fast and amphibious tank designed to meet the needs of Plan 1919. It had suspension and a power-to-weight ratio twice that of the Medium Mark A, and hence could reach 25mph. Three variants were built called the 'D', 'D Star' and 'D Two Star' and it is thought that five Ds were built and one each of the other variants. The first prototype ran in March 1919 and was demonstrated at Roundhay Park in Leeds in May 1919. It is reported that the demonstration started with the vehicle driving directly towards the assembled VIPs at 20mph and swerving away at the last minute. The concern caused by this manoeuvre was made worse by a number of wooden sole plates coming loose and a number of VIPs broke ranks and fled.

The second two variants were both larger than the first and 'D Two Star' had a more powerful engine (300hp compared with 240hp). The second two variants were also built to be amphibious and in 1920 one prototype completed a series of trials, which included repeated crossings of the River Stour near Christchurch using its tracks for propulsion. This trial was carried out at the site of the Experimental Bridging Company, which eventually became the Military Engineering Experimental Establishment.

Previous British tanks had lacked suspension, but a system was essential to running at higher speeds. The challenge was providing an affordable and effective suspension for the multiple road wheels then used, seen as necessary for maintaining the track profile and ensuring uniform pressure on the tracks. The solution developed was based on a continuous 'wire rope' system, which was lightweight and gave an excellent ride but was vulnerable to damage. Another issue with the Medium D was that it was designed around Plan 1919 requirements and therefore was very long for trench-crossing but narrow to fit the rail-loading gauge. It was armed only with machine guns and did not have a fully rotating turret; this meant that there were detractors in the army who also claimed it was unreliable.

Meanwhile Johnson and his team were given little direction on requirements to enable the design to be refined. The team also designed a light tank, called the 'Light Infantry Tank'. This was similar in appearance to the Medium D and had the same cable-based suspension but was smaller. It also attempted to achieve large radius turns by bowing the tracks. Lieutenant Colonel Johnson then went to India to assess the requirements for a tank suitable for use on the North West Frontier. As a result he designed a 7-ton light tank mounting a machine gun and called the 'Tropical Tank'. This tank was also amphibious as demonstrated when it swam across Fleet Pond. Four vehicles were built by the Ordnance Factory at Woolwich, the fourth being a supply tank variant. This too was amphibious and demonstrated on Fleet Pond in June 1922. Two of the Tropical Tanks were sent to India for trials, but they proved to be unreliable and underpowered. In August 1922 the supply variant was handed over to the 9th Field Brigade Royal Artillery for user trials, and as a result two more prototypes were built but aimed at use as field artillery tractors rather than supply tanks. These were of similar design to the 'Tropical Tank No. 4' but had conventional coil suspension, based on that used on the Vickers Medium Tank. The resulting vehicle went into a limited production run of eighteen as the Dragon Mark I for use by Field Brigades of the Royal Artillery for towing 18pdr guns. One of the prototypes was trialled in India where there were problems with the water-cooled engine; this led to subsequent Dragons being fitted with an air-cooled engine. The Dragon was subject to ongoing development with the final version, the Mark IV, seeing action in France with the British Expeditionary Force (BEF) at the start of the Second World War.

Johnson's small design team worked to requirements set by the War Office. Meanwhile the Master General of Ordnance (MGO) organisation had its own ideas and in 1921 it placed a contract with Vickers to design and build a tank. The resulting platform was technically inferior to those being designed by Johnson, but had the one advantage of being armed with a 47mm gun in a rotating turret, rather than the fixed machine guns on the 'D'. The vehicle had a number of defects and was rejected. However, it led to the design of what became the Vickers Medium Tank. A total of 160 of these were ordered in 1924 and formed the backbone of the army during the interwar period. This tank only had 6.5mm armour (later increased to 8mm in places), a petrol engine located within the crew compartment and, despite only having a crew of five, was armed with a 47mm gun and six machine guns. One small but significant development introduced on the Vickers Medium was the use of a single stamped unit for the sole plate and connecting bracket of the track. Tracks used on previous in-service tanks had an all-riveted construction and hence were prone to breaking.

The contract with Vickers used up all the available funding in the estimates for tank design and so Johnson's tank design department was reduced in size and the remnants transferred to a design department at Charlton Park near to the Royal Arsenal, Woolwich. There the department was known as Design Department (Mechanical) and worked alongside DD(V) – vehicles, DD(S) – small arms, DD(L) – ammunition, DD(C) – carriages and DD(G) – guns. The decision to focus tank design in industry and run down the experienced and innovative Department of Tank Design (DTD) was a significant factor that resulted in Britain becoming a backwater in tank design until the Chertsey establishment was established.

A further contract was placed with Vickers-Armstrong in 1924 for a heavy tank and this resulted in the design and build of the A1 E1, or Independent, a 31½-ton tank with multiple turrets. It had some advanced features including hydraulically assisted controls and a laryngophone communication system for the eight-man crew. It was a long vehicle to give good trench-crossing capability but narrow enough to be transported by rail, which gave rise to structural problems with steering loads. Only one pilot model was built, which was delivered in 1926, and it was eventually abandoned due to its high cost. It was used for experimental purposes until retiring to the Bovington Tank Museum in 1935.

The need for an advisory committee to oversee matters related to tanks and mechanical warfare vehicles had been recognised, and in 1920 the Mechanical Warfare Board was set up to bring together military requirements and technical expertise from learned bodies and universities. A Mechanical Transport Advisory Board was also set up at that time to address requirements for wheeled vehicles.

An impressive list of members of the Mechanical Warfare Board dated 31 December 1930 included:

Lieutenant General Sir Web Gillman (MGO)
Major General Peck (Director Mechanisation)
Brigadier Croft (Commandant RTC centre)

Professor W.E. Dalby (Institute of Civil Engineers)
Sir Henry Fowler (Institute of Mechanical Engineers)
Brigadier K. Laird (Inspector Royal Tank Corps)
Mr Legros (Institute of Automotive Engineers)
Captain Lewis (Design Department, Royal Arsenal)
Professor W. Morgan (University of Bristol)
Mr Newton (Military College of Science)
Lieutenant Colonel Barnes (MT advisor India Office)
Dr W. Eccles (Institute of Electrical Engineers)
Professor C. Inglis (Cambridge University)
Dr W. Ormandy (Institute of Petroleum Technologies)
Mr D. Shave (London General Omnibus Company)
Sir Thomas Stanton (National Physical Laboratory)

A number of committees were eventually set up to support the Mechanical
Warfare Board including the Tank and Tracked Transport Technical Committee.
This was formed in 1925 under the chairmanship of Colonel S.G. Picton DSO
with the object of 'advising on the details of design of tanks and all tracked and
semi-tracked transport'.

From 1 April 1934 the Mechanical Warfare Board was reorganised to
become the Mechanisation Board. The Board had two main subcommittees: 'A'
committee covering Armoured Fighting Vehicles and 'B' committee covering
Motor Transport (MT) vehicles. The terms of reference of the board were:

1. To act in an advisory capacity on technical problems in connection with
    mechanisation of all types of vehicles for army requirements;
2. To carry out investigation, research and experiment and to put forward
    recommendations as to the development in design of mechanised vehicles
    for all types of army requirements;
3. To secure liaison with the Mechanical Engineering Industry so that the
    army may be in close touch with engineering progress and commercial
    production;
4. To direct the technical work of the Mechanisation Experimental
    Establishment.

The terms 'A Vehicles' for Armoured Vehicles and 'B Vehicles' for Logistic Vehicles,
which originated with the two subcommittees, are still in use.

One area where British industry was active in the interwar years was light
tanks and machine-gun carriers. They were developed mainly by Vickers-
Armstrong, using private venture funds, due to their low cost and hence good
export potential. Although DTD had little input to the designs the light tanks and

associated tankettes and machine-gun carriers were the subject of much testing at the Tank and Tracked Transport Experimental Establishment at Pinehurst Barracks at Farnborough. These light tanks had an interesting heritage, which started in 1924 when a First World War tank commander, Major G. Le Q. Martel, built a one-man tank in his garage. At the same time Captain J.V. Carden, who had served with the Army Service Corps and had experience of Holt tractors, built a one-man tracked carrier. This was built in a London garage owned by Captain Vivian Loyd. Captain Carden met with Major Martel who shared ideas and encouraged him to further develop the concept. The result was a series of Carden-Loyd tankettes. In 1928 Vickers-Armstrong took over the small Carden-Loyd company, which by coincidence was based at Chertsey, and there Carden continued to work as Technical Director. By this time the original company had developed the Mark V tankette, which was a two-man vehicle that could run on tracks or on rubber-tyred wheels in a tricycle arrangement.

Vickers-Armstrong improved the design as the Mark VI of which 325 were supplied to the British Army and around 100 were sold to other nations. In 1932 Vickers-Armstrong used the Carden-Loyd Mark VI tankette as the basis for a light tank with a rotating turret and this resulted in a series of light-tank designs aimed initially at an Imperial General Staff requirement raised in 1929. Around half of the British Army tanks in France during the German invasion were later marks of the Vickers light tank. The Carden-Loyd vehicles were also further developed into the Universal Carrier of which 40,000 were built during the Second World War. One of the most significant contributions of the Carden-Loyd series to armoured vehicle design was in the field of track design. The track life of early vehicles was very limited and hence a number of early designs of Carden-Loyd vehicles could run on wheels or tracks. Carden-Loyd continued to evolve track design until a version consisting of cast-iron track links with track guides on each side became the model for track design in many countries.

At the instigation of General George Milne, the Chief of the Imperial General Staff, it was agreed in October 1925 that an Experimental Mechanized Force should be set up. Milne disagreed with the pure tank theorists, and aimed to organise the force as a balanced capability of all arms, so far as resources allowed. After the units concerned had completed their training on their new equipment, the force officially came into existence at Tidworth on 27 August 1927 ready for trials on Salisbury Plain. Colonel R.J. Collins, whose professional background was light infantry, was appointed to command the Experimental Force. It was mainly equipped with the Vickers Medium Mark I and II[*] and light tanks. Although the

---

[*] The Mark I and Mark II were similar, the main visible difference being the Mark II had skirting plates to protect the suspension.

Vickers Mark IV Light Tank. (Copyright W. Suttie)

Vickers Medium with its 6.5mm armour was not battle-worthy, its range, speed and reliability made it very suitable for these trials. The layout of the vehicle also enabled close interaction between the crew members. The trials soon showed how a mechanised force could overwhelm a conventional force but highlighted the need for the infantry to have suitable transport to keep up with the tanks.

The lessons learnt with respect to mechanised doctrine resulted in the publication of Colonel Charles Broad's booklet *Mechanised and Armoured Formations* ('The Purple Primer') in 1929. Broad argued that tanks should be used to exploit their firepower and shock action, and be deployed in an attack either independently or in co-operation with infantry and cavalry formations. Later trials in 1931 demonstrated the value of radio for command when a force of eighty-five medium and ninety-five light tanks were controlled by voice commands from Charles Broad, now promoted to Brigadier. In 1931 the army agreed to form an independent tank brigade comprised entirely of tracked vehicles. Thus by the early 1930s Britain had established herself as a leader in doctrine for mechanised warfare. However, it failed to develop the equipment to realise the doctrine and it was other nations, in particular Germany, who acted on the clear lessons.

Throughout this period there was a general lack of available finance for equipping the army in general and, despite the evidence from the exercises, mechanisation in particular. There remained some resistance to mechanisation from the traditional Arms and a belief that horses provided better mobility than vehicles. Even among some supporters of armoured vehicles there was a view that losing horses from the army could discourage recruitment.

3

VEHICLE TESTING IN THE INTERWAR YEARS

A Tank Testing Section was formed at Pinehurst Barracks, Farnborough in September 1921. It existed on a 'temporary basis' for the purpose of 'testing any experimental track machines', chiefly those from DTD&E. The initial complement was thirty-two, one captain, three subalterns and twenty-eight other ranks. A single vehicle was allocated for unit transport – a Crossley Tender. The section was attached to the 2nd Battalion Tank Corps, who were resident at the barracks, and who were responsible for regimental matters. Technical direction came from the Director Royal Artillery in the War Office.

The first commander was Captain H.M. Hordern RA who was sent from Woolwich. He was supported by Lieutenants Williamson and Skinner from the resident 2nd Battalion Tank Corps and Lieutenant Sheryer from the Workshop Training Battalion, Bovington. The section was provided with a single building, which was the store, workshop and office – so the clerical work was carried out in one corner. No storage or benches had been provided.

Initially the section had two Medium D tanks from Charlton Park, which had arrived on 31 August 1921. Over the next twelve months further machines were received and the list of vehicles became:

Source	Vehicle
Vickers Crayford	Medium D
Ordnance Factory (OF) Woolwich	Medium D Tank No. 2
OF Woolwich	Medium D Tank No. 3
DTD&E	Light Infantry Tank
DTD&E	Tropical Tank No. 1
DTD&E	Tropical Tank No. 4
DTD&E	Ammunition Carrier No. 1
Vickers Erith	Vickers Tank No. 1

By December 1922 the section was up to strength, but it was recognised that the need for day-to-day administration to go through the 2nd Battalion was unsatisfactory, and hence on 9 December 1922 a recommendation was made that the section should become a self-contained unit. Thus on 1 April 1923 the section was given the status of a Company and became independent of the Battalion 'except for rations, accommodation and discipline'. The unit took over offices and two hangars at Pinehurst Barracks vacated by the RAMC Medical Store. At this time it was organised into two subsections, a driving and maintenance subsection and a workshop subsection.

The facilities available were improved when Lieutenant Oddy visited the DTD&E at Charlton Park to select suitable machinery and further material was obtained from Bovington workshops in March 1923. As the workload on the section increased a request for more manpower was submitted in October 1923 and implemented in May 1924.

The section was soon requested to test private venture vehicles and the list of vehicles to test in 1924 included:

Source	Vehicle
Armstrong Ltd Coventry	Small Dragon
Vickers Sheffield	Peerless Lorry
Vickers Crayford	Ingoldby Transporter No. 1
Austin	Austin Tractor
Vickers Sheffield	18pdr Tractor Mounting
H.G. Burford London	Burford Kegresse*
Vickers Sheffield	Indian Tank No. 59
Vickers Sheffield	Indian Tank No. 60
V Medium Bn Larkhill	Mk II Dragon No. 41
V Medium Bn Larkhill	Mk II Dragon No. 44
Crossley Motors	Crossley Kegresse

The 'Indian Tanks' 59 and 60 were based on the Vickers Medium Tank and had the transmission of the Mark I and a Hull that resembled the Mark II. The turret only mounted machine guns. The two tanks were delivered from Vickers Ltd in Sheffield for testing in October 1924 and were then shipped to India about a month later. The two tanks arrived in India in January 1925 and were formed as a detachment under Lieutenant J.T. Crocker, Royal Tank Corps (later General Sir John Crocker). For four months they toured India, making a series of long road marches at the end of each of which they gave mobility demonstrations to local infantry in the area.

---

* Kegresse were a make of rubber tracks fitted to a number of vehicles for cross-country use.

On 30 June 1925 the designation 'Tank Testing Section' was changed to 'Tank and Tracked Transport Experimental Establishment'. By this time the unit was responsible both for testing of experimental machines and for Acceptance Tests of production vehicles on behalf of the Chief Inspector of Artillery (CIA). The increased workload meant that in 1926 'Hangar No. 5' was obtained from the RAF for storing up to thirty-one vehicles undergoing acceptance testing. In addition CIA staff were trained to carry out the acceptance tests.

A course for the acceptance tests was defined and included:

a. A gradient of 15° at least 50yd long – a hill about 300yd north of the Ely Inn on Hartford Bridge Flats;
b. A water splash 18in deep with hard bottom – a ford over Blackwater River ½ mile south of the Railway Halt at Sandhurst;
c. One or two ditches etc, but no trenches, tree trunks or 'stunt' obstacles.

A road test to include:

d. One mile of level road (gradient not greater than 1 in 50) – Hartford Flats west of Ely Inn.
e. Six miles of road where the gradient nowhere exceeds 1 in 15 – from AA Box at Blackwater to a milestone on the Basingstoke side of Hartley Row;
f. A continuous down slope of 1 in 12 of half-mile length for brake tests – on the Hale–Odiham road near Beacon Hill.

In light of the growing mechanisation of the army, and the importance and visibility of the unit, it was requested to put on a demonstration of tanks and other vehicles for the Dominion Premiers attending the Imperial Conference. This occurred on Saturday 13 November 1926 and attendance also included Sir Laming Worthington-Evans, Secretary of State for War, Mr Winston Churchill, Chancellor of the Exchequer and Mr Leo Amery, Colonial Secretary. The demonstration took place on Old Dean Common, north of the Staff College at Camberley under very wet and cold conditions.

Vehicles in the demonstration included:

Light Tank Mark I (Likely to be the Vickers Medium which was initially called 'Light');
Three-Man Tank;[*]
Two-man Martel half-track;

---

[*] A3E1 three-man machine-gun carrier which had been delivered to T&TTEE on 29 March 1926.

One-man Martel half-track;
One-man Carden-Loyd (two versions);
Armstrong Siddeley Dragon machine-gun carrier;
Burford Kegresse half-track;
Morris ½ track;
Dragon Mark II with QF 18pdr;
Dragon Mark III with 6in howitzer;
Burford Kegresse with QF 18pdr;
Morris half-track with QF 18pdr;
QF 18pdr self propelled mounting;
QF 13pdr self propelled mounting.

One vehicle delivered to the unit for testing in 1926 was the A1 E1 Independent. In 1931 an Army Officer named Lieutenant Norman Baillie-Stewart obtained photographs and specifications of this vehicle from the Aldershot Military Library and he passed copies of these, along with information on other equipment, to German agents. He was subsequently court-martialled in 1933 under the official secrets act and convicted of treason. As the country was not at war at the time he was given a five-year prison term in the Tower of London and was the last British citizen to be imprisoned there. The information he provided may have inspired the Germans to design the Neubaufahrzeug tank, which, unlike the Independent, did see limited use in the Second World War.

Captain Hordern, who had run the unit since its inception, was awarded the OBE in the King's Birthday Honours list on 3 June 1927. He was replaced on 31 March 1928 by Lieutenant Colonel A.W.C. Richardson DSO RTC; by this time the complement had reached eight officers, 104 other ranks and three civilian draughtsmen. On 1 January 1929 the unit was renamed the 'Mechanical Warfare Experimental Establishment' (MWEE). It was stated that:

> This change of title anticipated a drastic change in the activities of the unit, as in April 1928, the experimental work in connection with all wheeled vehicles previously carried out by the RASC Training College was taken over, and the unit became responsible for all experiments, and trials in connection with every type of Mechanical Vehicle, whether tracked, semi-tracked, or wheeled, prior to their introduction into the service.

A start was made at this time on two new buildings, an up-to-date store and an office, to replace the wartime huts that had been occupied since 1921, and these new buildings were planned to be completed by August 1929.

In April 1928 the unit was requested to provide a demonstration for their Majesties King George V and Queen Mary. The date of the demonstration was to be 17 May and so much urgent work was required to lay on the resulting large-scale demonstration of in-service and experimental vehicles. The demonstration was held in the Miles Hill area just off the Fleet to Aldershot road. It was kept as secret as possible and more than 100 civilian and military police secured the area. The King, accompanied by members of the Army Council, the Commander in Chief Aldershot Command, his staff and members of the Royal Suite rode over from Aldershot. They were joined at the demonstration point by Her Majesty the Queen who had travelled separately by road from Aldershot. The demonstration started as soon as they arrived and consisted of:

a. March past of around 50 vehicles at speed along the main Fleet–Aldershot road. Machines were grouped in their various categories with 500yd between each group and 100yd between each vehicle. At the saluting point, which had been prepared by the Royal Engineers, machines saluted by turning their guns or turrets towards their Majesties and dipping them. The wheel-cum-track machines[*] halted at the saluting point to demonstrate the ease with which they could change from wheels to tracks and vice-versa;

b. Cross-country runs by selected machines;

c. Hill climbing demonstrations by selected machines;

d. All vehicles formed up for presentation.

The King and Queen were reported to appear keenly interested in the performance of the various machines and were driven up one of the minor slopes of Miles Hill in a Morris six-wheel staff car. The demonstration passed without any hitches or breakdowns and on return to barracks the unit was congratulated by the Director of Mechanisation Major General P.C. Peck CB DSO. The small hill south of Miles Hill from where their Majesties witnessed the demonstration was christened King Hill.

With both the War Office and the newly constituted Technical Subcommittee of the Mechanical Warfare Board requesting trials and experiments, the increased workload led to another request for an uplift in establishment. Only half of the increase requested was approved so from 1 April 1929 the unit consisted of eleven officers and 160 other ranks. With the increase in numbers the unit was reorganised into:

a. Headquarters and administrative wing;

b. Technical wing;

---

[*] There was much interest in such machines due to the very short life of tracks at that time.

c.   Driving wing;

d.   Technical Stores Section;

e.   Workshops.

In view of continuing British interests in India, the Far East and the Middle East, a lot of emphasis was placed on ensuring that vehicles were suitable for these environments. The Long Valley area was used for trials as during dry periods it was sandy and could replicate abrasive sandy conditions in the Middle East. However, it was necessary to carry out some trials in theatres of interest. An extended trial was carried out in Egypt in the early part of 1932. A Convoy consisting of a Crossley light six-wheeled lorry, a Commer 'Raider' four-wheeled 30cwt lorry, a Morris-Commercial RS 12cwt four-wheel van and a Riley 9HP car left Cairo on 16 January for a long-distance test run to Southern Sudan. The outward route followed the Nile Valley to Rejaf, a distance of 2,830 miles. The return journey to Cairo went along the shores of the Red Sea via Port Sudan, a distance of 2,241 miles. The convoy returned to Cairo on 16 April 1932. Varied conditions were experienced during the journey including mud roads, hard gravel, sandy soil, very heavy sand, black cotton soil, trackless desert and hilly ground. Terrain and environmental data were obtained to inform requirements for cooling, tyre performance and general durability, with the report noting that 'modern British vehicles of the types developed and specified by the War Department should be capable of operating under most conditions likely to be encountered in any theatre of operations'.

The MWEE undertook a second convoy in Egypt in 1933. This time the vehicles were:

Commer Raider 30cwt lorry;
Crossley forward-control 30cwt War Department six-wheeled lorry;
Hillman Wizard four-seater open car;
Morris RS type 12cwt four-wheel van;
Morris Minor 8hp car with standard two-seater body;
Morris C type 30cwt four-wheel lorry.

The Commer Raider 30cwt lorry and the Morris RS 12cwt van had also been part of the 1932 experimental convoy, but this time had different tyres in order to note any improvements in performance. The convoy left Cairo on 25 March and followed a 3,557-mile route across varied terrain. The outward route followed the Nile Valley via Asyut, the Selima Oasis, Dongola, El Obeid, Costi and Khartoum. The return route was via Atbara, Abu Hamed, Wadi Halfa, Luxor and Asyut with Cairo reached on 4 June. The performance of the vehicles was reported as generally satisfactory with all of them completing the route.

During the forty-one running days a total of only eight hours were lost due to mechanical defects. There were a few cases of overheating and these were mainly attributed to the obstruction of radiators by grass seed and air filters by sand. An important aspect of the test was an investigation of the behaviour of various types of wide-section low-pressure tyres and the information obtained was to prove invaluable in the future.

In 1934 MWEE was renamed again, becoming the Mechanisation Experimental Establishment (MEE).

4

REARMAMENT

Throughout the 1920s and 1930s the development of tanks was not well co-ordinated, which, in light of the acute funding shortages, was far from ideal. The formation of the Mechanisation Board in 1934 was an attempt to improve matters. The person responsible for tank development was the Director of Mechanisation at the War Office who controlled MWEE and the Design Departments at Woolwich. The Mechanisation Board could acquire tanks from three sources:

a. In-house designs by the Superintendent of Design at Woolwich;
b. The Board placing contracts directly with industry;
c. Procuring private venture vehicles from firms such as Vickers.

This meant the funds available to DD(V) at Woolwich were very limited. The situation was not helped by the General Staff frequently changing requirements for armour, vehicle speed and armament. Hence when rearmament started in the 1930s the status of tank design in Great Britain was at a low.

The lack of focus and clear requirements resulted in fifteen different tank projects during the period from 1934 to the start of the Second World War. One factor that influenced the subsequent inadequacies of British tanks during the Second World War was the policy to focus on three classes of tank:

Small light machine-gun-armed tanks for reconnaissance;
Cruiser tanks with an emphasis on mobility;
Infantry tanks with an emphasis on protection but requiring a low top speed.

The requirement for three classes of tank was formally endorsed as policy in the 1937 Annual Report of the Mechanisation Board.

The emphasis on either mobility or protection meant that firepower was often neglected, even though the proponents of mechanised warfare recognised that the best counter to tanks would be other tanks. The overall balance of performance of the resulting tanks was often poor and even though some did have reasonable attributes the army tended to buy light tanks because they were cheaper and were seen as having utility for operations throughout the British Empire.

In 1926 the Superintendent of Design had started work with Vickers to develop the A6 Medium Tank, which was intended to replace the Medium Mark II. A design driver was a weight limit of 15.5 tons which led to the nickname of '16 tonners'. A mock-up was completed in March 1927 and the first two of three prototypes were delivered to MWEE in June 1928 for trials. Various engines, both petrol and diesel, and turret arrangements were tested, but overall the vehicle was considered inadequate leading to a redesign. The new design, called the Medium Mark III, had a revised turret and improved armour. Three Medium Mark IIIs were built, one by Vickers and two by the Royal Ordnance Factory at Woolwich, but it was considered too expensive and no further production was undertaken. Development activities on the Mark III stopped in 1931. One novel feature of the vehicle was that it had a very early implementation of a 'collective protection' system. This is a system where filtered air is provided to the crew compartment to provide ventilation in a chemical warfare environment. Trials of the 'Porton Filtration Unit' were carried out in June 1931 and Major R.A. Hepple of the Royal Army Medical Corps, noting the clearance of the smell of oil and 'fug' when the unit was running, reported that, 'The installation of the Porton filtration unit caused a distinct improvement in hygienic conditions in the fighting chamber, and will undoubtedly have a beneficial effect on the health of personnel of the Royal Tank Corps.' The three Medium Mark IIIs were taken into service by the HQ of the Tank Brigade and one was fitted out as a Command Tank.

In 1929 the Chief Superintendent of Design started work on an experimental medium tank and the Ordnance Factory at Woolwich produced three prototypes of what was the A7 Medium Tank. Development of this vehicle stopped in 1937, but it helped form the basis of the A12 Matilda Infantry Tank, which was developed by the Vulcan Foundry.

In 1934 Sir John Carden of Vickers-Armstrong designed the Cruiser Mark I (A9), which was intended as a cheaper alternative to the A6. Design of a heavier but slower version with thicker armour (A10) was started soon after. The resulting vehicles ended up very similar to each other, but both went into production as the Cruiser Mark I (A9) and Cruiser Mark II (A10). They saw action in France and the Western Desert although numbers built were limited as by the time production contracts were ready (1937 for the A9 and 1938 for the A10) work was underway on the superior A13.

After years of limited funding the remains of expertise in tank design was to be found in Vickers-Armstrong and DD(V) at Woolwich, but when rearmament started a number of other contractors were brought in to develop tanks. These included Bedford, Leyland, the LMS Railway works, Nuffield Mechanisation, the Vulcan Foundry and Harland and Wolff. Nuffield Mechanisation was one of the more prominent of these companies. It had been formed by the Morris Motors group to build aero-engines, but orders did not materialise so the organisation turned its attention to tanks.

In September 1936 Lieutenant Colonel Martel, in his role of Assistant Director Mechanisation, visited army manoeuvres in the Soviet Union where he was particularly impressed by the performance of the Soviet BT3 tanks. The design of this tank had been based on the M1931 tank designed by John Walter Christie in the USA, two of which had been bought by the Soviets. The War Office therefore asked Nuffield Mechanisation to act as their agent in buying a Christie vehicle. Following receipt of this request Mr Oliver Boden, an ex-Vickers employee who now worked for Nuffield, contacted Christie and arranged to buy a vehicle for £8,000. The vehicle bought was the M1932, an improved version of the M1931 which had been offered to the US Army. They had turned it down mainly due to frustrations in trying to work with Christie. To meet US regulations the basic vehicle was exported to the UK as an agricultural tractor with the more war-like parts said to have been sent separately as 'grapefruit'. The vehicle reached the UK on 17 November 1936 and it was delivered to MEE for trials. Tested over 687 miles, of which 327 were cross-country, the vehicle was reported to have reached a speed of 63.4mph on a slightly downhill run. Despite the impressive automotive performance it was assessed that, as it stood, it was unsuitable to meet British Army requirements. It was, however, used by Nuffield Mechanisation as the basis for the A13 Mark I or Cruiser Tank Mark III.

The A13 was wider and higher than the M1932, in order to mount a 2pdr gun, and was 2 tons heavier. The basic concept was defined by January 1937 and an initial order for sixty-five followed a year later in January 1938 with the first vehicles being delivered in December that year. The A13 Mark I was followed by the A13 Mark II, which had an improved turret and was the first vehicle to use spaced armour. The A13 Mark I and II saw action in France and the Western Desert. The final version of the A13, the Mark III, also called the Covenanter or

TOG 2 Turret, as used in protection trials, showing a mantlet designed to mount three coaxial weapons. (Crown Copyright-MOD)

Cruiser Mark V, was designed by the LMS Railway Company with input from the Mechanisation Board. Delivery started in 1940 when tanks were needed quickly after the fall of France, but it proved to be very unreliable and although over 1,700 were built it was only ever used for training.

Meanwhile Vickers-Armstrong had developed the A11 Matilda 1, which met a request for a tank 'built down to a price' and cost only £6,000. The requirement for the A11 stated that the 'heaviest possible armour was essential' although it was only required to have a top speed of 5mph and was armed with a machine gun. A total of 139 were built and some saw action in France.

Work on two experimental heavy cruisers was started in 1938, neither of which went into production. The A14 was built by the LMS Railway Co., who had design support from the DTD, and the A16 was built by Nuffield Mechanisation. The A16 weighed over 21 tons and used a heavier version of the Christie suspension. An interesting aside with the A16 was that when a major design problem arose with the vehicle Thomson and Taylor, a Brooklands-based racing-car firm who had been involved in the design of the Bluebird Land Speed Record car, was asked to help; they very quickly carried out some redesign work and built some components. Later the prototype was used to investigate transmission and steering problems in the A13s and became the first tank fitted with a 'Merritt' controlled differential steering system.

One in-house design by the DTD was the A20, which met requirements for an assault tank with a long track length for crossing trenches. The prototype was built by Harland and Wolff, but development was subsequently taken over by Vauxhall Motors and became the basis of the A22 Churchill. Another project of interest was the TOG (The Old Gang) tank designed by the Special Vehicle Design Committee. This committee included a number of those involved in the development of the original First World War tanks including Swinton and designers at Fosters of Lincoln. It was a slow-moving unwieldy 70-ton vehicle with solid suspension conceived to attack the Siegfried Line. The project was dropped when it became apparent that the nature of warfare was very different from the defensive trench warfare of the First World War. The DTD had some involvement in the TOG programme and, for example, supported the design of the TOG 2 turret. This was manufactured by Messrs Stothert & Pitt Ltd under a contract placed by William Foster and Co. The turret was made from 3in armour plate supplied by the Admiralty with an inner layer of 0.5in steel. DTD provided advice on design and testing. For ballistic trials purposes the turret was fitted with an obsolete mantlet designed to mount a 2pdr gun, 3in howitzer and a machine gun. This mantlet had been designed to meet a requirement for armament that had been seriously proposed as an alternative to mounting a 6pdr gun in cruiser tanks and would have been a nightmare for the crew. Trials, which included attacks by 6pdr anti-tank rounds and 25pdr proof shot, demonstrated the ability of the inner skin to provide protection against secondary fragments should the outer shell be damaged or bolts dislodged.

5

TANK DEVELOPMENT IN THE SECOND WORLD WAR AND THE ROLE OF THE DTD

At the start of the Second World War the majority of tanks in service were light tanks and efforts to address inadequacies in the quality and availability of vehicles was hampered by a lack of resources as aircraft and ships were given priority. The expenditure on tanks in the build-up to rearmament was:

1931	£357,000
1932	£309,000
1933	£315,000
1934	£501,000 (The year Germany started rearmament)
1935	£772,000 (The year Italy invaded Abyssinia)
1936	£842,000 (The year Germany reoccupied the Rhineland)
1937	£3,625,000

The £500,000 spent in 1934 represented only about 1 per cent of the total army budget. Further problems had arisen from the office of the Master General of the Ordnance (MGO). At the time of rearmament the MGO was General Elles who had originally commanded the Tank Corps in the First World War; however, instead of being an advocate of tanks he was convinced that the development of anti-tank guns had so reduced their utility he was unwilling to commit significant funds to their procurement. It was only when it was demonstrated that the Infantry Tank Mark I was proof against 37mm and 47mm anti-tank guns that procurement started in earnest.

Following the Experimental Force Trials in 1927 and development of the doctrine captured in the 'Purple Primer' it had been agreed in 1933 that a single Tank Division be formed although even by the start of the Second World War it was still not fully equipped. The British Expeditionary Force in France was equipped with 342 light tanks, seventy-seven Matilda 1s, twenty-three Matilda 2s and 150 Cruisers consisting of twenty-four A9s, thirty-one A10s and ninety-five A13s. Even at this stage the inadequacies of British tanks were recognised by some; before deploying to France Brigadier Vivian Pope, the adviser of armoured vehicles at the General Headquarters of the British Expeditionary Force, wrote to the War Office to say, 'We must have thicker armour on our fighting vehicles and every tank must carry a cannon. The 2pdr is good enough now, but only just. We must mount something better and put it behind 40 to 80mm of armour.' His concerns were well founded and during the fighting leading to the fall of France the light tanks were all but useless, and although the Cruisers showed some utility they suffered from a lack of armour. Only the infantry tanks had any significant success when on 21 May 1940 fifty-eight Matilda Mark Is and sixteen Matilda Mark IIs took part in a counter-attack. This caused much confusion amongst German forces, who found them largely impervious to their anti-tank guns, and it delayed their advance to the extent that it made the withdrawal to Dunkirk and subsequent evacuation possible. Unfortunately the counter-attack itself was not supported and could not be sustained.

Following the fall of France a very limited number of tanks were left to defend the United Kingdom. Exact numbers are not clear but probably consisted of around 407 light tanks, 141 cruiser tanks and 140 infantry tanks. Therefore the priority became re-equipping the army to defend against invasion. In 1938 the Secretary of State for War had put forward a proposal that led to the formation of the Ministry of Supply. This was set up with the Liberal MP Leslie Burgin, previously Minister for Transport, as Minister for Supply from July 1939 to May 1940. A key principle behind the thinking and policies of the ministry was that successful businessmen would have the skills for mobilising industry for war. Organisations within the War Office concerned with the Design, Development and Procurement of weapon systems were transferred from the War Office to the Ministry of Supply – with the office of MGO placed in abeyance. Thus the responsibility for delivering tanks was separated from the War Office and hence from direct contact with the operational user. This resulted in the situation where the priority of the Ministry of Supply was to meet the production targets it was being set and it did not want to put delivery at risk by the design changes or new designs being requested by the War Office. Existing contracts and production lines were kept running, leading to the delivery of more light tanks that were already known to be largely useless.

Meanwhile the Mechanisation Board was evacuated from Woolwich to a small Victorian Manor House near to Egham, called Woodlee, and the Design Sections DD(V) and DD(M) to Riverbank Flats in nearby Staines. Hence these departments had moved close to their eventual home on Chobham Common. At that time the Mechanisation Experimental Establishment remained at Farnborough.

In order to facilitate the delivery of enough suitable tanks a new body – the Tank Board – was formed on 29 May 1940 to act as the interface between the

War Office and the Ministry of Supply. It was suggested that Major General Hobart, who had played a key role in the mechanisation exercises, should be put in charge of 'tanks'. In 1938 Hobart had formed the 'Mobile Force Egypt', the forerunner of the Desert Rats, but had been dismissed into retirement due to his unconventional ideas. In 1940, when the suggestion was made, he was a Lance Corporal in the Home Guard. The idea of such an advocate of mechanised warfare in that role was too much for the Army Council so they offered him the post of the Command of Royal Armoured Corps (RAC) with the caveat that this post had no authority over tank design. Hobart turned that post down but went on to form the 79th Armoured Division, which, with its range of engineer assault vehicles, played a key role at D-Day. The role of the Command of the RAC was then taken by Martel, who by then had been promoted to General, and he focused on training suitable commanders for armoured warfare.

After reviewing the situation for several weeks, the Tank Board made recommendations that resulted in the dismissal of the Director General of Tanks and Transport along with certain members of his staff. He was replaced by a new DG, Mr Geoffrey Burton, who immediately set up a Directorate of Tank Production and appointed one of the members of the Tank Board, Mr A.A.M. Durrant – formerly Chief Engineer London Transport – to the post of Director of Tank Design. At the same time a new department (TT2) was formed within the Ministry of Supply at Euston House in London to address wheeled vehicles.

Considerable difficulties faced the new Tank Board, chief among them being:

- The imminent danger of invasion, which made it imperative for any tanks, regardless of performance, to be produced in quantity as quickly as possible;
- The War Office hastily changing its priority from a preponderance of assault tanks for static warfare in France to a preponderance of cruiser tanks for operations in North Africa;
- The Ministry of Aircraft production having an absolute priority in the deployment of labour, machine tools and materials;
- The available production facilities being committed to the building of Matilda, Valentine, Covenanter and Crusader Tanks despite these all having known limitations.

The situation was not helped by the range of new manufacturers, often in the rail and automotive industry, who had no background in armoured vehicle design and manufacture.

The Department of Tank Design lists the following principal staff members:

Deputy Director General Tank Design   Mr A.A.M. Durrant
Deputy Directors   Col W.M. Blagden RT
                                      Mr L.F. Little

Principal Technical Officer	Mr D.M.F. Sheryer
Senior Technical Officers	Maj. H. de J. Keays RAOC
	Maj. R.G. Shaw RAOC
	Maj. D.M. Rycroft RE
	Mr N. Niblett
	Mr W.J. Semmons (Later to become DD(Wheeled Vehicles) at FVRDE)
	Mr A.T.G. Priddle
	Mr A.E.H. Masters (Later to be Director FVRDE)
Superintendent	Maj. J.L. Morton RAOC
Assistant Superintendents	Mr A.T. Sweeney
	Capt. J.J. Davis Dorset Regt
	Lt H.F. Barnard
	Capt. K.C.C. Hunter RAOC
Senior Design Officers	Mr A.A. Sykes
	Mr D.C. Brown
	Mr W.J. Mesher
	Mr G.W. Patchett
	Mr A.C. Lock
Officer in charge technical records	Capt. C.E. Iliffe RAOC

The Directorate of Tank Production rapidly expanded, but the Department of Tank Design, which consisted mainly of some staff from DD(V) at Woolwich and the Mechanisation Board, was not given any priority. The accommodation the units had moved to in Egham and Staines was unsuitable, and since these locations were classed as outstations they could only offer low salaries, and hence did not attract the best engineers. Attempts to secure more staff and better facilities were largely unsuccessful and the best new recruits were staff on loan from industry.

One member of DTD of note was Leslie Little, who had worked for Vickers-Armstrong at their Chertsey factory. He had a number of far-reaching ideas. In particular he believed running gear should be as efficient as possible and some of his ideas were incorporated into the Tetrarch light tank, which had hydro-pneumatic suspension and a steering system based on bowing the tracks. The Tetrarch had been developed by Vickers-Armstrong in 1937, intended as the Light Tank Mark VII. Unlike previous light tanks it was armed with a cannon – the same 40mm 2pdr as contemporary Cruiser tanks. In May 1938 the prototype was delivered to MEE who, following testing, recommended a number of design changes. The situation regarding production was subject to change reflecting the often confused direction at that time. In November 1938 an order for 120 vehicles was placed. In July 1940 this was cut to seventy, but since materials had been procured and production started for more than seventy, the number was revised up to 220. Eventually 177 were built and a number were supplied to the Soviet Union. The vehicles in British Army service were eventually used as airborne tanks flown in gliders in support of D-Day.

After the fall of France the General Staff priorities for tanks were:

- More cruiser tanks and less infantry tanks;
- A better gun than the 2pdr;
- Thicker armour on both cruiser and infantry tanks.

Design of the Cruiser Mark VI, the A15 Crusader, had been started in 1938 by Nuffield Mechanisation as their own development of the A13, and it first saw action in June 1941. Despite the request for a better gun than the 2pdr this was the weapon fitted to the Crusader Mark I on the basis that changing production to the 57mm 6pdr, which had been available in 1938, would delay delivery. Meanwhile the German Army carried on up-gunning their Panzer IIIs from 37mm to 50mm and, soon after the start of the Russian Campaign, started to up-gun Panzer IVs to a higher performance 75mm gun. The Crusader Mark III was eventually fitted with the 6pdr, but that version did not reach troops until August 1942.

One tank fielded in large numbers was the Valentine. This had been designed by Vickers-Armstrong using much of the technology used on the Cruisers Mark I and II. A proposal for this vehicle had been submitted to the War Office on St Valentine's Day 1938 – hence the name. A production order was placed in July 1939. No pilot models were built, as the automotives were already proven, and the first production model was ready in May 1940. Like other British tanks at that time it only had the 2pdr gun.

As already stated DD(M) had designed the A20, which was being used by Vauxhall as the basis for the A22 Infantry Tank. This was required to have similar

A22 Churchill Tank.
(Copyright W. Suttie)

levels of protection to the Matilda II but with an increased gap-crossing and step-height capability. The design of the A22 was well advanced and could not be readily changed and the Tank Board considered abandoning the project in favour of manufacturing more Cruiser tanks. It was, however, the first tank to be specifically designed for mass production and it met the Prime Minister's personal insistence on a requirement for 500 assault vehicles; in light of the PM's support it became known as the Churchill. Design had started in July 1940 and due to the urgent need for tanks it was planned to be in production within a year. The first vehicle was running by December of that year, but due to the haste with which it had been designed and lack of tank experience within Vauxhall there were reliability problems. It was not until August 1942 that the Churchill was used in action. Like the Crusader it was initially fitted with the outmoded 2pdr gun, but by October 1942 six Churchills with the 6pdr gun reached the 8th Army in North Africa. The Churchill was the first tank to be fitted with a Merritt regenerative gearbox, which improved the effective power when steering.

Meanwhile Nuffield Mechanisation, design parents of the Crusader, were tasked with designing a new Cruiser tank with heavier armour and a three-man turret mounting a 6pdr gun. The DTD were given specific instructions to keep away from the design process. Having been relieved, for the time being, of any responsibility for the design of new tanks, and having limited facilities to do so anyway, the DTD focused on trying to overcome the shortcomings of existing tanks.

The DTD undertook work to deal with reliability issues associated with the Matilda II. When it was designed use was made of a pair of commercial vehicle engines because at the time there was no suitable engine of sufficient power available. It had been wrongly assumed that a reliable truck engine would be suitable in a tank environment, and also no account was taken of issues related to coupling two such engines together. The problem was ultimately solved by the use of a different engine in a rationalised layout. Another problem with the Matilda was gearbox reliability as it had been designed for use in a 16-ton vehicle, not one of 26 tons. A Wilson epicyclic regenerative gearbox was developed for the Matilda, which would have improved reliability and manoeuvrability, but it was not put into production because the Ministry of Supply believed the change would slow down production. Instead some later production vehicles were fitted with a ratchet mechanism inside the crew compartment to enable a manual gear change should the unreliable air-servo fail. Much work was also done on the very unreliable Covenanter, but by the time the issues had been resolved the tank was well out of date and even more unsuitable for operational use.

Even when modifications for defects had been developed in a timely manner and had been accepted by the Ministry of Supply they had to be introduced to existing production runs without disrupting delivery; this meant solutions took inordinately long to be fielded.

The unsatisfactory nature of tanks being issued to units was soon recognised by the politicians. Also there was an insistent claim from the Special Vehicle Development Committee (SVDC) that there should be more control over British tank design and production. The result was further changes in the departments concerned although for the interim the DTD was still not authorised to undertake its own designs.

In October 1940 Mr Herbert Morrison, who replaced Leslie Burgin, left the Ministry of Supply and Sir Andrew Duncan took over as the Minister responsible. The chairman of the Tank Board was replaced by Sir James Lithgow and its membership expanded to include representatives from industry and the Chairman of the SVDC. In addition to chairing the Tank Board, Sir James Lithgow took on responsibility of Controller General of Mechanical Equipment over the head of Mr Geoffrey Burton who then concentrated on production rather than his wider R&D role. A new post of Director General of Mechanical Equipment was created and filled by Mr James Weir.

None of these reorganisations strengthened the position of the DTD and in many ways gave more power to the manufacturers. One example of the issues faced by DTD was that it repeatedly argued for the introduction of welding into the fabrication of tank hulls, but this was strongly and successfully opposed by industry even though the benefits had been demonstrated on armoured cars. It was not until the Cromwell went into production in 1943 that welding was used for tanks.

MEE at Farnborough was renamed in May 1941 to become the Experimental Wing, Department of Tank Design. It consisted of two sections, 'A' and 'B', responsible for tracked and wheeled vehicles respectively.

In June 1941 Lord Beaverbrook replaced Sir Andrew Duncan at the Ministry of Supply, which set in process further changes with the departure of Sir James Lithgow and Mr James Weir and the appointment of Mr Oliver Lucas as Controller of Research and Development of all weapons and transport. Geoffrey Burton became chairman of the Tank Board and Mr H. Ainsworth was appointed to the new post of Controller of Tank Design. Mr Ainsworth was in the USA at the time of his appointment, having been appointed by telegraph without an interview. On his return to the UK he was dismissed by Lord Beaverbrook having officially been in post for three days. Then in December 1941 Mr W.A. Robotham of Rolls-Royce was appointed as Chief Engineer Tank Design and put in charge of research and development of armoured vehicles. Lord Weir became the fourth Chairman of the Tank Board in around nineteen months and the DTD was reorganised. The impact on the ability of the DTD to carry out its work can be imagined as each change brought the need to familiarise the new management with the issues and challenges.

A statement to a House of Commons sitting on 1 July 1942 listed the following as members of the Tank Board:

Chairman	Viscount Weir
War Office Representatives:	Lieutenant General R.M. Weeks (Deputy Chief of the Imperial General Staff)
	Major General D.G. Watson (Assistant Chief of the Imperial General Staff)
	Major General A.W.C. Richardson (Director Armoured Fighting Vehicles)
	Major General E.B. Rowcroft (Director Mechanical Engineering)
Ministry of Supply	Sir William Rootes (Chairman of the Supply Council)
	Sir George Usher (Director General Tank Supply)
	Mr Oliver Lucas (Controller General of Research and Development)
	Mr W.A. Robotham (Chief Engineer Tank Design
USA Liaison	Colonel G.A. Green

In September 1942 Viscount Weir was replaced by Commander E.R. Micklem who, coming from Vickers-Armstrong, was the first Chairman of the Tank Board to be appointed because he was familiar with tanks. He was given the post of Controller of Armoured Fighting Vehicles. The heads of the firms of Vauxhall Motors, Nuffield Mechanisations and Leyland Motors made representations to the Minister of Supply, who was once again Sir Andrew Duncan, for the removal of Mr W.A. Robotham as Chief Engineer Tank Design and the suppression of DTD. These demands were not met in full and the DTD continued to function although still with limited terms of reference and with further reorganisations. The stated function of the DTD was to 'deal with projects that had been accepted for production, addressing such defects that might arise during production or service and acting in an advisory capacity to manufacturers through the resident engineers appointed by Controller AFV' – these 'resident engineers' were not under DTD control.

The association of tank research and development with Chobham Common and the birth of what became the 'Chertsey establishment' came in 1942. The DTD was transferred the short distance there from Egham to a purpose-built establishment constructed on the site of what was a small RAF camp (RAF Chobham). During the week 22–29 June 1942 'A' section of the Experimental Wing of the DTD, together with the workshops, was also moved to the site. The experimental wing was given the title Fighting Vehicle Proving Establishment (FVPE), with a charter to carry out development testing of armoured vehicles on behalf of the DTD and manufacturers, and acceptance testing on behalf of the War Office. In addition to the area already occupied by the camp, around 37 acres of adjacent common land was requisitioned for vehicle testing. Before the move started plans were already in hand for the first specialist test facility to be built at the site, a cold chamber for testing vehicles, and this was commissioned in 1943. The new site at Chobham Common also housed the School of Tank Technology (STT), which was part of the Military College of Science. The STT ran its first course in December 1942. On at least one occasion during the war the Chertsey site was bombed – when a hangar door was left open and the bomber spotted the stray light.

In addition to the site at Chobham, the DTD had a 'Tank Armament Research Wing' at Porton Down. This section occupied a large hut (Building 102), a 'universal' concrete hut, which was used as an Optical Laboratory (Building 11), and two hangars for vehicle storage. The section also took over the conference room in the Porton Headquarters Building.

As previously noted there was a lack of expertise in the field of tank technology and design, making the School of Tank Technology courses very important but challenging to staff. Co-location with the DTD helped as it gave ready access to the few available experts. To support the courses both in-house experts and those from industry were brought in to lecture and write course material. E.W.E. Micklethwaite generated textbooks on mobility and tracked vehicles and H.E Merritt was brought in to lecture and provide textbooks on gearboxes. The STT textbooks formed the basis of much of the material used at the Armour School later set up at Bovington camp when the school at Chertsey closed. Another benefit of co-location at Chertsey was having access to captured German equipment that was brought there for evaluation. Reports on technical aspects of captured equipment were generated by the school for use by students and the wider technical community. An example of such a report is an unreferenced document by Major W. de L.M. Messenger RTR of the Armament Section SST dated June 1944. This compares the design and performance of muzzle brakes fitted to the German 7.62cm PAK,* 7.5cm KWK40 as fitted to the Panzer IV and the 8.8cm KWK36 as fitted to the Tiger. Following the end of the war teaching material was supplemented by translations of German technical information. An example of this is FVDD Running Gear Branch Report ST12 dated 12 December 1945. This is a translation by a Mrs Hamilton of SST of a paper presented by Dr Lehr of MAN to the German Ministry of Armaments and War Production on 28 January 1944. The paper is entitled 'The springing and damping of the suspension of the armoured fighting vehicle'. As well as suspension design theory and results of tests on German vehicles and test beds it includes brief comments on the T34, Crusader and Sherman suspension solutions.

Meanwhile the development of a suitable cruiser tank by industry was complicated by the lack of a stable policy on tank power units. It was recognised

---

* A modified Russian 7.62 Model 1936 Field Gun.

Centaur gun-firing trials at Porton Down – part of experimentation to reduce the obscuration. (Crown Copyright-MOD)

that at around 320–330hp the Liberty engine then in use in Cruiser tanks did not have enough power for the heavier better-protected tanks being envisaged. The problem was taken on by W.A. Robotham at Rolls-Royce cars who was keen to keep his design and development team of automotive engineers together. He set about looking at whether existing Rolls-Royce aero engines could be used in place of the Liberty engine. The team first considered an unsupercharged Kestrel engine with a modified carburettor and ignition settings, but, although it showed potential to provide more power than the Liberty engine, it could not meet longer-term requirements for engines of up to 600hp. The team then looked at the Merlin engine. The supercharger, reduction gears and other ancillaries required for use as an aero engine were removed and modified Zenith carburettors fitted. This resulted in a significant reduction in cost and complexity. The Merlin had an advantage in that it could readily be fitted in the space occupied by a Liberty engine, and hence a Crusader tank was thus modified with the new engine – a procedure that took five months. In September 1941 it was sent to the DTD for testing. Initial test runs were promising with the vehicle reaching speeds of up to 50mph and so further tests were carried out with the vehicle covering 3,600 miles. These tests confirmed that the gearbox and suspension of the Crusader could not cope with an engine of twice the power it was designed for. Rolls-Royce was therefore asked to not only develop the tank version of the Merlin but also other automotive ancillaries. Rolls-Royce agreed to this on the condition that they were financed with an 'open credit of one million pounds' and would be free from external interference. Lord Beaverbrook himself sent a telegram agreeing to these conditions, the first of which further distanced the DTD from tank development work.

Robotham set up a facility at the Rolls-Royce plant at Clan Foundry at Belper to undertake development work and a member of his staff identified some waste ground some 5 miles away at Allestree that was suitable for vehicle testing. As already mentioned at this time Robotham was also appointed Chief Engineer Tank

Design within the Ministry of Supply. A key challenge for the Rolls-Royce team was how to keep the engine cool within the confines of a tank engine bay and so they developed a new layout for the radiators and very efficient fans and drives. In 1943 work on the engine was transferred to Rover under an agreement that allowed Rolls-Royce to focus on the development of the Whittle Gas Turbines.

Despite the successful development of what was called the Meteor engine there was still concern that building this would direct resources away from the Merlin aero-engine version, and also a significant investment had been made in the facilities to manufacture the Nuffield Liberty engine. Hence the choice of engine for new Cruiser tanks switched between the use of an uprated Liberty engine and the Meteor engine, a state of affairs which led to three similar tanks being built, the Cavalier, Centaur and Cromwell. Each had different engine and gearbox configurations and between them had Nuffield Mechanisation, Leyland Motors, Birmingham Carriage and Wagon Co. and Vauxhall all involved at various times in design and production. The Cavalier was the first Cruiser to be designed during the war and was meant to take on board operational lessons. It was based on the Crusader but had wider tracks and thicker armour. It used the same power train and so had many of the same mechanical limitations. This was followed by the Centaur, which went into production in late 1942. This tank should have had the Meteor engine, but it was decided that none could be spared and so it reverted to the same Liberty engine as the Crusader and Cavalier. It did, however, have a new Merritt-Brown gearbox, which improved performance and reliability. Finally the Cromwell went into production in early 1943 with the Meteor engine and the Merritt-Brown gearbox. Although a very mobile and reliable tank, even when fitted with a 75mm gun from late 1943, it was outclassed by contemporary German Tigers and Panthers.

During the period of rearmament and the early war years the policy had been to fit anti-tank guns to tanks. A change in policy was issued on 3 January 1943 when the General Staff requested that more tanks be fitted with a dual-purpose gun with

Comet. (Copyright W. Suttie)

both an Anti-Tank (AT) and High-Explosive (HE) capability. This decision was based on operational experience in North Africa with US-supplied tanks. These had a dual-purpose 75mm gun and around 50 per cent of the ammunition fired was HE. The new policy resulted in the development of a 75mm weapon, which used many components from the 57mm 6pdr but could fire the two types of ammunition, including US 75mm ammunition. The new gun started to be fielded in October 1943 and was eventually used on the Churchill, Cromwell and Valentine.

The last in the line of cruiser tanks using Christie suspension was the Comet. This mounted a version of the 76.2mm 17pdr anti-tank gun (called the 77mm), which at last provided an accurate and potent weapon for taking on enemy tanks.

As stated the main development activities and trials of DTD at Chobham were focused on addressing problems associated with in-service vehicles. The scope of activities is reflected in establishment reports issued in 1944, which cover a range of topics including:

- Reliability;
- Alternative drivers' seats;
- Road wheel tyres;
- Removal of top rollers;
- Towing trials of a Crocodile Trailer;[*]
- Wheel lock nuts;
- Tracks for use on ice.

One piece of important work carried out by the DTD was the fitting of the 17pdr gun to the Sherman. This had been claimed to be impossible by some but was successfully carried out by the DTD. The resulting vehicle, the Sherman Firefly, was one of the most potent available to the British Army after the D-Day landings, and such was the effectiveness of the gun that the German Army were given orders to seek out and destroy the Fireflies as a priority over the normal Sherman variants. The work at the DTD was led by W.G.K. Kilbourn who had worked as an engineer at Vickers. The main challenge was that the recoil of the 17pdr was too long to accommodate in the Sherman Turret. To address this problem a new recoil system was developed, which consisted of two new cylinders, one each side of the gun. The gun was rotated through 90 degrees to allow loading from the left – rather than from on top. Other modifications designed by the DTD included replacing the hull machine gun and assistant driver position with ammunition stowage, provision of a hatch for the loader and moving the radio to an armoured box on the rear of the turret. Production of the Firefly started in early 1944 and around 342 had been delivered by 31 May ready for the D-Day landings.

---

[*] The Crocodile was a flame-thrower version of the Churchill tank.

In industry some further developments of infantry tanks were undertaken that reached pilot-model stage including the A33, based on the Cromwell, the A38 Valiant, which was a development of the Valentine, and the A43 Black Prince, which was a development of the Churchill. However by 1944, when the Valiant pilot was built, the concept of the heavy 'Infantry' tank was seen as obsolete. The lack of knowledge within industry and inability to understand operational lessons and requirements was illustrated by the Valiant. This had a very poor driver's station, which was too small when operating closed down, and ground clearance down to 7in. One other heavy-tank development was the A39 Tortoise, which had a 32pdr gun with limited traverse in a fixed superstructure. At 78 tons and with a range of 50 miles it was not very practical, but six were built and used on troop trials and experimentation after the end of the war.

In August 1943 the DTD was at last authorised to start design work on a 'heavy cruiser tank' designated A41. The requirements were driven by the user needs and included:

- An armament that was capable of defeating the German Tiger tank, which was just coming into service, and also able to fire HE;
- Armour that was proof against the German 88mm gun;
- Attention to be given to improved mine protection compared with existing vehicles;
- A high top speed was not needed, but there was a requirement for high-agility cross-country;
- A high-speed reverse gear.

The DTD worked with the design parents, AEC Ltd, and the first mock-up was available nine months later in May 1944. By May 1945 the first six prototypes were rushed to Germany but arrived just too late to see action.

Another very important area of equipment development in which the DTD played a key role was that of specialist Royal Engineer and other vehicles that

Early Mark of Centurion with Mono-Trailer. One limitation of Centurion was its range; FVRDE investigated a number of ways to increase its range, including use of this trailer. (Crown Copyright-MOD)

would be key to the success of D-Day. The Armoured Vehicle Royal Engineers (AVRE), based on the Churchill tank, was developed by the DTD. Lieutenant Colonel George C. Reeves, an Assistant Director at the DTD, had been an observer during Operation Jubilee – the raid on Dieppe. The analysis of that raid concluded that in future operations infantry should secure a firm beachhead before armour was landed, but he met with his staff on 27 August 1942, just eight days after the operation, and came to a different conclusion. They generated a report that was sent to the War Ministry with a recommendation for 'exploring the possibility of developing devices to enable obstacles to be surmounted by a tank or destroyed by a tank crew without being exposed to enemy fire'. A more detailed assessment was undertaken with significant input from Lt John James Devonan, a Canadian officer attached to the DTD; he had lost some close friends among the Canadian forces who took part in the operation at Dieppe. A report was issued on 6 October 1942 recommending the development of an Engineer Tank and including some initial concept drawings. The report helped set in train the development of the basic AVRE vehicle, with a demolition gun, and a wide range of other vehicles including mine-clearing, bridging, trackway laying and demolition-charge emplacement vehicles. These became famous for equipping the 79th Armoured Division and are referred to as the 'Funnies'.

The DTD was also closely involved in the development of the Duplex Drive (DD) swimming tanks. Systems were trialled on a number of different vehicles including the Valentine tank, but best known is the solution integrated on the Sherman Tank and used on D-Day. Although the US did not embrace the AVRE concept in the same way as the British Army, following visits of DTD staff to the US they did adopt the DD Sherman.

The DTD was also involved in the development of the successful Churchill Crocodile Flame Thrower tank – proposing and developing it at a time when the official policy was to focus on man-portable devices or those based on the small Universal Carrier.

Duplex-Drive Sherman with flotation screen lowered. (Copyright W. Suttie)

6

VEHICLE TESTING DURING THE SECOND WORLD WAR

Whilst the 'A' section had moved to Chobham and had become FVPE, the 'B' section of Experimental Wing DTD remained at Farnborough and took over the hangars and workshops vacated by 'A' section. The establishment, which came under the control of the Directorate for Wheeled Vehicle Design and Production, was named the Wheeled Vehicle Experimental Establishment (WVEE) and consisted of:

Commanding Officer	Lieutenant Colonel
Chief Technical Officer	Major
Experimental Officer (4)	Captain
Workshop Officer	Major
Stores Officer	Captain
Adjutant	Captain

158 Warrant Officers, NCOs and other ranks
162 Civilians including fitters, electricians, carpenters and drivers

WVEE was tasked by TT2 of the Ministry of Supply and was responsible for testing all wheeled load-carrying vehicles, artillery tractors, tank transporters and wheeled armoured vehicles, including half-tracks. Prototypes were sent for testing at WVEE and once a new type of vehicle had been accepted into service production examples were sent there again to compare the performance with that of the prototypes.

In addition to those produced in the UK large numbers of vehicles were now being imported from the USA and Canada and these required testing. The tests by WVEE enabled comparisons to be made with equivalent UK types and to establish load-carrying or tractor capabilities. Other tests at WVEE included those associated with remedies for defects and short comings with in-service vehicles.

One area of specific focus at WVEE was tyre testing, especially with the advent of synthetic rubber. This work was carried out for the Ministry of Supply and for the tyre industry itself. Typically testing included a mix of 80 miles on roads and 20 miles off-road for every 100 miles run. The off-road testing was carried out on a rough road circuit at Hawley. Running was undertaken at high speed on all terrains, often with vehicles running in convoys to enable direct comparisons of different tyres and vehicles under the same conditions. Tyre testing remained a major activity long after WVEE moved to Chobham.

Another activity for both WVEE and FVPE was the test and evaluation of captured enemy vehicles.

When the Tank Testing section had been formed in 1921 at Pinehurst Barracks much of the vehicle automotive testing was carried out on land adjunct to the Barracks. By the Second World War a number of sites were available in the Farnborough area centred on what was known as Long Valley. These included:

Miles Hill	Test slopes
Ively Farm	Cross-country course
Ively Road	Concrete brake-test course
Jersey Brow	Articulation course
Ball Hill	Corrugation course and test courses
Long Valley	2-mile sand circuit (when dry)

A number of defined road-test circuits started from Farnborough and were used by both wheeled and tracked vehicles. The '100 mile road run' went from Farnborough via Hook, the Basingstoke bypass and Stockbridge to a turn-round point at Lopcombe Corner at the Junction with the A30 and A43. Some heavier vehicles were diverted from the A30 at Micheldever going via Andover and Middle Wallop. The route had a good road surface and none of the hills exceeded 1 in 15. This route continued to be used long after the move to Chobham and the opening of the Longcross Test Track in 1953. The 'Hindhead Route' was about 40 miles long and ran from Farnborough via North Camp, Ash Vale, Ash, Tongham, Tilford, Rushmoor and Beacon Hill to the A287 and then back to Farnborough via Hindhead, Haslemere, Whitley Camp, Godalming bypass, Hogs Back, Ash and North Camp. This was an undulating route with a total of 14.1 miles ascending and 12.2 descending with gradients up to 1 in 9. Variations of this route had extensions via Petworth, Bordon and as far south as Horndean. Shorter circuits ran round what was known as the Pirbright Triangle for repeated sharp-turn tests and for testing track life on different road surfaces. Another area where vehicles were sometimes sent for tests was the 'Mountain Course' on the B4246 between Abergavenny and Blaenavon in South Wales. The hill used there was about 3 miles long with a ruling gradient of 1 in 10 and some stretches up to 1 in 6. Heavy vehicles and tank transporters made repeated ascents and descents along the road, turning at each end, but lighter vehicles could use a road to the south to undertake complete circuits.

The following table gives an insight into a typical trial, in this case cooling system trials on a Cruiser Mark VI (Crusader). It shows part of the data record made. The vehicle was run under 'approach march' conditions with the turret hatch open, driver's hatch closed and engine bulkhead doors open. Cooling water outlet temperatures were measured every five minutes during the run and every two minutes when ascending long hills.

Time	Miles	Water outlet temp °F	Remarks
10.15	0		Start at MEE Farnborough
10.20	0.4	95	
10.25	1.2	125	
10.30	2.7	130	
10.35	4.7	135	LH Bulkhead door opened
10.40	5.8	130	Stopped to remove driver's screen
10.45	7.5	132	
10.50	8.0	120	
10.55	8.8	130	
11.00	–	132	Stopped to lower jammed RH bulkhead door
11.05	–	125	Frensham Pond
11.10	–	130	Beginning Beacon Hill
11.12	–	134	Uphill
11.14	–	135	Uphill
11.16	–	140	Uphill
11.18	–	146	Uphill
11.20	–	150	Uphill
11.22	–	148	Top of hill (Hindhead)
11.25	17.2	130	Downhill
11.30	18.4	115	
11.35	19.5	120	
11.40	20.2	124	
11.45	22.5	124	Wrong road, stopped to enquire
11.55	–	125	Restart
12.08	–	138	Start of hill leading to Fernhurst

12.10	–	140	Uphill
12.15	28.1	118	Fernhurst village (Downhill)
12.20	29.3	129	Bottom of hill
12.22	–	132	Uphill
12.24	30.4	135	Top of hill
12.30	31.7	118	Downhill to Midhurst. Stop to adjust fan and inspect fan arch
14.45	32.5	105	Restart for return run

The records indicate that the vehicle was at times averaging over 27mph, although the reaction of the person asked for directions is not recorded.

Work at FVPE focused on tracked vehicles and at its peak during the Second World War around 150 different vehicle tests were being undertaken at the site. One notable aspect of testing on Chobham Common was that of mine-clearance tanks, such as those fitted with flails. The trials involved the use of live mines and resulted in at least one fatality when a mine-clearing tank missed a mine and subsequently reversed over it. Many years later, in the early 1990s, the site was evacuated when an anti-tank mine was discovered by workmen digging near to the establishment canteen; that particular mine turned out to be inert.

The picture below is a composite of two aerial pictures of Chobham Common in 1945 and shows the extent of the area used for vehicle testing. The main site is at the top-right of centre with Chobham Lane running east to west below it. The Sunningdale to Chobham road runs from top to bottom towards the left-hand side of the picture.

FVPE also had a Middle East wing to support trials and evaluation in desert environments and this remained open until January 1948.

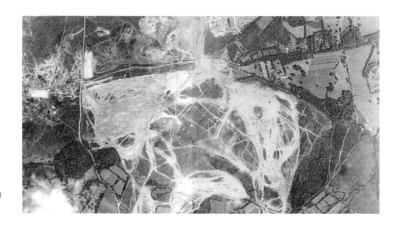

Chobham Common in 1945.

The establishment was also a focus for testing captured equipment, either on site or with staff supporting vehicles on trials at other establishments. The establishment maintained a display of equipment and held visitors' days, including a major event after the war in July 1946 advertised as an 'Exhibition of German and other vehicles and equipments'. This event included mobility demonstrations of some vehicles. As well as captured equipment the displays included full-scale wooden mock-ups of enemy vehicles including a Panther and an Elephant. After the war the vehicles were disposed of, either being scrapped or sent to museums. Even though the vehicles themselves soon went, many components such as engines and gearboxes could be found in the corners of laboratories and workshops many years later.

It is very likely that the German E100 heavy tank prototype was one of the vehicles brought to Chertsey as photographs of the E100 attributed to the School of Tank Technology, which at this time was at Chertsey, are in the Bovington Tank Museum records. It is possible that the tracks, which were not on the vehicle when captured, were fitted at Chertsey before the vehicle was transported to Bovington. At the 1947 RAC conference trials of the A41 Tortoise (FV101) were discussed noting that the army had no requirement for the vehicle in service but wanted to understand the capabilities and limitations of such heavy vehicles in the event of being deployed by potential enemies. It was further stated that the E100 was being restored to running order in order to assess even heavier vehicles. The E100 was later disposed of. There is one unconfirmed report that it was

A Tiger at Chertsey. This picture is taken from a 'Motion Study' Report dated December 1947, which examined the crew positions and weapon-loading arrangements of the German Tiger 1, Tiger 2 and Panther tanks. The work was carried out with the help of staff and facilities at FVDD. After trials at Chertsey, the vehicle pictured was donated to the Bovington Tank Museum and it appeared in the 2014 film *Fury*. (Crown Copyright-MOD)

not welcome at Chertsey as it was so heavy it kept sinking into the ground and was difficult to move. Once at Bovington it was equally unwelcome and Derek Talbot, who later worked at Chertsey, recalls seeing it sat on a multi-wheel trailer of German origin, the said trailer with a number of burst tyres.

Testing of foreign vehicles continued to be a feature of work at Chertsey with a focus on vehicles from the former Soviet Union when the opportunity arose. This was particularly the case following the First Gulf War when there was a hangar full of captured Iraqi vehicles. A 1954 FVRDE report outlines tests of medium anti-tank mines against the T34 tank. Photographs of the trials vehicle show it still with prominent German markings showing that it was an example that had been captured by the Germans during the war and subsequently brought to Chertsey.

Supporting the vehicle trials at the Chertsey establishment was a range of test facilities. By the end of the Second World War the permanently installed test plant included a vehicle dynamometer, two engine test cells, a suspension and wheel test rig, a cooling-fan test tunnel, an engine air-cleaner test cabinet, a shock-test machine, a burst-test spindle, high- and low-temperature test cells, a torque-converter test rig and equipment for investigating the welding properties of armour plate.

7

CHOBHAM COMMON

The Chertsey establishment was built on the north-east side of Chobham Common. It used areas of the common for tank testing and mine-clearance trials during the Second World War with the result that major portions of the common had to be ploughed and reseeded after the war.

The common itself is a 1,400-acre (6km²) area of lowland heath, which is a National Nature Reserve and the area between Burma Road and the establishment security fence designated a Site of Special Scientific Interest (SSSI). A wide variety of plants and wildlife, including the following, have been recorded on the common:

- 26 species of mammal including the nationally rare Water Vole;
- 116 species of bird with the common being a nationally important breeding area for the European nightjar, woodlark and Dartford warbler. It is also one of few places in the UK where the black redstart has nested;
- 9 species of reptiles and amphibians including the smooth snake and nationally rare sand lizard;
- A wide variety of invertebrate fauna being one of the best sites in the UK for spiders, hymenoptera (bees, wasps and ants) and ladybirds. 23 species of dragonfly and 33 species of butterfly including large colonies of the rare silver-studded blue have been recorded;
- 390 species of plants.

There was much of interest to be found on the main establishment site, including great crested newts that were resident in ponds and adders that were often seen sunning themselves on the quieter paths or resident in vehicles left in long-term storage outside. Dartford warblers nested in one of the hangars for several years and there was also a hobby nesting on the site. Water voles lived in the small stream that flowed towards the Wentworth Golf Course. Five different species of native wild orchid were recorded on site as well as some uncommon grasses and fungi. Most important was the rare Deptford Pink (*Dianthus armeria*), threatened with extinction, and the Wall Bedstraw (*Galium parisiense*), both of which were carefully monitored annually and steps taken to ensure that the right conditions for their continued existence were maintained.

It is believed that, like other inland heaths, Chobham Common was created when early farmers cleared the primary woodland that once cloaked the country. This exposed and degraded the fragile soils that underlie the site, creating the conditions favoured by heath land. After the initial clearance the area would have been kept free of trees by grazing and fuel gathering. The area was probably occupied during the Neolithic period and the Bronze Age, and there is evidence of Bronze Age earthworks on the common. There are three scheduled ancient monuments on the common, a Bronze Age round barrow and two earthworks known as the 'Bee Gardens'. These are so called because there is a local tradition that in the Middle Ages the earthworks protected the beehives at a time when beeswax was used to pay taxes to the Chertsey Abbey where it was used for making candles. It is more likely that the earthworks are much older and part of an enclosure for livestock.

In the seventh century, the Manor of Chobham was granted to Chertsey Abbey by the Crown and remained in the possession of the abbey until its surrender to Henry VIII in 1537. On 20 July 1614 the Manor of Chobham was conveyed to Sir George More, reverting back to the Crown on his death. On 19 November 1620 the Manor was then granted to Sir Edward Zouch and again reverted back to the Crown on his death. George II granted the Manor to Walter Abel for a term of 1,000 years and Lord Onslow derived his title to the Manor from Walter Abel. The Manor then comprised 1,075ha (2,658 acres) of arable land and 677ha (1,672 acres) of grassland with Chobham Common forming part of this lease.

Even prior to the building of RAF Chobham and its subsequent conversion to the home of the DTD and FVPE the common was associated with the British Army. In 1853, from April to August, the common was used as a large temporary camp for the army before shipping the troops to the Crimean War. This was established at the insistence of Prince Albert who wrote to the new Commander in Chief, Lord Hardinge, urging upon him the need to do something about the training of the army. As a result divisional scale exercises were carried out. According to *Punch* magazine at the time, conditions were very unpleasant due to wet weather. For instance, there were cartoons of soldiers with frogs' legs, and of soldiers fishing while sitting in their tents. Despite this the 'grand military picnic', as it was called by some detractors, was seen as a success and a writer of the period stated it 'was sufficient to prove the need for a permanent school for field operations where officers might learn to handle large bodies of men and where the men might learn to rough it, and to draw more upon their own ingenuity for comfort'. Thus the exercises on Chobham Common directly resulted in the establishment of the 'Camp at Aldershot' – the first permanent garrison in the United Kingdom for the concentration or training of troops on a large scale. Aldershot later became the home of the British Army. The Aldershot site was selected by Lord Hardinge who rode out from Chobham over all the commons and heaths around Ash, Aldershot and Farnham to select a suitable site. The area fitted the strategic need to be within reach of the South Coast where the threat of French invasion intermittently loomed. Lord Hardinge recommended that Aldershot Heath should be selected, the proprietors agreed to sell for £12 an acre and a tract of nearly 10,000 acres was thus purchased early in 1854.

Queen Victoria reviewed the troops at Chobham on 21 June 1853, and in 1901 a cross was put on the spot to mark the occasion and also act as a memorial to the late monarch. At the same time a cannon was presented to Chobham village to commemorate the visit. The current cannon is a replacement for the original which was sacrificed to the metal salvage collections of the Second World War.

It is believed that the common was used for training during the First World War and in a number of areas of the common, including just north of the Victoria memorial, there are alternating banks and depressions thought to be First World War training entrenchments. In 1952 a stone was erected in Chobham Place Woods by Sir Edward le Marchant, in memory of the troops who trained there.

The Queen Victoria Memorial.
(Copyright W. Suttie)

IN MEMORY OF THE NOBLE LIFE OF QUEEN VICTORIA WHO REVIEWED 8129 OF HER TROOPS ON THIS COMMON JUNE 21ST 1853

AFTER A REIGN OF 63 YEARS SHE RESTED FROM HER LABOURS JANUARY 22ND 1901

THIS CROSS IS ERECTED BY 400 PARISHIONERS 1901

Many years later First World War trench scenes were recreated on Chobham Common for the filming of the video for Paul McCartney's *Pipes of Peace*.

There were other associations between the area and military activity in the Second World War. There was an ammunition dump adjoining the common at Childown and an Italian prisoner-of-war camp on part of the common now owned by the Sunningdale Golf Club. In a coincidence a British POW camp in Italy was recreated nearby for the film *Danger Within*. During the war the area was patrolled by two platoons of the Local Defence Volunteers: the Chobham No. 1 platoon was later stationed in the Round Pond woods and No. 2 platoon at Benhams Mill. No. 1 platoon patrolled the area from Sunningdale railway bridge to Longcross and Burrow Hill and No. 2 platoon covered Chobham village and the surrounding area. Many years later an episode of *Dad's Army* was filmed in the area and shots included the Walmington-on-Sea company patrolling along Burma Road running up the side of the establishment.

As well as a strong association with the army, Chobham Common had also previously been the venue for scientific experimentation. The July 1907 issue of *Auto* magazine, a precursor to *Flight* magazine, records how the Aeronautical Society of Great Britain met on Chobham Common for experiments and a display of scientific kite flying. As well as kites a Mr Jose Weiss was present with some model gliders and a Mr Cave with some small hydrogen-filled rubber balloons, which were used to carry instruments aloft. The gliders, which were launched from high ground or released from kites, enjoyed varying degrees of success with *Auto* reporting: 'Much that took place was extremely amusing, and for those who are making a study of this intensely interesting problem there was a certain amount that was really instructive.'

As indicated above, from the 1950s onwards the common was frequently used as a film or television location. Other films made on the common include *Lawrence of Arabia*, *Carry On* films and Hammer Horror films. After vehicle testing stopped the common gradually recovered, becoming the natural habitat it is now, and when it was declared a National Nature Reserve any filming activities had to be approved and steps taken to ensure no damage was done. The common has been used more recently as a location for television series such as *Spooks* and *Silent Witness*.

Burma Road runs parallel to the south-west boundary of the establishment from Chobham Lane towards the railway line and a roundabout was built at the end of the lane when the M3 was constructed. For a while this road was used as a camp for travellers. It is said that they were evacuated when there was a fire on the common and a narrow chicane was placed at the end of Burma Road to prevent their return. The more colourful legend goes that following some suspect disappearances of metal from the site a tank was driven up and down the road until the incumbents took the hint and left.

8

POST-WAR EVOLUTION OF THE CHERTSEY ESTABLISHMENT

At the end of the Second World War TT2 Branch of the Ministry of Supply, which had addressed wheeled vehicle requirements, was wound up and some of its staff absorbed into the DTD to form the Wheeled Vehicle Division. The DTD itself was renamed the Fighting Vehicles Design Department (FVDD). In 1946 WVEE merged with the Fighting Vehicle Proving Establishment, which it joined at Chobham. Facilities continued to be used at Pinehurst and the Long Valley area continued to be used for tank cross-country testing. Also in 1946 the small group of scientists and engineers who had formed the Tank Armament Research Wing at Porton moved to join the main FVDD site at Chertsey, among them Mr C. Dunbar who was later to become Director of FVRDE. The buildings they vacated were put to other uses, but now, apart from the HQ building where they occupied the conference room, none of those they occupied remain on the Porton site.

In 1948 FVDD was renamed the Fighting Vehicles Design establishment within the following organisation:

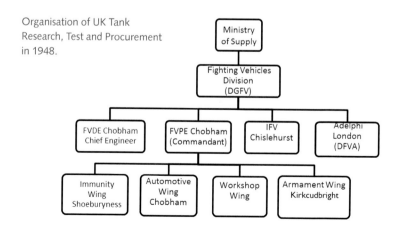

Organisation of UK Tank Research, Test and Procurement in 1948.

For four years the two establishments, FVPE and FVDE, existed side by side on the Chobham site until 1952 when they were amalgamated to form the Fighting Vehicles Research and Development Establishment (FVRDE) with Mr A.E. Masters as Director. Also in 1952 the School of Tank Technology moved to Bovington and with this move the large collection of Allied and foreign armoured vehicles that had been tested at the establishment was also transferred, a number to become part of the Tank Museum collection.

One of the major projects at this time was the construction of the facility adjacent to the main site that became the Longcross Test Track. When the Chobham site was occupied in 1942 the common adjacent to it was used for a variety of purposes including automotive trials, mine clearance and explosive trials. Churchill tank track marks and craters from mines exploded by flails were exposed on the nearby Oystershell Hill[*] area during the hot summer of 1976 when much surface vegetation was destroyed by fires. The main site had been leased by the Ministry of Supply and 37 acres immediately adjacent to the establishment requisitioned by the War Office for use by the School of Tank Technology and later by the research wing of FVRDE. In 1950 the Ministry of Supply purchased the adjacent Longcross Estate (to the east of the main site), less the Barrow Hills building and the stables on the site, with a view to building a test track there.

The area occupied by the establishment was within the designated 'green belt' area and soon after the war there had been opposition to the 'Tank Factory' remaining in the area. Therefore when the application to build the test track was submitted there was much opposition from local residents who complained about the noise and dust generated by vehicle testing. Planning objections also came from the Ministry of Health, which argued that several hospitals in the vicinity were adversely affected by the activities of FVRDE. A Public Local Enquiry was held in June 1950 and in the resulting report it was recommended that the establishment should be moved to a new site unless for reasons of State this was impracticable.

In January 1951 the Lord President's Committee ruled that essential additional facilities, including a test track, could be built at Chobham, but the establishment should move to a new site within five years. In June 1952 the Minister of Supply asked the Home Affairs Committee to postpone the move as the new works, which had only just been authorised, could not be completed until 1955 – a year before the proposed move. The Home Affairs Committee agreed that the move could be postponed but required the search for an alternative site to continue. At this point the Treasury questioned the justification of building new facilities if the establishment was to move. The question was referred back to the Home Affairs Committee in March 1953 when the Ministry of Supply pointed out that

---

[*] So-called because of oyster fossils found there.

the estimated cost of the move (about £6 million) could not be found within the defence vote, even if an alternative site could be found. It also pointed out that the continued uncertainty was having an unfavourable impact on the efficiency of the establishment. The debate was closed in December 1953 when in reply to a House of Commons question the Minister of Supply stated that 'although the government had not reached a final decision about the permanent location of the establishment, it must be recognised, in view of the expenditure which would be involved in transfer to another site that it would be impracticable to remove the establishment from Chobham in the foreseeable future'. The local authorities accepted the situation and Surrey County Council eventually gave planning permission to build thirty-three houses for service officers and other ranks on the Longcross Estate area. Thus the part of Chobham Common that had been requisitioned in 1942, and occupied by the main buildings, was retained, the Longcross Estate area developed as the test track and the soft running area that had been leased given up and returned to common use. The test track was built in stages with stage 1 being the main track and stage 2 the suspension courses and test slopes, with other facilities following.

In 1957, with Mr A.E. Masters still as Director, FVRDE was organised into ten branches, each run by an Assistant Director (AD), grouped under four Deputy Directors (DD):

DD (Research) AD Basic Research
  •   AD Applied Research
  •   AD Research (Materials)
DD (Tracked Vehicles)   AD Project Co-ordination (Tracks)
  •   AD Turret and Sighting
  •   AD Power Plant
  •   AD Running Gear
  •   AD Electrical
DD (Wheeled Vehicles) AD Project Co-ordination (Wheels)
DD (Trials and Development Services)
  •   AD Development Trials

In January 1960 Mr Dunbar took over as Director FVRDE. He had been a member of the Tank Armament Research Team that had been transferred from Porton to Chobham in 1946. He was succeeded by Mr David Cardwell who took over as Director in May 1967.

In May 1968 the research division was disbanded and its functions distributed to other branches so that R&D could be more closely aligned. The branches were:

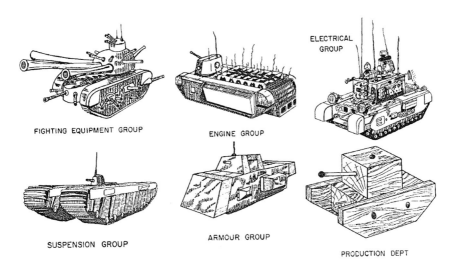

The 'Specialist Menace' picture. Generated in the 1950s but often used as a reminder of the need for a balanced design. (Crown Copyright-MOD)

DD Automotive
- Power Train
- Mobility

DD Operational Equipment
- Fire Control and Weapon Mounting
- Fighting Equipment and Electrical
- Armour and Materials

DD Vehicles
- Combat Vehicles
- Concepts
- Logistic Vehicles

DD Trials and Services
- Trials Design
- Field Trials

In addition to the ADs running these branches an AD Plans reported directly to the Director.

On 4 July 1969 the importance of the establishment was recognised by a visit by the Duke of Edinburgh. By 1970 around 1,200 staff worked on the site and on 1 April that year FVRDE was amalgamated with the Military Engineering Experimental Establishment (MEXE) at Christchurch to form the Military Vehicles and Engineering Establishment (MVEE). MEXE was the centre of R&D for equipment for the Royal Engineers. Christchurch had been a centre

FVRDE support to trials. In this case an FVRDE Centurion and crew assess the effectiveness of the Swynnerton cratering device. (Crown Copyright-MOD)

for research into bridging since 1919 and MEXE was formed in 1946 when the Experimental Bridging Establishment based there was combined with the Experimental Demolition Establishment and the Experimental Tunnelling Establishment, both of which had been relocated to Christchurch.

Under a new rationalised structure an additional post of Deputy Director (Projects and Research) was created and three of the previous Chertsey DD posts formed a new level of management called 'Head of Division'. An additional branch (Special Projects) was created, tasked with designing and developing a vehicle to exploit the newly 'invented' Chobham armour and this reported directly to DD (PR). The branches were now:

DD (Projects and Research)
- AD/Concepts
- AD/Vehicle Engineering (Special Projects)

Head of Vehicle Engineering Division
- AD/Vehicle Engineering (Combat)
- AD/Vehicle Engineering (Logistics)

Head of Operational Equipment Division
- AD/Fire Control
- AD/Armour and Materials
- AD/Fighting Equipment and Electrical

Head of Automotive Division
- AD/Mobility
- AD/Power Plant

DD (Trials and Evaluation)
- AD Trials Design
- AD Field Trials

DD (Engineer Equipment)
- AD Plant Roads and Airfields
- AD Bridging
- AD Power
- AD Mechanical
- AD Materials Research

In 1972 there was an addition to the site with the arrival of Vehicles Branch, Technical Group of the Royal Electrical and Mechanical Engineers (REME). Within this branch there were a number of Maintenance Advisory Groups that were responsible for 'Ease of Maintenance' assessments, the generation of maintenance documents and addressing in-service repair and maintenance issues for vehicles and other equipment. The branch was also responsible for developing repair and recovery techniques and assisting the Operational Requirements Branch in sponsoring REME equipment, such as recovery vehicles. The origins of the branch lay in the Military Services Branch FVRDE but it was based at Woolwich. There had long been an aspiration to relocate the branch to Chertsey, but financial constraints prevented this until there was a decision to extend the Tate Gallery! The extension required the demolition of the Milbank Military Hospital and the decision was made to relocate this to Woolwich at the new Queen Elizabeth Hospital. This was to be built on the site occupied by the Vehicles Branch organisation, hence the finance was found for new buildings at Chertsey.

Co-location had clear benefits with ready access between platform designers and maintainers. It also made easier some different activities, for example a surplus Chieftain tank was subject to attack by a HESH round so that Vehicles Branch REME could undertake an assessment of what was required to repair it. The branch remained at the site until 2005, just after the last government staff from the rest of the establishment left. It had become the Vehicles and Weapons Branch

Chertsey Gate Guardian.

in 1982, part of the Army Technical Support Agency (ATSA) in 1995, and finally part of the Defence Logistics Organisation (DLO) from 2000 until 2005.

In January 1975 there was a further rationalisation of senior posts within MVEE and regrouping of branches which became:

DD (Projects and Research)
- AD/VE (Special Projects)
- AD/Management Services

Head of Future Systems Division
- AD/Concepts
- AD/Armour and Materials
- AD/Future Studies

Head of Sub-Systems Division
- AD/Fire Control
- AD/Power Plant
- AD/Mobility
- AD/Fighting Equipment and Electrical

Head of Vehicle Engineering Division
- AD/VE (Combat)
- AD/VE (Logistics)
- AD/VE (Main Battle Tank)

Head of Engineering Equipment
- AD/EE (Support)
- AD/EE (Military)
- AD/EE (Bridging)

DD (Trials and Evaluation)
- AD/Technical Facilities
- AD/Trials

At this time David Cardwell was still Director; other key staff managing vehicle development activities were D.H. Troughton (DD/PR), S. Oleman (H/VED), A. Martin (H/SSD) and J. Ellis (H/FSD). Also of note was the AD/Main Battle Tank, David Beavan, who was the last remaining engineer who had served in tanks in the Second World War. He had fought at El Alamein, Sicily and Italy. He then fought in Northern Europe from D-Day plus two through to the armistice, including the liberation of Belsen. David Beavan was not the only member of staff who had an association with Belsen; David Dodds, one of the drivers at Chertsey, was a Royal Engineer in the Second World War and was involved in burying the bodies there.

At this time the VE (Special Projects) Branch became dedicated to the development of tanks for Iran under project 4030 with other activities reintegrated with the Concepts Branch.

David Cardwell carried on as D/MVEE until 1976, then following five years as Controller Establishments and Research (CER) he was appointed Chief of Defence Procurement (CDP) in 1980 and subsequently knighted. He was followed by Ian H. Johnson (1976–78) and John Ellis (1978–85). In 1978 when John Ellis became Director there were 814 non-industrial staff and 946 industrial staff across the whole of MVEE.

Since the Second World War, due to the work of the establishment, the UK had become recognised as world leading in the development of innovative and effective armoured fighting vehicles. In 1959 the Ministry of Supply was abolished and FVRDE became part of the War Department. With the formation of the Ministry of Defence (MOD) in 1971 the establishment became part of the Procurement Executive (PE) within the MOD. The PE embraced all three services, whereas the Ministry of Supply had not. Within Chertsey the Future Studies and Concepts branches studied long-term equipment concepts and developed the initial concept designs for new vehicles. Once approved for development the Vehicle Engineering Branches would take over responsibility for the design and would then work with the rest of the PE and industry where detailed design and production was undertaken.

The workshops at MVEE had the capacity to build vehicle test rigs and prototypes but often the latter would be built by industry. The subsystems branches carried out research into future technologies and supported new platform design and development. Throughout the process MVEE remained the design authority responsible for delivering almost all the platforms that were procured to meet army requirements. The main UK armoured vehicle manufacturers who worked

Defence cuts have been a constant issue, as this January 1975 cartoon from the MVEE news shows.

with Chertsey were GKN, responsible for medium AFVs like FV432 and Warrior; Alvis, responsible for light AFVs including the Saladin, Saracen and the CVR(T) range; Daimler, designers and manufacturers of Ferret and designers of Fox; Royal Ordnance Factory (ROF) Nottingham, who primarily manufactured large-calibre guns, but built some light vehicles, including the Combat Engineer Tractor and later Fox, when ROF Leeds was focused on delivering the Iranian order; and ROF Leeds and Vickers, responsible, often in parallel, for Main Battle Tanks (MBT) and variants.

In 1982 the Conservative government made the decision that design authority should be vested in industry who would take responsibility for the 'Post Design Services' of existing platforms and the design of new platforms. This effectively reduced the role of the establishment back to an advisory one similar to that of the DTD in the 1930s and early 1940s. The establishment was to continue to lead research and act in what was called the 'intelligent customer' role for the Ministry of Defence. The decision resulted in three significant challenges. Firstly, although the UK armoured vehicle industry was very competent, no supplier could match the depth of design and subsystem experience at MVEE. This is a situation that has remained the case even with the subsequent amalgamation and rationalisation of the major UK players. The problem was recognised at the time and an attempt was made to force some members of MVEE to transfer to ROF (Leeds), but few moved. In some cases industry did address specific shortfalls in their own capability by subcontracting work to the establishment. The second issue was that due to the commercial pressures on industry there was, and remains, a strong tendency to be risk adverse and hence avoid the kind of significant innovations in design or manufacturing processes associated with Chertsey. This situation could be compounded by the policy of the MOD to attempt to seek value for money through competition, including promoting competition from overseas suppliers. The third issue was that the natural route for exploiting new technologies from research into products became constrained. The one area where design authority was not fully transferred to industry was armour, for which Chertsey retained full responsibility. This has remained largely the case since and the armour team within government still retains design authority for some UK armour solutions.

A further, and significant, change happened on 1 April 1984 when MVEE and PERME (Propellants, Explosives and Rocket Motor Establishment) at Waltham Abbey became part of the Royal Armaments Research and Development Establishment (RARDE) at Fort Halstead in Kent. Therefore, MVEE ceased to exist as a separate establishment and became the Vehicles Department of RARDE, of which it was now an outstation. This was much to the dissatisfaction of the Chertsey staff who considered weapons to be just another subsystem to be fitted to or carried by platforms and were of the rather tongue-in-cheek opinion that MVEE should have taken over RARDE with the Fort Halstead site renamed MVEE (East). RARDE, however, was the larger establishment and had a wider

FV432 with prototype Granby bomblet protection net in the Chertsey workshops. (Crown Copyright-MOD)

spectrum of tri-service work. The title of D/MVEE was lost and John Ellis was the last in that post. In 1985 Colin Evans took over the role of what was now called Deputy Director (Vehicles) (DD(V)).

In 1989 Julian Walker became DD(V) and head of the Chertsey establishment. Previously he had been in charge of the Special Projects Branch that had developed the 4030 vehicle and which evolved into the Challenger tank and had then been H(VED). When Julian Walker was head of the establishment some significant activities started on 14 September 1990. On that day the government announced that the 7th Armoured Brigade would be deployed to Saudi Arabia as part of the build-up of the Gulf War coalition force to liberate Kuwait following the Iraqi invasion. On 22 November the government announced that in addition to the 7th Armoured Brigade the 4th Brigade, a divisional HQ and supporting elements from 1st (British) Armoured Division would also be deployed for what was called Operation Granby. In this operation many of the vehicles and technologies developed at Chertsey were put to the ultimate test for which they had been designed, war fighting.

From the initial September announcement until British forces entered Kuwait on 25 February 1991 Chertsey was involved in what many staff regarded as its final significant activity, technical support to the operation. The deployed forces were equipped with vehicles that had been designed to fight a defensive war in north-west Europe, but they were now being deployed to fight an offensive war in a desert environment. The changed operational requirements resulted in over 100 key technical projects being undertaken by Chertsey staff under tight timescales to ensure the invasion force had the required capabilities and the best possible levels of survivability. These included:

- Development and trials of solutions for crossing oil pipelines and breaching Iraqi defences;
- Testing all vehicles in the climatic chambers at Chertsey to check they would operate in the hot desert climate. As a result of these extensive trials recommendations were made for replacing subsystems and components if they failed, hence helping to ensure better reliability in theatre. Trials also informed different ways of using equipment when quick modifications could not be identified. In addition some items of equipment that would have been totally unsuitable were identified and so not shipped out;
- Testing of air-conditioning units and solar shields;
- Development of a wide-area, vehicle-mounted smoke-generating system;
- Design of additional armour packs for Challenger, Warrior, CVR(T), Centurion AVRE, Chieftain AVRE, Chieftain AVLB, and other vehicles;
- Build of the Warrior armour packs, for which a production line was set up and a paint shop created in one of the Climatic chambers;
- Development of roof nets to provide protection against bomblets;
- Development of a system for crossing burning oil-filled ditches. The selected solution was based on a sledge-mounted fire-suppression system, pushed into place by a Centurion AVRE and used to create a break in the fire so that a combat bridge could be layed. The initial testing of the Centurion and sledge was undertaken in very un-desert-like conditions in pouring rain at Long Valley. Once developed the full solution was tested at RAF Manston in Kent where a representative ditch was built and filled with oil. The oil was set alight, the flames suppressed and a bridge laid by a Chieftain bridge-layer. Despite the huge plume of very black smoke there were no complaints from the surrounding population;
- Navigation systems, including a sun compass, which used the tank's fire-control and GPS systems;
- Battery vent systems;
- Armoured charge bins;
- Thermal imager lens protection solutions;
- Trials of alternative tyres and studies to optimise tyre pressures;
- Assessment of rack-mounted fuel and water carrying tanks;
- Build of remote-control systems for vehicles for mine-breaching operations.

The role of the Chertsey staff in supporting Operation Granby was recognised by a number of awards, with a CB awarded to Julian Walker, an OBE to Tom Packard, a MBE to Gerald Whiteing and a BEM to Colin Andrews. There were also personal visits to the site by Major General Jeremy Blacker (ACDSOR(Land)) and Major General Patrick Cordingley – who commanded the 7th Armoured Brigade during the operation – who both came to personally thank the staff involved for all that had been done to ensure victory and minimise the risk casualties.

Left: Trial of the burning ditch suppression system, with AVLB launching the bridge. (Copyright W. Suttie)

Above: Granby Warrior packs being painted in the Chertsey Test Laboratory. (Crown Copyright-MOD)

Supporting operations was an important role of the establishment until its closure and is a legacy that continues in the organisations that have followed it. Support was provided during the Falklands conflict and operations in the Balkans; more recently ex-Chertsey staff have supported operations in Iraq and Afghanistan.

The next significant organisational change came on 1 April 1991 when the Royal Signals Research Establishment (RSRE) at Malvern, Royal Aerospace Establishment (RAE) at Farnborough and Bedford, RARDE (Fort Halstead, Chertsey and Christchurch) and the Admiralty Research Establishment (ARE) at Portsdown, Portland, Rosyth, Holton Heath, Funtington and Haslar became the founding members of the Defence Research Agency (DRA). The Chertsey site became part of the 'Military Division' DRA with Julian Walker as Deputy Managing Director of Military Division (Chertsey). Until becoming part of an agency the establishment had been 'vote funded', which meant it had a fixed budget from the MOD to carry out its required tasks. This meant the resources were fixed and prioritisation of tasks often had to be made. With the move to Agency status as part of the DRA the establishment operated under a 'trading fund' and so was only funded for the actual tasks carried out. Out of this funding all fixed (overhead) and project specific tasks had to be covered. Trading fund status therefore required much more financial control and a more business-like focus. The Chertsey staff had, until recently, been used to working as a design authority under the discipline of defined time and cost constraints associated with vehicle projects, and hence the impact of the new regime was not as great as on some other establishments.

One other significant change at this time was that control of the research programme was moved from the research establishments to the Operational Requirements Branches in the MOD. Until this time the establishment had been largely responsible for formulating its own research programme, within the available funds. The research aimed to respond to inputs from the military community on key capability needs and to developments in the threat. A summary of the complete research programme of each establishment was presented to the Controller Establishments and Research (CER) each year under the savings and enhancement process. This enabled some rebalancing of the programme, but overall the user community had no direct control of the finances or activities. Direct control by the military user ensured that the research remained focused on operational needs and that there was no 'science for science sake', neither of which were significant issues at Chertsey with its traditional strong links to development projects. It did, however, result in changing priorities as the military staff in the MOD changed and there was the constant need to convince the user of the importance of longer-term research into future technologies. The dangers that might arise were highlighted by a story from colleagues at the Malvern site: during the early days of the development of thermal imagers the establishment was told by senior army representatives that they could see no need for such technology as it did not have a role within the then existing tactics and procedures, which limited the scope of night operations. At other times the military staff had too much confidence in future technologies, one example being the head of the Requirements Branch who insisted that all work on conventional guns and supporting integration should stop and all funding on weapon aspects be focused on Electro-Magnetic (EM) guns – a technology that over twenty years later is still a long way from being suitable for land platform use. Of concern to Chertsey staff was that some funding on vehicle-related research was reduced so that funds could be transferred to the EM gun project.

In 1992 as part of further rationalisations the former MEXE site at Christchurch was closed and the remaining technical staff relocated to a new building on the Chertsey site with just the bridge test facility remaining at Christchurch.

The formation and operation of the DRA was seen as a success by government and so other defence establishments were brought in to form a bigger agency made up of four Technical Divisions: the DRA, the Chemical and Biological Defence Agency, the Centre for Defence Analysis and the Defence Test and Evaluation Organisation. Formed on 1 April 1995, the new enlarged organisation was called the Defence Evaluation and Research Agency or DERA. Of course management went to a lot of trouble to explain that the new name should not be pronounced as 'dearer' despite the increasingly commercial focus of the organisation. A clear goal of DERA was to reduce duplication and inefficiencies across all the establishments and hence reduce costs. The trials and test activities at Chertsey were brought under the DTEO and thus separated from the vehicle research division; such a split between the research and test activities had only previously existed prior to 1952 when FVDE and FVPE, both on the Chertsey site, had merged to form FVRDE.

Further reorganisation in 1997 broke down the four divisions with the Chertsey site becoming part of the Land Systems sector, which along with Air Systems, Sea Systems and Command and Information Systems came under Managing Director Programmes. Land Systems sector consisted of two departments at Chertsey, Mission Sustainability under Nick Warner and Combat Vehicle Concepts under Alex Mckie. There were three other departments in the sector, which were the Airspace Management and ISTAR* System departments at Malvern and the Land Battle Management department at Fort Halstead. This structure was again revised in 2000 with Chertsey then becoming part of Land and Weapons, which was part of the Future Systems Technology Division. By this time DERA had built a new facility on the western side of the Farnborough airfield.

The final chapter in the story of the Chertsey site started on 24 July 2000 when the Secretary of State for Defence announced the creation of a Public-Private-Partnership (PPP) for DERA. In a move that resulted in much speculation in the press regarding personal motives, the senior DERA management, who had been brought in from outside of the civil service, pushed for this to be implemented as a complete privatisation of DERA. Full privatisation was explored but seen as unacceptable, not least because the US Government stated they would not continue valuable government-to-government exchange activities with a commercial organisation. Loss of links with the US was something that would have impacted particularly on armour research where there had been strong collaboration since the exchange of information on Chobham armour. The resulting solution was a split of DERA with a quarter of the staff remaining within government and the rest being transferred into a newly formed private company. The government-retained portion became the Defence Science and Technology Laboratory (Dstl) and the privatised portion QinetiQ, which formally came into existence on 1 July 2001.

The impact on the Chertsey site reflected the wider division of staff between the two organisations. The armour, concepts, vulnerability assessment, signature management and foreign-vehicle assessment teams went into Dstl along with a number of technical experts covering specific aspects of vehicle technology. The other technical teams covering areas such as sighting systems, mobility, gun and fire control, training systems, vetronics (vehicle electronics) and crew systems went into QinetiQ. As part of the split the Chertsey site, including the workshops

---

* Intelligence, Surveillance, Target Acquisition, Reconnaissance.

The Gate Guardian being
removed.

and test tracks, was gifted to QinetiQ. The QinetiQ management quickly sought
to sell the main Chertsey site for profit, closed the workshops and started to move
the technical staff to Farnborough. This left Dstl in an unsustainable situation
unable to cover the overheads of the site with the much smaller number of staff.

Under DERA it had been planned for the staff at Chertsey to move to
purpose-built premises at the main DERA site at Farnborough. This was close
to the site of the original Pinehurst Barracks where the Tank Testing Section had
formed in 1921 and the areas around Ively Road where much vehicle testing
had been carried out up until 1946. No progress had been made before the
QinetiQ/Dstl split despite plans having been drawn up. When Dstl was formed
proposals were made for a new Dstl building in that same area but these too did
not go ahead. The end of the site as a centre for military vehicle research and
development happened very quickly. With QinetiQ staff being relocated in April
2002 Dstl announced it would withdraw from the site with the bulk of the staff
vacating the site by the beginning of September. The armour team was relocated
to Porton Down where it continues to undertake world-leading armour research
and where it benefits from direct access to the Porton ranges to carry out armour
and mine trials – something not possible in the confines of Chobham Common.
The bulk of the rest of the Dstl staff were relocated to the old RARDE Fort
Halstead site[*] where, working alongside the operational analysis and wargaming
staff, they continued to give expert advice to the MOD.

---

[*] At the time of writing Dstl is moving off of the Fort Halstead site and the Dstl staff involved in Land
Platform analysis have already relocated to Portsdown.

View of the main entrance to Longcross Studios, with the Engineering Test Laboratory building renamed as 'Stage 1'. (Copyright W. Suttie)

The one exception to the immediate move was the foreign-vehicle assessment team of around sixteen who remained on the site until January 2004 awaiting the completion of vehicle hangars at Fort Halstead. This team were relocated to various hangars and buildings including the old Vehicles Branch REME hangars (Building 14) and with offices in the old Property Service Agency building (Building 118).

When the last of the staff left, the great history of Chertsey as a world-leading military vehicle research and development establishment ended. The former Vehicles Branch REME did continue on the site for a little longer – before vacating in 2005 – and during this period the site was called DLO (Defence Logistics Organisation) Chertsey.

The final move from the site involved much activity including the removal of the Gate Guardian; this was a prototype Chieftain on a plinth by the main entrance, which according to legend had been driven onto the plinth when its use as a trials vehicle ended. It is said that until the late 1970s soldiers from 'A1 Section' – the heavy tank section – would run up the engine on a monthly basis to ensure it still ran. This vehicle was an early prototype that had an extension welded to the rear of the hull associated with changes to the power pack. This vehicle and other experimental vehicles found new homes, and a number live on at the Tank Museum at Bovington where they remain as a testament to the work of the Chertsey establishment.

At the time of writing in June 2014 the establishment remains in use as a film set called Longcross Studios with most of the infrastructure still standing. The test track is still available for hire but business is mainly for commercial use. Planning permission for the build of houses and offices has been submitted for both the main and Longcross sites and redevelopment work on the main site has just started.

9

DEVELOPMENT OF THE CHERTSEY SITE

In 1942 the new Chobham Common home of the DTD and FVPE was the site of an RAF camp. At that time there were buildings used to store aero engines and other parts to supply the Vickers-Armstrong bomber factory at Brooklands. One building, Building 99,* which became known as the Admin Building, was used throughout the life of the establishment. Other buildings from the original RAF camp situated at the north end of the site between the railway and Chobham Lane were used as the 'establishment loft' to store anything that might possibly be useful in the future. These buildings were demolished when Chobham Lane was realigned during the construction of the M3 motorway. As well as the administration offices and typing pool, Building 99 eventually housed the drawing office, library, a board room and the director's suite of offices. In the early days the 'walls' between offices in the central section were moveable screens and it was not uncommon for someone to return from leave to find that their office had been reduced to the size of their desk.

On 21 September 1942 a railway station, called Longcross Halt, was opened adjacent to the site and on 8 November a siding into the establishment was opened, branching off the line at the London end of the station. This was used to deliver vehicles, stores and coal for the boiler house. In 1943 a railway crane was delivered to the establishment, primarily for measuring the centre of gravity of vehicles. The use of the siding declined after the war and it was removed on 19 November 1961. The first attempt to remove the track ended in failure; the crane on an FV1119 6×6 recovery vehicle was used to try to lift the first section, but the track stayed put and the vehicle fell on to it. Between 1971 and 1974 another siding was put in place near to the station, this time for delivering materials for the M3 construction site.

---

* The building numbers referred to in this section are the official numbers used at the site; key buildings referenced are shown in the site plan at the end of this section.

By the end of the war a number of buildings had been added for use by the DTD, including the tropical and cold-weather test chambers (Buildings 18 and 20), a six-bay workshop building (Building 24), the main vehicle hangars (Building 43), built in 1942 with three bays but extended by a further two bays in 1944, a heavy machinery workshop (Building 44) and a subsystem test laboratory (Building 27). In addition there were other smaller buildings including stores, offices and a vehicle preparation hangar.

Some additional work was carried out at the end of the war when the site had a temporary additional role as a demob camp. It is thought that at this time a large commercial-style cinema building was built. Even after its use as a cinema for troops at the demob camp ended it continued to be used and during the days of FVRDE it hosted shows performed by the FIVE Club (the establishment social club) and the annual Children's Christmas Party. The building remained until the late 1970s by which time it was in a state of disrepair and was finally demolished to make way for new offices.

The approval in 1953 for building the test track and the return of some of the common area to public use left the establishment occupying 129 acres. The lower picture on page 88 shows 'West Block', which housed the Research Wing offices. It consisted of a main two-storey block and a number of single-storey wings, which were added to with time. A musty corridor linked it to the cinema and Building 99. This complex was always referred to as 'West Block' and when replaced the new building was called 'The New West Block', until it received a new, permanent name. Two wings are shown in the 1958 plan but others were added later. New buildings constructed during the 1950s included vehicle workshops, to replace a smaller Second World War building, a tyre test bay (Building 10), an office attached to the environmental chambers (Building 19), a goods-in building and a health centre.

During the 1960s there were further additions including a fire station and new reception, a trials office and a building housing the recovery section (Building 103). An interesting addition to the site, built in 1965, was the 'Rotunda' (Building 64). This was a purpose-built building large enough to house a Main Battle Tank and with room to fully traverse the turret. This was used as a laboratory for developing gun and fire-control systems. When built its location provided a long sight line to the far side of Chobham Common, but the view was gradually obscured by trees over subsequent years. The Rotunda was often used to house and operate an equipment facility called the 'Hull Motion Simulator'; a motion platform that could support a full Main Battle Tank turret and simulate a wide range of hull motion inputs for gun and turret stabilisation trials and gun and fire-control system development.

One building constructed during the 1970s that was directly linked to a programme at the site was Building 114, known as the International Building. It

The Rotunda.

West Block, prior to the
construction of the M3.

had a suite of conference rooms on the ground floor with Interpreters' booths and offices on the first and second floors, and was built to house the project team for the Anglo-German Future Main Battle Tank project. The building was planned to be the first of four to be built round a quadrangle and replace the old inefficient and inadequate Admin Building 99. The Anglo-German project never got beyond the initial studies phase and so the other three buildings never materialised. The old Admin Block continued to be used until the end of the establishment, although a new roof was built over the eastern end of the building, covering that part of the building used by the administration staff. They had worked for many years enduring frequent leaks and the noise of water dripping into buckets!

Other additions in the 1970s included a new reception building at the station entrance, the buildings and hangars for Vehicles Branch REME, the provision of additional office space in the form of Portakabins to house the 4030 project team, additional vehicle hangars and a new canteen. In 1976 Building 118 was constructed to house the Property Services Agency (PSA) team who were responsible for site maintenance. As previously mentioned this building, which consisted of an office wing and a wing of small self-contained stores, had the honour of providing the offices that housed the last team of staff working on the site, including their group leader who had the old paint store as a large but spartan office.

On 21 October 1974 another new building was formally opened, the Computer Centre (Building 108). Until the provision of this facility there were no in-house computer facilities at Chertsey and use had to be made of those at other establishments, mainly those at the Royal Aircraft Establishment at Farnborough, or at a computer bureaux. The building was handed over by the Department of the Environment (DOE) on 1 July 1974 and the computer, an ICL 1903T, delivered the next day. After installation and commissioning it came into formal use on 28 August. A remote card reader and printer were provided at Christchurch. The computer centre was run by a team of fifteen headed by Dr John Brittan.

Another significant milestone for the site was the laying of the foundation stone for the new Engineering Test Laboratories (Building 17) on 31 July 1974. When finished it provided a range of state-of-the-art engine test cells, shock and vibration rigs and other test equipment. It was followed around two years later by the start of construction of two new climatic chambers, built to reduce the need for expensive overseas testing. The climatic chamber complex consisted of three buildings, 121 the complete vehicle climatic chamber, 122 the plant room and 123 the altitude chamber. The complex was fully commissioned in March 1982.

The International Building.

Other changes came with the building of the M3, which opened in 1974. This passed between the main and test track sites, running parallel with Chobham Lane. At one stage consideration was given to a junction by the establishment to enable easier access for large vehicles such as tank transporters, but this proposal was not taken forward. A new bridge between the main site and test track was built to cross Chobham Lane and the M3, replacing the bailey bridge that just crossed Chobham Lane.

One small but significant building that was completed in August 1980 was the splash range, which allowed testing of armour systems designed to defeat small arms threats. Such armour systems were developed by the establishment for use on lighter vehicles including VIP cars.

After becoming part of the DRA/DERA there were two significant new buildings. Firstly the West Block buildings were knocked down and replaced by a new building – the Sir David Cardwell Building (Building 124). This was long overdue as by the end of their life many of the West Block spurs had scaffolding on the inside holding them up. Then in 1992 Building 138, 'The Christchurch Building', was built to house the staff who had moved to Chertsey following the closure of Christchurch.

The final major new building on the Chertsey site was an electromagnetic compatibility (EMC) test chamber (Building 125) completed in 1987.

Along with the developments on the main site there had been ongoing changes on the other side of Chobham Lane, where the establishment owned or built other buildings and facilities in addition to the test track. As part of the estate a

M3 during construction, showing the new bridge between the main site and test track.

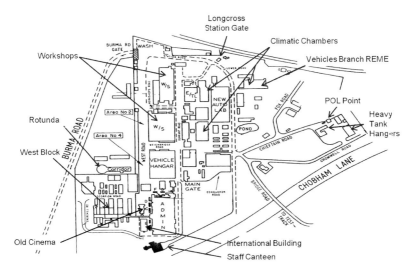

Chertsey site in 1983.

The Sir David Cardwell building.

number of houses were procured including Fairfield, Heathlands, Little Paddock, Holly Lodge and Tanglewood House. Fairfield became the officers' mess and Trials Officers lived in huts in what had been the vegetable garden. The purchase of the Longcross Estate in 1950 did not include the main house, Barrow Hills, which at that time was being used as a school. Barrow Hills had been considered for military use in 1947 when, at the behest of the Ministry of Supply, GEC had looked at purchasing it to house a facility to develop a fighter aircraft radar system as there was no room for the team at their Wembley laboratories. This did not happen, but in 1953 Barrow Hills was taken over by the establishment when the school, which was part of St Georges Weybridge, closed and moved to Witley. There it has kept the 'Barrow Hills' name. The cellars of Barrow Hills were then used for archives from the main site with the rest of the building converted for use as the officers' mess. Much renovation of the house was required, but the first officers moved in on 15 December 1953 and a house-warming party was held the following February. Fairfield then became the home of the Chertsey staff

social club – known as the FIVE (FIghting VEhicles) Club. During the 1960s
the Director, Mr C. Dunbar, lived in Little Paddock. In the early 1970s married
quarters were built between Heathlands and Little Paddock (Albury Close)
and in the grounds of Holly Lodge and Tanglewood House (Holly Close and

EMC Test Facility.

Aerial shot of the main site, with the M3 running from centre top to centre right. The picture can be dated as just prior to 1992, with the U-shaped Cardwell building right of centre but work on the Christchurch building not started.

The Staff Canteen gave good views of the M3, which ran to the right of this picture. Upstairs was the canteen and kitchens and downstairs became the FIVE Club and Senior Staff Mess.

Barrow Hills.

Tanglewood Close). In 1976 Fairfields and Heathlands were demolished to make way for a new barrack block including the warrant officers and sergeants' mess and the FIVE Club moved into Little Paddock. The Longcross Barracks were formally opened to soldiers in October 1978 by Colonel Derek Ivy with Brian Clark, who went on to become a full-time driver at the establishment, the first occupant in. The NAAFI at the barracks was named 'The Track and Wheel Club'.

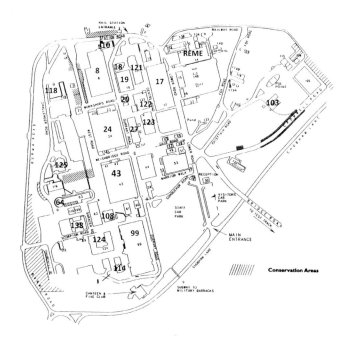

Chertsey site at the time of closure with key buildings numbers.

10

CHERTSEY FACILITIES

Drawing Office and Workshops

A vital contribution to the success of Chertsey came from the activities of the Drawing Office (DO) and Workshops.

A number of draftsmen transferred from Woolwich when the establishment moved to the Chobham Common site and the DO continued to provide vital support until the final days of the establishment. It was housed in Building 99 and at its height had over 100 staff, but by the final days of DERA there were only around twenty.

One legendary aspect of Chertsey life was the annual DO dinner, the first of which was held in March 1960. As well as the meal and drinks there were infamous songs and sketches for entertainment. Guests were invited to attend from both the other branches in the establishment and contractors employed during the year. Usually if a member of staff from 'the Branches' was invited, it meant that person had made some foolish mistake during the last year which needed to be highlighted. The contractors were invited to pay for the wine with

The Drawing Office in Building 99. (Crown Copyright-MOD)

the meal! The after-dinner entertainment was the highlight of the evening and sketches and songs were written and performed to a high standard. A main feature was the presentation of a Golden Cockerel to the individual from the branches deemed to have made the major 'cock-up' of the year. In return the branches presented a very large pencil to the draughtsman who had performed the most noteworthy misdemeanour.

The workshops had extensive facilities with pattern/model makers and carpenters, a well-equipped main workshop, and heavy armour, light armour and wheeled vehicle workshops. The workshops had the capability, if used to the full, to build around one and a half Main Battle Tanks per year. Some of the most impressive facilities were those in the heavy machine shop for machining hulls and turret rings. Facilities included a Scheiss vertical borer brought to Chertsey from the Krupps munition factory in Germany after the Second World War, complete with Swastika markings. It has been suggested that when it was first installed the lights in Longcross dimmed when it was switched on. The vertical borer was complimented by an Asquith Horizontal Borer. This was the largest single machine in the workshops and could be used to machine a complete Main Battle Tank hull. Prototype vehicles were assembled in the fabrication shop where there was a travelling crane. A larger 70-ton travelling crane, which could lift complete vehicles, was available in the tank shop.

In addition Chertsey ran a comprehensive apprenticeship scheme, which ensured a good supply of skilled craftsmen and engineers to work in the workshops and design departments. The apprentice workshop was located opposite the heavy tank shop and there apprentices faced a very regimented regime. In the 1960s apprentice master was Ernie Jordan, an ex-RSM, and his assistant was Bill Robinson, an ex-machinist from the tool room in the main workshops. Under the

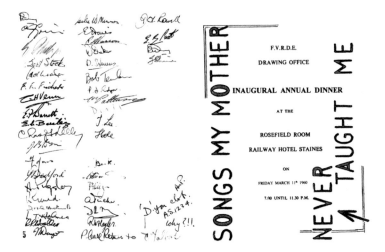

Signed song sheet cover from the first DO Dinner.

SONGS MY MOTHER NEVER TAUGHT ME

F.V.R.D.E.

DRAWING OFFICE

INAUGURAL ANNUAL DINNER

AT THE

ROSEFIELD ROOM

RAILWAY HOTEL STAINES

ON

FRIDAY MARCH 11ᵗʰ 1960

7.00 UNTIL 11.30 P.M.

ex-RSM discipline ruled and apprentices all had to clock in and cleanliness was maintained rigorously. They were all on the 'pipes and plates' rota every Tuesday when the copper pipes in the toilets and the brass plates on the main door had to be polished. Every few weeks the floor had to be polished and then for a day or so they had difficulty not slipping over as it was so shiny. On Wednesdays they were bussed over to Malta Barracks in Aldershot in an olive green army bus for PT, to be shouted at by two ex-PTIs from B Vehicle section.

The apprentices were all issued with an army toolbox containing the appropriate tools. When they started each apprentice was presented with a slab of black mild steel. From this only using hand tools, except for drilling five holes, they had to produce a gleaming '5-square block'. This had to be within one thousandth of an inch accuracy for all dimensions with a line of five square holes and one square plug that fitted each hole perfectly. 'Perfectly' meant that the plug had to push gently through each hole with no light visible around the plug and it did not fall out even if shook. To achieve this it meant at least three weeks' work using just files and a scraper. In the following months the apprentices made a name plate, calipers, centre punch, scriber, surface plate jacks and other tools. After their initial training in the apprentice shop, apprentices were sent to the main workshops to complete their training, spending several weeks in each section under the eye of an apprentice master. The sections included sheet metal, rig bay, pattern shop, foundry, machine shop, pump room, engine bay, gearbox bay, electricians and vehicle workshops. With such a scheme running it was not surprising that the establishment had a good supply of very competent engineers and craftsmen.

Each year, apprentices were able to compete with other MOD apprentices from Research and Development establishments and REME workshops in the Tom Nevard Cup Competition. This included making a fairly complex test piece from drawings, which was judged at the Tom Nevard exhibition held in the Duke of York HQ in Chelsea.

The pattern-making and carpentry shop always played a key role in equipment development, making initial models of concepts and then full-size mock-ups. Full-size mock-ups of parts or complete vehicles were used to check the feasibility of concepts, equipment locations and for ergonomic assessments. When urgent tasks requiring one-off items came up it was common to explain the requirement to the carpenters who then built a full-size model. This could then be used as a basis for manufacturing the required parts – this approach often being quicker than the drawing office generating manufacturing drawings.

Keeping on the right side of the workshops was important to the success of projects. One legend concerned a project engineer who went into the workshop manager one Friday with a broken propshaft and demanded that an identical one be made for the following week; the workshop is said to have obliged and made an identical broken propshaft.

Examples of items made by an apprentice, including the '5-square block'. (Photo courtesy of Paul Fenne)

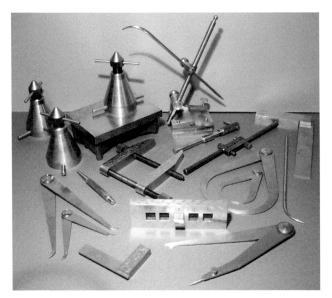

Example of pattern makers' skills – a scale model of a T94 for scale radar measurements. (Crown Copyright-MOD)

The Longcross Test Track

Construction of the Longcross Test Track started soon after planning permission was finally granted in 1953. The track itself was designed to be suitable for continuous use by Class 60 tanks and is said to have cost more than the equivalent length of a six-lane motorway. By 1954 it was partially completed and on 30 September that year a vehicle exhibition was held on the circular skid pan, arranged to coincide with the Commercial Motor Show. Visitors to that exhibition included:

- President of the Society of Motor Manufacturers and Traders;
- Director General, Fighting Vehicles;

- Vice Chairman, Nuffield Organisation;
- General Manager, Leyland Motors;
- Director, Dennis Bros;
- Sir William Routes, Chairman Routes Group;
- Chairman, British Overseas Airways Corporation;
- Sir Rowland Smith, Ford Motor Company;
- A.G. Wilson, Self-Changing Gears;
- Rear Admiral Slattery, Sea Plane Works Belfast;
- Representatives of Egham Council;
- Representatives from Joseph Sankey, Autodrome, Girling, Hobbs Transmissions.

The exhibition was a success and further events, again coinciding with the Commercial Motor Show, were held at regular intervals. Details of the 1962 show states that 150 vehicles were on display, fifty of which were used in demonstrations. Visits to the workshops were also available.

Notable exhibits in 1962 included:

- Multi-fuel engines from AEC and Rootes;
- A Land Rover with flotation bags, which, along with the Alvis Stalwart, gave swimming demonstrations;
- FV4008 Centurion with swimming kit;
- An Antar Tank Transporter carrying a Centurion on the tilt test platform;
- The Vickers Hover Land Rover;
- A Land Rover with Cuthbertson tracks;
- The TV1000 6×6 demonstrator.

Newly built skid pan hosting a vehicle exhibition, 30 September 1954.

Demonstration of a Land Rover with flotation bags at a vehicle exhibition at Longcross.

Longcross test track.

These exhibitions continued until 1972 as a showcase for British industry. On at least one occasion representatives from the Soviet Union attended and a story is told concerning the demonstration of vehicles swimming or wading through the wading pit. The last 'vehicle' was a 'stop me & buy one' tricycle; when it disappeared from sight and did not reappear the audience realised that this was a typical British joke and wandered off to the rest of the exhibition. The Soviets remained watching with concern until the joke was explained to them. The 'ice cream sales man' was perfectly safe as he was part of the safety diving team and had an oxygen bottle in the ice cream box.

Once built the test facilities remained in use largely unchanged through the life of the establishment and were still available for use at the time of writing although mainly for commercial testing and media events rather than for testing military vehicles. One of the impacts of the closure of Chertsey has been the loss of the ability to undertake repeatable trials over a known test course so that the performance of all vehicles can be reliably compared against a common baseline.

The utility of the test track was due not only to the facilities but also the skilled trials team including the vehicle drivers and the readily available backup from the workshops.

As previously mentioned, following on from wartime evaluation of German equipment, foreign vehicles, especially of Soviet origin, were tested when the

Ex-Iraqi BMD-1 on test at Longcross. This picture was provided by Brian Clark, a Chertsey test driver who, at the time, could fit inside such a confined vehicle.

Laying the pave course. In this photo dated November 1955 the Bailey bridge, which gave access from the main site, is visible in the background.

opportunity arose. A large number of vehicles captured during the First Gulf War were assessed on the test track and so some of the test drivers became proficient in driving a very wide range of vehicle types.

The track facilities are listed in Appendix C.

Throughout its life the test track was used for non-military purposes, for example for press launches of new vehicles, auto club days out, test drives and television and film productions. Those familiar with the test track know that the main course was the route taken by the Batmobile to the Bat Cave and the straight and level the scene of a car chase in *The Sweeny*. Other TV programmes filmed on the test track include *Spooks*, *Holby Blue* and *Echo Beach*. Use of the test track for launching new vehicles began early in the life of the facility, most notably for the press launch of the Mini in 1959.

Despite the concerns of local residents about the potential noise from the test track the only time there were significant complaints was when the McLaren Formula 1 team, with Nigel Mansell driving, used the test track for testing an automatic gearbox.

In the 1990s a member of DERA management proposed shutting the test track down. One of the aims of setting up DERA was to improve the cost effectiveness of MOD research and facilities through commercial exploitation and the test track made a good return through the large amount of non-MOD work undertaken. Fortunately sense prevailed and the closure did not go ahead at that time.

In 1999 the test track hosted the Defence Systems and Equipment International (DSEi) exhibition, exploiting the large available display area and close proximity of Longcross Station. Through the week that the exhibition was on there was a protest camp at the entrance to the establishment in Chobham Lane and unusually staff were required to use the Burma Road entrance.

Despite strict safety controls the test track was sadly the scene of tragedies. One was the death of the motorcyclist Alan Aspel, who was the editor of *Motor Cyclist Illustrated* and *Two Wheeler Dealer* among other publications. He died following a crash at the Guild of Motoring Writers/Institute of Motor Cycling Test Day in May 1979. This led to a ban of motorcycles using the test track. In another incident in 1980 two military members of the Chertsey trials staff, Gunner Ken Lilley of the Royal Artillery and Trooper Michael Allen of the Lancers, were killed when the CVR(T) they were crewing drove into the side of a Chieftain at high speed. They were both in their 20s and had recently returned to the main site after supporting SP70[*] cold weather trials in Norway. This accident was very sad for those at Chertsey, especially for the trials staff and drivers who were close friends with those killed.

---

[*] SP70 was a UK-German Self-Propelled Gun project.

Challenger 2 on the tilt platform. (Crown-Copyright-MOD)

Other Test Sites

In addition to the Longcross test track the establishment operated a number of other trial sites both local and further afield.

Bagshot Test Track

Situated about 8 miles south-west of the main site, this was mainly used as a rough-road test track for wheeled vehicles. It had a 3.7-mile rough-road main track that could accommodate vehicles up to the size of tank transporters and a narrower, steeper 'alpine course', which was 3.5 miles long and with gradient up to 1 in 2.7. The tracks were similar to the type used in some motor sport events like the RAC Rally and so the facility was sometimes used for testing and setting up rally cars. It was said that the Chertsey test drivers could always drive round the courses faster than the professional drivers as they knew the track so well.

Long Valley

Long Valley had been used for tracked vehicle testing since the days of the Tank Testing Section in the 1920s and it remained a tracked vehicle test track for Chertsey throughout the days of FVRDE and MVEE. Situated 17 miles south-west of the main site it was noted for the 2km 'Valley Bottom', which was used for heavy tracked vehicle running and was very muddy when wet and dusty when dry. In addition to the Valley Bottom there was a 4-mile sand and gravel course for wheeled vehicles and a 4-mile rough-road course. This area is still used for vehicle testing as part of the facilities used by the Army Trials and Development Unit (TDU) for Combat Support Vehicles.

Chieftain ARV trials at Long Valley, towing a prototype Chieftain hull with a Windsor Turret.

Hurn and Barnsfield Heath

These adjacent sites were the home of the Plant and Mechanical Handling Test Centre and other facilities that were part of the Christchurch establishment and so became part of the joint facilities with the formation of MVEE. The sites had a test track, suspension courses, a tilt platform and areas for testing earth-moving equipment and other plant. It is currently owned by QinetiQ and at the time of writing is still in use.

Kirkcudbright

Situated on the coast in south-west Scotland this was a 5,000-acre firing range with a 560km^2 sea safety area. It was used for main armament and gun and

Barnsfield Heath. (Crown Copyright-MOD)

Challenger 1 at the Central Firing Point at Kirkcudbright. (Crown Copyright-MOD)

fire-control equipment testing. It had a static range of 3.5km and a figure-of-eight test track for firing on the move.

As well as being used for testing conventional tank guns and associated gun and fire-control equipment it also became home to the UK electromagnetic gun test facility for which a purpose-built hangar was provided. The facility was built to support joint UK and US activities and the local press reported that a 'death ray' weapon was being tested there that was so dangerous that even the US would not allow testing in their home country. As a result of these rumours as soon as the hangar was finished there was a complaint from a local farmer that the testing was causing his best cows to die. His accusations were shown to be unfounded when he was invited to see the, as yet, empty hangar.

The benefits of the well-calibrated courses at Longcross, Bagshot and Long Valley were illustrated in a paper by David Cardwell. The paper, called 'Accelerations of Military Vehicles During Cross Country Operation', was presented to a symposium on vehicle ride at the Advanced School of Automotive Engineering at Cranfield in July 1962. This paper described work using the test track facilities to determine the loads that internal equipment was subject to in different classes of vehicle. With the usual FVRDE thoroughness comprehensive trials were carried out on a range of wheeled and tracked vehicles covering different weights and suspension types. The tracked vehicle trials were carried out on the Cambridge Carrier at 7.5 tons, Centurion Mk3 at 48 tons and Conqueror at 65 tons. It is interesting to note one comment in the paper where the author states that he considered the 65 tons of Conqueror to be the likely maximum of a tank and that future tanks would be 'considerably lighter'.

Climatic Chambers

In the early days of the DTD at Chertsey a tropical chamber and cold climatic chamber were built and were widely used. The tropical chamber was 12m by 6m and could operate at up to 71°C. The arctic chamber was 10.9m by 9.8m and could

Main entrance to the Complete Vehicle Climatic Chamber.

operate down to −40°c. These chambers were used for testing of equipment and for habitability trials. They were, however, very cramped especially with a vehicle the size of a Main Battle Tank inside and struggled to maintain test temperatures with vehicles running, hence the cold chamber trials tended to be limited to cold-start tests.

In 1982 the new climatic chamber facility was commissioned. It consisted of two chambers, which were larger and more capable than the existing ones. The two chambers and capabilities were:

The Complete Vehicle Climatic Chamber (CVCC)

- Chamber footprint: hexagonal 19.8m across flats;
- Height: 14.0m;
- Temperature range: −40°c to +52°c;
- Solar load: Up to 1,500W/m^2 – overhead and side arrays computer controlled to simulate diurnal cycles;
- Wind speed: Up to 26.8m/s (60mph);
- Dynamometers and wild heat dissipation to allow testing of vehicles with engines of up to 1,120kW (1,500hp).

The facility was used for testing a wide range of equipment, including, as discussed elsewhere, the majority of vehicles deployed in the First Gulf War. The ability to control the environment made it ideal for thermal signature trials, which could be carried out without the problems caused by the changeable British weather. In addition to land equipment the facility was also used for other systems including a Lynx Helicopter and a London Underground carriage.

The Climatic and Altitude Chamber (CAC)

- Footprint: 20m x 5.6m;
- Height: 5.6m;

- Temperature range: −57°c to +72°c;
- Altitude: Up to 4,300m (14,000ft);
- Wind speed: Up to 13.4m/s (30mph);
- Solar load: Up to 1,500W/m²;
- Dynamometers and wild heat dissipation to allow testing of vehicles with engines of up to 1,120kW (1,500hp).

The CAC altitude performance was based on the requirement for vehicles to drive over high mountain passes under extreme weather conditions.

The establishment had a wide range of smaller test chambers including environmental cabinets that could operate at up to 150°c, humidity cabinets, an altitude cabinet (up to 30,000ft) and salt spray cabinets.

Engineering Test Laboratories

An important goal of setting up the Department of Tank Design establishment on Chobham Common was to provide a facility for testing components and the Engineering Test Laboratories (ETL) remained an important part of Chertsey facilities throughout its life.

In addition to running the climatic chambers ETL carried out the testing of fans, filters, tyres, engines and suspension units. They also carried out shock and vibration testing of a wide range of components and subsystems intended for use on vehicles.

A focus of early work was fan and air-filter testing and the DTD carried out extensive research to develop a consistent test method. This resulted in a DTD specification, which later formed the basis of a British Standard (BS1701).

Tyre testing facilities enabled the performance of tyres to be consistently assessed at different speeds and loads. Other tests assessed the resistance of tyres to impacts and included a 'spike test'.

The establishment had always operated a number of engine test chambers with associated dynamometers. In 1961 there was major rework of the facilities

Chieftain in the Complete Vehicle Climatic Chamber. (Crown Copyright-MOD)

with water brake dynamometers being replaced by eddy-current dynamometers. An additional dynamometer rig was added at this time, making use of space previously occupied by the water cooling towers for the old dynamometers. In addition to engine dynamometer test rigs a whole vehicle rig, large enough to take a Main Battle Tank, was available. Initially the rig was in part of the main ETL facility, but there were issues with noise levels and so through the 1960s a replacement facility was used. This was a dynamometer tunnel built in an old wading pit where, because it was largely below ground level, noise levels were significantly reduced.

Specialist rigs for testing components included those for:

- Constant velocity joints;
- Gear trains;
- Torsion bars;
- Final drives;
- Chassis dynamics;
- Bursting tests for brakes, clutches and fans;
- Vertical and lateral shock testing of mounts and subsystems;
- Vibration tests.

In 1974 there was a major upgrade of ETL facilities with the build of the new test facility building which contained six state-of-the-art computer-controlled dynamometer test bays large enough to house engines or vehicles. The new building also housed the wide range of shock and vibration test rigs relocated from older buildings.

Sadly one fatal accident happened early in the life of the new ETL test building. On 6 January 1977 an Auto-Lab Technician, Duncan Morrison, was crushed when a transfer box (part of a power pack test rig) was being moved on a trolley out of a test cell. A wheel of the trolley snagged and the unit toppled off pinning Mr Morrison against the wall.

Tyre Test Rig. (Crown Copyright-MOD)

11

EQUIPMENT, CONCEPTS, DESIGNS AND DEVELOPMENT

Tank Concepts and Development

During much of its life the Chertsey establishment was the design authority for British military vehicles. In practice this meant it was responsible for the design and development of many vehicles, principally armoured vehicles. Even where the main design and development work was carried out in industry, as was usually the case for logistic vehicles, the establishment often had an important advice or support role. The establishment was responsible for production test specifications, testing of production vehicles and approval of subsequent modifications. Chertsey also carried out technical trials and testing in support of the equipment acceptance process.

The first significant product associated with Chertsey was the A41 Centurion tank, which the DTD started to develop in 1943. Twenty Mark Is were built and then the Mark II was the first full production version. It had thicker armour than the Mark I and a new-design cast turret that incorporated a cupola with all-round vision for the commander. A key innovation introduced early to the Centurion was the use of electrical stabilisation in elevation and azimuth for the main weapon.

In 1944 Field Marshal Montgomery stated that the army should move away from infantry and cruiser tanks to a single 'Capital' or 'Universal' tank that was capable of both roles; this decision finally addressed the policy on different types of tanks that had partly been responsible for British tanks being generally inferior to contemporary German vehicles for much of the war. At that time, as well as the A41, another new tank project was underway – the A45. This was being developed as an infantry support tank to complement the A41. It was to be fitted with a 20pdr gun, rather than the 17pdr on the A41, and had a design weight of 55 tons. Due to the work load at the DTD, English Electric was appointed as the main contractor to help development. The prototypes were planned to be completed by mid-1946 and when the first was built it was fitted with an A41 turret. An unusual feature was a remotely controlled machine gun on the front track guard; this was due to the hull machine gun and associated gunner, which was a common feature of British tanks of that time, being removed to allow more ammunition to be stowed.

In light of Montgomery's request the decision was made that a new Universal Tank (called the FV201) would be based on the A45, rather than on the Centurion, which was designated as the interim Universal Tank until the FV201 had been fielded. The decision was driven by the view that the A41 could not carry the required levels of armour protection or be readily adapted to the other proposed specialist variants. At the 1947 RAC conference it was stated that the FV201 would benefit from a lower ground pressure, improved ammunition storage, a hull machine gun, improved gun and fire control, thicker armour and an additional crew member in comparison with the Centurion, although an increase in weight was also recognised. The planned variants (with FV200 series designations) included a turreted and non-turreted Armoured Vehicle Royal Engineers (AVRE) (FV202 and FV203), Flail Tank (FV204), Assault Personnel Carrier (FV212), Bridge Layer (FV208), Recovery Vehicle and Beach Recovery Vehicle (FV209) and self-propelled guns and artillery tractors (FV205, FV206, FV207, FV210, FV211). In addition, the tank version was to be capable of being fitted with a dozer blade or be converted to a flame thrower variant in the field. A mock-up of the modified A45 design to meet the FV201 requirement was completed by June 1947 and a mild steel prototype was running by January 1948. The mock-up was then modified to represent the DD version. Work also started on other variants with the ARV and AVRE being the most advanced. Building of prototype flame-throwing equipment went ahead, the dozer blade design was built and tested, and a mock-up of the bridge laying equipment had been fitted to a Centurion. There were, however, questions about its performance and other issues arose concerning the variants; for example the flail tank required a longer hull to accommodate the engine and gearbox to drive the flail drum and neither the DD swimming version nor the bridge layer could be operated from the new Tank Landing Craft Mark VIII. Therefore in 1949 it was decided that the Centurion was to be adopted as the 'Universal Tank' until new designs could be developed. The decision was endorsed at the Royal Armoured Corps conference in November 1949. Work on the various variants of the FV201 stopped with the requirements to be met by solutions based on the Centurion or Churchill hull.

By the 1950s the process for developing a new equipment began with the generation of a General Staff Operational Requirements Document, called a GSR. From this a technical document known as the 'Military Characteristics' was developed. FVRDE would then undertake concept and technology demonstration activities from which the basic design was developed. Once this

Conqueror tank
(from the rear
with the turret
reversed). (Crown
Copyright-MOD)

was approved it was usual to appoint a design parent, from either industry or
the Royal Ordnance Factories, who would undertake the detailed design and
final prototype build working alongside FVRDE. This basic process was followed
throughout the life of FVRDE and MVEE until the time when the establishment
ceased to be the design authority for military vehicles.

There remained a requirement to defeat heavy Soviet tanks at range as the
Centurion was viewed as being 'out-gunned' by the Joseph Stalin III tank.
Following the 1949 RAC conference work started on developing requirements
and concepts for the new heavy tank and consideration was given to reducing
the turret crew to two men with the commander also acting as the gunner. In
1951 it was agreed that the FV201 would be used as the basis for this heavy tank
and would mount the US L1 120mm gun. The result was the FV214 Conqueror
tank. The hull required limited changes, the main one being an increase in the
power of the Meteor engine from 650hp to 810hp to cope with the increased
weight – which was eventually 65 tons. The increased power was achieved
through the use of direct fuel injection. More challenging was the design of a
completely new turret to mount the 120mm gun and stowage to carry enough
of the bulky ammunition. In order to demonstrate and prove the new engine
and give the army experience of operating such a heavy vehicle while the turret
was developed, it was agreed that a small number of FV214 hulls would be fitted
with an adaptor ring to take a Centurion Mark III turret; the resulting vehicle
was the FV221 Caernarvon. This was called the 'Interim Tank' by FVRDE and
four prototypes and ten pre-production vehicles were running by June 1953.
Following extensive testing of four Conqueror prototypes at FVRDE twenty
Mark Is were issued to the British Army of the Rhine (BAOR) early in April
1955. The Conqueror was the first tank to use the concept of a 'Hunter-Killer'
mode where the Commander could acquire a target, then automatically hand it
over to the gunner to engage, while he then searched for the next target. FVRDE

then developed the Mark II, which had a simplified crew interface for the gun and fire-control system.

A total of 180 Conquerors were built. A number of variants were planned including the FV215, intended as a super-heavy self-propelled anti-tank gun mounting a 180mm gun to defeat the expected successor to the Soviet Joseph Stalin III and T10 tanks; it only reached the wooden mock-up stage before work on it stopped in 1957. The only variant to reach production was the FV219 Armoured Recovery Vehicle (ARV).

In light of the threat from Soviet heavy tanks one variant of Centurion that reached prototype stage, but did not enter production, was the FV4004, called the Conway. This had a tall turret mounting the L1 120mm gun and was developed as a potential stopgap while the Conqueror was being developed. In support of the proposed FV215 super-heavy Self Propelled (SP) anti-tank gun the chosen weapon, the 180mm L4, was mounted on a Centurion hull in 1955 for trials. Although the resulting vehicle, the FV4005, was never intended to go into production, it can still lay claim to being the largest-calibre self-propelled anti-tank weapon ever made.

Improvements were continually developed for the Centurion and later production versions were up-gunned from the 17pdr to the 83.8mm 20pdr

FV4004 Conway. (Copyright W. Suttie)

FV4005. (Crown Copyright-MOD)

gun with earlier production vehicles modified. Later, in 1959, the fleet was again up-gunned to the L7 105mm. The Centurion was recognised as one of the world's best tanks and was purchased by Australia, Canada, Denmark, Egypt, India, Iraq, Israel, the Netherlands, South Africa, Sweden and Switzerland. In UK service it operated with distinction in Korea where its agility was used to good effect. At the Royal Armoured Corps conference held in November 1957 a representative of the 8th Hussars reported how it could reach places the lighter Cromwell Tanks and Oxford Carriers could not get to and how the 20pdr gun was accurate enough to target pillbox observation slots. The Israelis also had much success using Centurions with various upgrades and considered it far more survivable than the later US M60s in service at the same time.

By 1953 a programme had started for a family of self-propelled guns and supporting command vehicles based on Centurion automotives and running gear, with five- and six-wheel variants planned. None of what was to be the 3800 series of vehicles made it past the prototype stage.

FVRDE also developed the Charioteer (FV4101), which started to enter service with Yeomanry regiments in 1953. The requirement was driven by the need to field anti-tank weapons at a time when work on the Conqueror was not proceeding as quickly as planned. There was a surplus of 20pdr guns of the type being fitted to the Centurion and so a stopgap vehicle to mount these was required. Comet tanks were still required and so FVRDE developed a modified version of the Cromwell with an enlarged turret ring and light two-man turret. It only remained in service for around four years although in 1959 FVRDE successfully tested a version at Kirkcudbright fitted with a 105mm gun.

Meanwhile work had begun on developing a successor to the Centurion, with the challenge of producing a vehicle that had the firepower and protection of the Conqueror but within a smaller, lighter platform. The army defined initial requirements for the new tank (Medium Gun Tank No. 2) in 1951 and Chertsey started to investigate concepts. Some work was undertaken on a 'cleft turret' concept, which dispensed with a mantlet and enabled a lower turret. In 1953 it was decided to investigate the use of liquid-propellant guns, but this approach was soon rejected and in 1954 it was proposed that a concept be developed based on a 105mm gun using bagged charges. The weapon requirement was then revised and the decision made that it should be a 120mm gun. This decision followed an assessment of the required performance to defeat an internationally agreed armour target designed to represent postulated future Soviet tanks. The work on the 105mm gun using bagged charges had shown promise and so was taken forward as the starting point for the new 120mm gun on the basis that it would save weight over more conventional gun designs. Meanwhile Chertsey had looked at a novel approach to minimising height – the use of a prone position for the driver. In 1956, to assess if this was feasible from an operational perspective, a test bed, designated FV4202, was built based on Centurion components. It had a meteor engine and mounted the 105mm bagged charge gun in a cleft turret and is sometimes referred to as the 40-ton Centurion.

In June 1956 a new concept was produced, which embodied the L11 120mm bagged charge gun, a reclining driver, a 90°V8 engine and an automatic gearbox. The weight of the vehicle was estimated to be in the region of 47 tons. At that time it was hoped that with development the weight could be reduced to 45 tons, which was still considered by the army to be the desired maximum weight for a MBT. Leyland Motors was appointed as the main design contractor and some detailed design work started. It was then decided that the UK 120mm gun and US 90mm smoothbore should be interchangeable in both the new UK tank, now designated the FV4201, and the T95 being developed by the US. This then led to a decision to have a common turret for the UK and US tanks.[*] The common turret required a significant amount of redesign, adding delays to the programme. At a UK/US bilateral meeting in 1958 it was reported that the FV4201 turret could be fitted to the T95 hull but further changes would be required to fit the T95 turret to the FV4201 hull. However, by that time the US was working on the XM60 and soon abandoned the T95, which had a complex hull with adjustable suspension. The much simpler XM60 entered service as the M60. There was an initial assessment of whether the XM60 could be fitted with the FV4201 turret, which concluded it was feasible.

In November 1957 the third version of the operational requirements document was issued and this revised the gun elevation and depression limits, which increased significantly from +15° and −7° to +20° and −10°. To accommodate this the height, and hence weight, of the vehicle had to be increased. Further changes to requirements included an increase in protection and the fitting of infrared night fighting equipment. Towards the end of 1957 the NATO policy of using multi-fuel engines was agreed, leading to a decision in January 1958 to fit an opposed-piston multi-fuel engine. The use of this engine required a redesign of the engine compartment – which added another ton to the overall weight. The changes of requirements and policy meant that the project was now falling well behind schedule and so Vickers-Armstrong was appointed as the second main contractor to take over design of the turret. A mock-up was built and an acceptance meeting held in March 1959. The first automotive rig, P1, had its engine installed in September 1959 and this was followed by another automotive rig, P2, in April 1960. In addition to the prototypes built for development trials a further six were ordered in June 1959 for user trials, along with two vehicles specifically for gunnery trials.

---

[*] A prototype T95 was built with a 105mm gun. The turret with a 120mm gun was referred to as the T96 turret and a proposed version of the T95 with the T96 turret was referred to as the T95E6.

Chieftain being loaded at Liverpool docks en route to the desert trials at Yuma. (Crown Copyright-MOD)

The prototypes, with initial delivery dates, were:

P1	January 1960	Automotive rig with dummy turret
P2	April 1960	Automotive rig with dummy turret
P3	August 1960	Gun and fire-control development rig, including IR equipment
P4	July 1961	Firing trials development vehicle
P5	April 1962	Development trials
P6	Nov 1962	After development trials was put on the plinth at MVEE
W1	March 1961	Initially at Bovington and then reworked for user trials in the BAOR
W2	April 1961	Fitted with a 'Windsor'[*] Turret and sent to Bovington for driver trials. This vehicle was the first to be modified with Centurion-type road wheels to give increased ground clearance
W3	April 1961	Initially sent to Kirkcudbright and then Lulworth before rework for user trials in the BAOR
W4	Dec 1961	FVRDE/User Trials at Bovington
W5	February 1962	Bovington
W6	April 1962	BAOR Germany
G1	January 1962	Lulworth for gunnery trials G2
	Nov 1962	BAOR Germany

---

[*] The Windsor Turret was a circular dummy turret without a gun to provide a representative turret weight for automotive trials.

FVRDE was involved in the build of the initial prototypes and carried out much re-working to keep the prototypes up to the latest standards, especially as the automotives were developed and improved. This placed a very high workload on the workshops.

The prototypes now weighed 49.5 tons and the weight further increased when larger road wheels, of the type fitted to the Centurion, were fitted to increase ground clearance. Heavier tracks were also fitted to meet the German Government requirement to operate with rubber track pads. A further weight increase came with the introduction of the Nuclear Biological and Chemical (NBC) Collective Protection system. By this time the estimated weight for production vehicles was 53 tons, which was considered too heavy. Some weight reduction was achieved by a reduction in the arc over which the frontal armour protection was provided, removing armour from the search light and the army agreeing to reduce high-explosive squash-head (HESH) stowage by six rounds. The increase in weight had led to gearbox and running gear reliability issues and the engine being underpowered; hence further redesign and development were required. Changes to the engine, strengthening the gearbox and fitting larger air filters, along with lengthening of the hull to incorporate these changes, added further weight. Forty Mark I vehicles were built for troop trials and the first of the full-production

A resident and well-kept MVEE Chieftain – as shown by the MVEE Crest on the toe plate – pictured at the top of the test slopes. The number of armoured vehicles based at Chertsey meant that in its later years it was a site liable to visits by Soviet Arms Inspectors under the arms limitations agreements. An event rehearsed for several times but one that never occurred. (Crown Copyright-MOD)

vehicles (Mark II) was delivered to 11th Hussars in November 1966 with ten vehicles a month being delivered from January 1967. The Mark II had the revised automotives and running gear, an NBC pack, a contra-rotating commander's cupola with improved all-round vision, revised stowage and a Browning ranging machine gun (RMG) in place of the M85 gun, and weighed 55 tons.

Despite the increase in weight, testament to the Chieftain design was the fact that the production Chieftains still weighed 10 tons less than the Conqueror yet had 388mm frontal armour compared with 258mm on the Conqueror. It also had better gun depression, which had been a shortcoming with the Conqueror. When fielded it was the best protected in-service NATO tank and remained so until 1980. The areal density of the armour – 3 tons per square metre – has never been bettered. The one significant area of weakness with the Chieftain was its power pack. The unusual two-stroke opposed-piston engine selected to meet the multi-fuel requirement proved unreliable in service – leading to the joke 'Chieftain is the best tank in the world provided it breaks down in a good fire position'.

Significant efforts were made to address the reliability issues of the L60 and these are discussed in a later chapter. One requirement for the power pack was that the engine, gearbox and cooling system be combined to facilitate rapid removal for repair; this did at least mean that replacing the pack was a relatively straightforward task and minimised vehicle downtime. The worth of the Chieftain was, however, demonstrated by the desire of Israel to buy it. They had considered the German Leopard tank, which was allegedly described as a 'good agricultural tractor' in comparison. In support of the potential sale, under a programme called HOTSHOT 1, vehicles undertook hot weather trials in Aden between June 1966 and September 1966. Then under HOTSHOT 2 they went to Israel for firing trials; the vehicles were therefore in Israel during the 1967 war. An unconfirmed story is that a message was sent to Israel saying, 'Make sure our tanks are nowhere near the border,' to which a reply came back, 'Don't worry we've moved the border.' The potential sale to Israel gave impetus to a number of improvements to the Chieftain, including those to the power pack to improve operation in desert conditions. A new NBC pack was developed and further improvements were made to the gun and fire-control equipment as it moved from a ranging machine gun to a laser-rangefinder-based system. The purchase was blocked by the Wilson government and Israel developed the Merkava tank instead. The Chieftain was subject to continual improvement and one of the most significant upgrades was the fitting of the Improved Fire Control System (IFCS) on the Mark VIII. The final major upgrades to the Chieftain, which significantly enhanced its capability, were the fitting of the Thermal Observation and Gunnery Sight (TOGS) and additional turret armour. The armour fit was named Stillbrew after Colonel Still and John Brewer – John Brewer being a senior member of Chertsey staff. As well

Chieftain Armoured Engineer Vehicle (Gun) Concept. (Crown Copyright-MOD)

as Israel the Chieftain was assessed by the Netherlands, with the potential sale supported by Exercise CRACKLE which ran from November 1967 to July 1968, and by Switzerland, supported by Exercise Royal Chief which ran from August 1971 to March 1972.

A number of Chieftain variants were planned of which the Armoured Recovery Vehicle (ARV) and Armoured Vehicle Launched Bridge (AVLB) went into production. Two armoured engineer variants were planned, Armoured Engineer Vehicle (Winch), AEV(W), which was based on the ARV and Armoured Engineer Vehicle (Gun), AEV(G), which was planned to mount a 165mm demolition gun in a modified turret. These AEV variants were never developed, which meant that the Centurion Engineer Tank was run on and saw service in the Gulf War. When the Challenger entered service some surplus Chieftain gun tanks were re-worked as Armoured Vehicles Royal Engineer (AVRE) with the turret removed and a frame for carrying fascines fitted.

Even with the design and development of the Chieftain well in hand there was still a significant amount of concept work ongoing at Chertsey. Much of this was driven by the perceived requirement for increased mobility of tanks on the nuclear battlefield; this called for lighter, faster tanks without compromising the firepower or protection.

In the early 1950s work had started on a vehicle called 'Contentious'. Contentious sought to take a radical approach to the provision of a tank destroyer capability providing the firepower of FV214 within a smaller, lighter and cheaper package (aimed to be one-quarter of the cost). The initial concept, which was reported on in a significant amount of detail in a 1953 report, was for a one-man tank. The running gear and power train were based on the FV400 series (Cambridge Carrier) but upgraded to carry additional weight. Gun, missile and rocket versions were considered but the gun option preferred. It mounted four 120mm guns each with a single round, but following user feedback this was revised to two 120mm guns each with a seven-round revolving autoloader. The

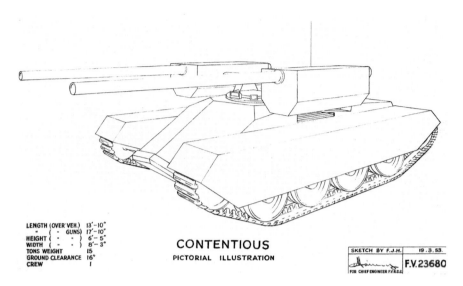

LENGTH (OVER VEH.)	13'-10"
" (" GUNS)	17'-10"
HEIGHT (" ")	6'-5"
WIDTH (" ")	8'-3"
TONS WEIGHT	15
GROUND CLEARANCE	16°
CREW	1

CONTENTIOUS
PICTORIAL ILLUSTRATION

| SKETCH BY F.J.H. | 19.3.53. |
| FOR CHIEF ENGINEER F.V.R.D.E | F.V.23680 |

Initial Contentious Concept for a one-man tank with two 120mm guns. (Crown Copyright-MOD)

guns were to be mounted on a cupola giving +/− 20° of traverse and +10/−5° of elevation. To meet the requirement for low cost, no stabilisation was fitted for firing on the move, but a ranging machine gun was planned to give a high probability of a first-round hit when static. The frontal armour was 6in thick but at 6ft 5in high and 8ft 3in wide (compared with 11ft 2in and 13ft 1in of the Conqueror) its small silhouette was expected to provide significant survivability benefits. The all up weight was estimated at 15 tons.

User feedback on the concept highlighted a number of concerns, including:

- The viability of a one-man crew;
- Vulnerability of the external guns;
- Lack of rounds (fourteen only) − the user expressed a preference for a single gun and more rounds;
- Accuracy of the guns − only likely to be accurate to 1,000yd;
- The need for improved mobility for the nuclear battlefield (the mobility would have been similar to that of the Centurion).

As a result, initial schemes were developed for a new two-man tank concept and these were reported in 1955. Following refinement detailed concepts were developed and reported in August 1959. The new concept, Contentious II, had a two-man crew and autoloader and mounted a limited traverse gun (+/−20°) in the hull, rather than a rotating turret. Gun elevation was to be achieved by tilting the whole hull through the use of adjustable suspension with a target of providing 18° of elevation. In order to assess the feasibility of this concept for gun aiming a Comet-based demonstrator was built with four road wheels and adjustable suspension. The calibre of the gun was to be a 120mm but 155mm or 160mm low-pressure guns firing HESH at a lower muzzle velocity were also considered. In addition a coaxially mounted 76mm gun (as fitted to Saladin) was proposed to provide a HE capability. The crew sat side by side and either crew member could drive or fire the gun with the proposed engagement cycle based on the commander taking control of driving on acquiring a target and slewing the vehicle so that the target could then be tracked by the gunner over the 40° arc of traverse. Missiles had again been considered for the main armament but rejected due to the low rate of fire – it was claimed that trials had indicated that Contentious II could hit sixteen targets in a minute. Frontal-arc protection was to be provided by two 40mm steel plates with a gap of over 1.2m between then. The slope of the plates plus 'ribbing' was claimed to improve performance against armour-piercing rounds. The large gap between the plates was to be utilised as a fuel tank, further enhancing protection. The total frontal protection was reported to be equivalent to 150mm of homogeneous steel armour. A polythene liner impregnated with Boron was to be provided to enhance protection against neutrons and reduce spall fragments if penetrated. The power pack was to be a multi-fuel engine of between 350hp and 500hp. It was recognised there were no suitable engines available, but an engine bay mock-up was built to start scoping the size and packaging requirements. The overall achievable weight was estimated to be around 20 tons, although schemes up to 30 tons were looked at, which had enhanced crew protection. Other novel features being considered included a photoelectric gun-control system and a pulsed-light ranging system. At the UK/US/Canadian armour conference in 1958 the UK reported that a test hull for Contentious, weighing around 13½ tons, had been used in air-drop tests from a Beverly aircraft. At the time the US were interested in the Contentious concepts as they were looking for a 25–30-ton vehicle to replace the M48. A wheeled variant, potentially with hydraulic drive, was considered as a follow-on from the initial tracked version and design data was carried across from the TV1000, which is discussed later.

Another concept that reflected a lot of the thinking from the Contentious studies was a Liquid Propellant (LP) gun concept. This had a two-man crew and like Contentious had a limited traverse gun. Unlike Contentious, gun elevation was achieved through elevating the complete crew compartment, which was a separate pod. A large-scale model of the concept was made and some forty years later, in the 1990s, this model was brought out of store when a team from RARDE at Fort Halstead visited Chertsey. They had come to argue a case for funding to undertake some concept design work for a liquid-propellant gun tank, claiming no work had been done. After their pitch the model, which had been hidden under a sheet, was revealed. It was pointed out that the main reason the concept was not taken forward in the 1950s – namely the highly corrosive nature of the propellant – had still not been addressed and so further concept work would be nugatory. This did not stop the Guns Division at RARDE from continuing to work on LP guns and concepts and only stopped after encountering 'unexplained events' with the propellant.

The Contentious project fed into another project – called Prodigal – which covered long-term concept and technology work for a family of 20–30-ton armoured vehicles to be fielded around 1970–75. Research addressed a number of the technology challenges highlighted by the Contentious studies, including autoloaders (with seven design concepts being assessed) and weapon accuracy. To improve accuracy trials were undertaken of a 105mm weapon with an additional barrel support mounted well forward of the main trunnion bearing. This line of study did not work, but the data and ideas it generated did lead to the very successful work on muzzle reference systems. An initial concept study report for Prodigal was issued in 1960, supported by a report on weapon options. This included an assessment of the US Shillelagh weapon system, which could fire gun-tube launched missiles.

In the 1960s, even before the Chieftain had entered full production, long-term concepts for a possible replacement started to be considered. An initial GSR, 1008, for Chieftain replacement was issued in June 1961. An emphasis continued to be placed on reducing weight while maintaining firepower and protection and so by 1966 FVRDE was evaluating a range of concepts in the 40–50-ton bracket. One potential way of reducing weight that was considered was replacing the manned turret with an unmanned external gun. This could significantly reduce the overall weight as a manned turret can typically be around one-third of the weight of an MBT. Such a configuration can also reduce the frontal area when in a hull-down fire position and enable the crew to be located where they are least

Two-man liquid propellant
tank concept model. (Crown
Copyright-MOD)

vulnerable – down in the hull. In order to explore the concept of an external gun, in 1968 FVRDE built the world's first external gun demonstrator. It was based on a Comet hull and mounted an 83.8mm gun with autoloader; it was called the COMRES 75. A key driver for the vehicle was to demonstrate the viability of a reliable autoloader as this is essential for such a concept.

Chieftain replacement was further addressed as part of the 'AFV for the 80's' project. Stages 1 and 3 of this project, which are described later, addressed the requirements for medium-weight vehicles and self-propelled anti-tank systems respectively; Stage 2 addressed the requirements for Main Battle Tanks. As part of the study six main concept designs were developed:

- Conventional 55-ton tank;
- Lighter 45-ton conventional tank with fewer stowed rounds and reduced protection levels;
- External gun concept with ready rounds and autoloader behind the gun;
- External gun concept with ready rounds and autoloader in the hull;
- 'Conventional' semi-fixed gun concept;
- Fixed gun concept with crew in an elevating pod.

By the time Stage 2 reported in February 1972, FV4211, described below, had already been built and the decision made to develop the next MBT as a joint venture with Germany; however the 'AFV for the 80's' concepts were fed into that programme.

The decision that the next MBT, called 'Future Main Battle tank', would be a joint venture with Germany was made in the late 1960s. It was based on the fact that at that time the two nations were both planning a Main Battle Tank replacement programme around 1985, the UK for Chieftain and Germany for Leopard I. In 1970 a meeting was held between the respective army chiefs and by 1971 there was general agreement on a General Staff Target. An Anglo-German technical symposium was held in May 1972 after which plans for a joint programme started to be drawn up. At this symposium the idea of an external gun was discounted, but much interest was expressed in a turret-less tank with the gun mounted in the hull. Some of the thinking was driven by the very compact Swedish S-Tank, two examples of which had been assessed by the army at Bovington in 1968. During 1973 an agreement was reached on a broad division of development responsibilities; however, the work-share situation was complicated by parallel work on a standardised NATO gun, which involved the US. Two sets of concepts were considered: turreted concepts with a weight target of 55 tons and semi-fixed gun concepts with a weight target of 48 tons. The main armament was to be either a 110mm or 120mm gun and power packs under consideration were Rolls-Royce CV12 and CV16 and the MTU871 and 873.

MVEE developed a semi-fixed gun concept that had some features first considered for Contentious. Unlike the S-Tank, which had a fixed gun, the MVEE concept allowed the gun to elevate from -10 to $+20°$ and traverse $+/-$ $2°$, allowing fine tracking without moving the hull. The concept was much better protected than the S-Tank and so weighed 54 tons compared with 39 tons. Meanwhile the army carried out a further assessment of the S-Tank with ten vehicles borrowed for trials in Germany (Exercise Dawdle) and it was concluded that the lack of turret and inability to fire on the move was too restricting. Despite this some further work was carried out on the MVEE turret-less tank concept, which adopted the German name of Casemate. A Casemate Test Rig was built based on Chieftain components. It made extensive use of aluminium to minimise weight but was wider than the Chieftain and had a modified engine compartment so that a ten-cylinder MTU engine could be fitted in place of the L60. The barrel was a dummy tube, although use of a 120mm gun was envisaged, as was the fitting of Chobham armour. The demonstrator was transferred to the Bovington Tank Museum in 1990 where it is often referred to as the JagdChieftain. It was less complex than the German contribution, which had two guns for improved first round(s) hit and attempted firing on the move by coincidence firing when zigzagging. The German turreted concepts included both conventional layouts and 'Driver in Turret' or DIT concepts. MVEE analysis of the German turret concepts concluded that they would exceed the 55-ton weight target, estimating both at over 60 tons. The DIT concept required a large turret and turret ring, and so would not have fitted inside the rail gauge for transportation.

Since 1970, in parallel with the FMBT studies, Germany had also been developing an improved version of the Leopard tank as a replacement for its M48 tanks. Named Leopard II in 1971, this vehicle incorporated the power pack and other technologies from the German/US MBT70 project. By 1976 the Germans had concluded that FMBT, as envisaged, would provide only limited benefits over Leopard II, especially as analysis of lessons from the 1973 Yom Kippur War had already led to an increase in armour protection on that vehicle. The increased protection was based initially on the use of multi-layer perforated armour in place of conventional sloped armour. However, following the release of details of Chobham armour under FMBT, a further redesign was made to incorporate this technology. With Leopard II well advanced Germany wanted to delay the FMBT project, but the UK needed to continue to develop a replacement for the Chieftain. The UK also saw that programme timescales were being put at risk due to continuing indecision regarding a common NATO tank gun. With the disagreement on timescales, work on the joint project was terminated in March 1977. The tenth and final Anglo-German FMBT Steering Group meeting convened in March 1978 at which was approved a 'lessons learnt' document. The fact that releasing details of Chobham armour to Germany resulted in them incorporating it in Leopard II, which in turn contributed to their decision to withdraw from the FMBT project, did not go down well at Chertsey.

Chertsey had been working on the development of Chobham armour since the 1960s. The flat armour pack configuration required a different approach to hull- and turret-structure design, and in 1971 to demonstrate this the world's first 'Chobham armour' tank, the FV4211, was built. It was based on Chieftain components but with a new hull and turret structure. The hull structure made use of aluminium to keep the weight within acceptable limits. The feasibility and suitability of aluminium for MBT hulls had been demonstrated on the 'Test Vehicle Aluminium (TVA) demonstrator. It was testimony to the excellent Chertsey design office and workshops that the demonstrator was built in only thirteen months. Originally the vehicle was considered as an interim replacement for Chieftain to field Chobham armour quickly and a number of prototype vehicles were planned. Ten turret castings were made and work on nine hulls started but only the one vehicle was completed. To ensure that a full set of Chieftain components were delivered for the first FV4211, ROF Leeds built a complete Chieftain vehicle using a rejected hull casting and this was delivered to MVEE for dismantling. The idea of putting FV4211 into production was dropped when work started on the UK/German FMBT programme, although it did form the basis of the UK 'Concept 2' developed for that programme. The single prototype continued to be used as a research platform.

As FMBT was an international project, with the added complexities of joint decision making and work share, it was known that it was likely to be subject to delays. This was borne out early in 1974 when at the request of the Federal Republic of Germany the concept phase was extended by eighteen months. Hence the possible need for an interim vehicle was identified. In July 1974 a proposal was made for a project called 'Kinship', which would use the experience on FV4211 to design a vehicle with Chobham armour based on reworked Chieftains. Like FV4211 Kinship was to have an aluminium hull to keep the weight within acceptable limits, the feasibility of which had been demonstrated previously on the TVA. It was soon recognised that the so called 'rework' was actually a very extensive exercise and would not be the low-cost option originally envisaged.

After the failure of the Anglo-German FMBT initiative the US XM1 programme, which developed into the M1 Abrams, was considered. This was rejected because it failed to meet the UK Staff Requirement; in particular the fire-control capability was inadequate and, even though it incorporated Chobham armour technology, the protection was inadequate. Hence in 1976 MVEE started work on MBT80.

The concept selected for MBT80 was a conventional four-man-crew turreted tank. It was, however, to have many advanced features. In addition to high levels

MBT 80

Artist's impression
of the MBT80.
(Crown
Copyright-MOD)

of protection based on the latest variants of Chobham armour, it was to have independently stabilised gunner's and commander's sights, a thermal imager (TI) with integrated rangefinder, digital gun and fire control with coincidence firing, a dynamic muzzle reference system, an advanced power pack and advanced electronics. The TI sight for the MBT80 was to be the STAMP (Sight, Thermal, Armoured, Periscope), with a CO_2 laser rangefinder, hence called STAMPLAR. It was not a fully panoramic sight but could be traversed over an azimuth range of $\pm90°$. Due to its size the unit, including large internal cooling system, was to be mounted on the loader's side of the turret. Therefore a Chieftain was modified to represent the internal volume in order to check that the loader could still operate with the resultant intrusion. The MBT80 programme defined a number of system development rigs including three turrets and a hull, which were due to be completed by 1981. The rigs included a trials turret, called the Fire Control Rig (FCR), to support the development of the gun and fire-control equipment. In addition development of the TN38 gearbox, to match the proposed 1,500hp engine, was also started. It was planned that nine prototypes would be delivered between April 1983 and October 1983 but none were completed. Production activities had been planned to start in 1986 with an in-service date of 1989 and, despite some unresolved technology issues, there was pressure to compress the programme and bring this forward to 1987.

Meanwhile MVEE had also been supporting Defence Sales in efforts to sell equipment to Iran. The establishment hosted a number of VIP visits including one by the Technical Advisor to the Iranian Minister of War on 24 November 1972 and the Iranian Vice Minister for War in March 1973. Initially efforts were focused on securing the sale of 800 Chieftains. However, although the Iranians wanted to buy Chieftain, they wanted a more reliable engine, automatic transmission and Chobham armour. The FV4211 vehicle had already demonstrated some of the features they were looking for and a significant order for Main Battle Tanks was subsequently secured, to be delivered in three phases covering:

FV4030/1: Chieftain with some minor improvements

FV4030/2: Shir 1: An improved Chieftain with:

- Improved Fire Control System (IFCS); the development of which came from fire-control research at Chertsey and was also implemented on British Army Chieftains;
- New hull back half to house a new power pack;
- Rolls-Royce CV12 engine;
- David-Brown TN37 Hydrostatic gearbox.

FV4030/3: Shir 2: A vehicle with a new hull and turret structure incorporating:

- Significantly improved protection using Chobham armour;
- The CV12/TN37 power pack;
- Improved mobility through the use of hydrogas suspension.

The size of the order was large, covering 200 Phase 1 vehicles – the only ones actually delivered to Iran, 125 Phase 2 vehicles and 1,250 Phase 3 vehicles. The FV4030/3, which was effectively a new vehicle, was developed within very short timescales compared with those normally associated with the development of complex armoured vehicles. Within five years of contract start six 4030/3 prototypes were running and the first production vehicles had started to work their way down the line at the ROF Leeds. This rapid development time was only possible due to the expert technical, drawing office and workshop staff and facilities at Chertsey along with the range of advanced technologies that could be drawn from the comprehensive research and demonstration programmes at the establishment. The Iranian order for Shir 2 placed the UK in the position of being the inventors of Chobham armour but possibly seeing the US (with the M1 Abrams) and Iran (with Shir 2) fielding vehicles protected by it first.

When work started on FV4030 a follow-up proposal to Kinship was considered, which drew on the experience of FV4211, Kinship and FMBT. This was for a UK version of FV4030, called project 4222. It was to mount a 110mm gun but be designed for this to be replaced with a 120mm gun if required. Like 4030 it would have Chobham armour, a CV12 engine and hydrogas suspension, but 4222 had a target design weight of 55 tons compared with the 60 tons of 4030. The weight reduction was to be achieved partly through the use of a combined steel/aluminium hull structure.

In March 1979 the change of regime in Iran meant the cancellation of the orders. By this time the 125 Shir 1s had been built and production of Shir 2 had just started with nine hulls fabricated, two of which, along with two turrets, had been passed to the assembly line. The loss of the orders presented significant problems to ROF Leeds, which had transferred work on the Combat Engineer Tractor and Light Weight Gun to other ordnance factories in order to work on the Iranian order. The factory now had no orders and production of MBT80 was

Khalid undertaking track durability trials at the Frome basalt mine. (Photo courtesy of Paul Fenne)

several years away. The factory did win some small commercial orders to bring in a limited amount of work but not enough to be viable. Then in October 1979 Jordan agreed to buy the undelivered Shir 1 vehicles and ordered a further 148, thus ensuring ROF Leeds would be viable at least for the near term; the Shir 1 vehicles went into service in Jordan as the Khalid.

Some problems with track life were experienced on Khalid and a suitable representative test area was required to test the durability of redesigned tracks. The solution to the test site was use of an open Basalt mine near to Frome in Somerset. At the time the mine was the largest in Europe and provided ample space for running the required thousands of kilometres.

On 14 July 1980 there was a Parliamentary Statement that a new tank, to be known as Challenger, would be brought into service to equip four armoured brigades in the BAOR. This £300m order for 237 Challengers used the opportunity to undertake a partial replacement of the aging Chieftain fleet with a vehicle based on 4030/3, thus exploiting the investments already made. As well as enhancing the BAOR until a full replacement of the Chieftain could be fielded it helped preserve around 10,000 jobs that had been put at risk with the loss of the Iranian order. A General Staff Requirement for Challenger was developed quickly by Patrick Cordingley, who was then a Major, but went on to command the Challenger-equipped Desert Rats in the liberation of Kuwait. The requirement was compromised somewhat by what was achievable based on the existing 4030/3 design but resulted in a number of changes. The most notable were fitting the Thermal Observation and Gunnery Site (TOGS) and revised stowage to take a longer armour-piercing fin-stabilised discarding-sabot

FV4030/4. This is a copy of a publicity picture taken of the vehicle at Long Valley. (Crown Copyright-MOD)

Challenger 1 prototype undergoing user acceptance trials near Tidworth. (Crown Copyright-MOD)

(APFSDS) round. The resulting vehicle, 4030/4, was accepted for service on 14 December 1982 with the proviso that remaining issues with areas such as the engine generator drive, laser range finder and gearbox were addressed. Challenger entered British Army service in April the following year with the Royal Hussars being the first regiment to be equipped.

The decision to procure Challenger clearly had implications for MBT80 and the same Parliamentary Statement announced that the MBT80 project, as then running, would be cancelled. However, studies and technology maturation work would continue to support the development of a vehicle that, in the longer term, would replace the remaining Chieftains.

In 1983, at the invitation of the government there, Challenger 1, along with Warrior, was successfully demonstrated in the United Arab Emirates (UAE) showing it was able to cope with the terrain and environment. The French AMX30 tank was run alongside Challenger but unlike Challenger was not able to complete the mobility test course despite being a lighter vehicle. Operational availability for both UK vehicles was high over trials which covered around 900km and the problems that did occur were assessed as being minor.

Although the Challenger 1* had a number of subsystems inherited from the Chieftain, it represented a significant step in terms of protection and mobility. The vehicle was used very effectively by UK forces in Operation Granby, the Liberation of Kuwait. In his thank you speech to Chertsey, Major General Patrick Cordingley highlighted that the performance of the Challenger 1 compared favourably with that of the more complex and more expensive US Abrams tank. He noted that despite issues with Challenger 1 reliability he still had 98 per cent of his vehicles operational at the end of the campaign. The high operational availability enabled UK forces to undertake more extensive training than the US forces once in theatre. The resulting high readiness of crews and vehicles enabled them to successfully take on and defeat the best-trained and best-equipped elements of the occupying Iraqi forces. The much longer range of the Challenger 1 across difficult desert terrain compared with the Abrams also contributed to its success. Exploiting the firepower and night-fighting capability there were confirmed kills of Iraqi tanks at night at ranges out to 4km. A testament to the tempo the Challenger 1 provided came near the end of the campaign when the Desert Rats were ordered to occupy positions across the Basra Road before the planned ceasefire time. Due to what appears to have been a misunderstanding of time difference between UK and Kuwait the Desert Rats were required to fight their way across difficult desert terrain and through enemy-held positions before the deadline, advancing 40 miles in well under two hours.

To address known shortfalls of 4030/4 the Challenger Improvement Programme was started in 1980 with the aim to bring it up to the standard of that planned for MBT80. The programme was to be in two phases with changes being brought into production in December 1986 and mid 1989 respectively. The initial project was soon modified to have a less ambitious programme of work, which was undertaken addressing both the Chieftain and Challenger fleets under the Chieftain/Challenger Improvement Programme (CHIP). The key capability areas where improvements were to be sought through the CHIP programme were:

---

* Although originally called Challenger, it was subsequently referred to as Challenger 1 following the start of the Challenger 2 project.

1. Firepower, including improved kinetic energy (KE) ammunition;
2. Gun and fire control to reduce engagement times and improve chance of hits against moving targets;
3. Automotive agility and manoeuvrability without loss of reliability;
4. NBC protection.

As well as ongoing gun and fire-control research Chertsey worked extensively on the automotive aspects, which included a new gearbox, improved main engine and auxiliary generators, hydraulic track tensioner, digital engine controller and double pin track. A major output from the CHIP programme was an improved gearbox, TN54, which although not fitted to the Challenger 1, was initially used on the Challenger Armoured Repair and Recovery Vehicle (CRARRV) and later on the Challenger 2 and the Trojan and Titan engineer vehicles. Other automotive aspects were also later exploited on the Challenger 2. Chertsey worked with Microflow Pathfinder, then at Farnborough, to develop the CHIP NBC filtration pack. This was three-quarters of the size of the existing No. 6 Mark II pack but provided the same air throughput and had improved integrity. It was retrofitted to Chieftain and Challenger 1 tanks and later used on the Challenger 2.

Meanwhile MVEE undertook a study into the longer-term requirements for a MBT to be fielded in 1995. Findings were presented at a conference hosted at Chertsey on 14 July 1981. A focus of the study was the benefits that a smaller vehicle gave in terms of survivability, hence the supporting concepts presented layouts that were the same size, or smaller than T72. The reduced size compared with the Challenger was achieved by either having only two men in the turret and using an autoloader, or by having an external gun with either a two- or three-man crew in the hull. In order to meet the 1995 in-service date it was recognised that development of the concept would need to start in 1984, followed by project definition in 1986 and full development starting in 1988. More in-depth studies were undertaken in 1983 and 1984 as the 'Future Tank Study'. The MOD placed contracts with consortia lead by Vickers, Alvis and ROF(Leeds) to carry out the work; the ROF(L) team included the MVEE Concepts Branch as they did not have their own concepts team. The Chertsey-generated concepts included:

- Concept A: Small turreted tank with carousel autoloader;
- Concept B: External gun;
- Concept C: Hybrid 105mm external gun/missile concept.

The Future Tank Study identified a number of technology areas where research and risk reduction was required; these were addressed by the Component Technology Demonstrator Programme (CTDP) and the Operation Demonstrator Programme (ODP). The CTDP had a number of strands including the integration of a gas

Chertsey Generated Future Tank Study
Concept C. (Crown Copyright-MOD)

turbine in a Chieftain, undertaken by ROF Leeds. This demonstrator was short-lived as it was found that the power pack could not survive reverse loads through the transmission – a fact only discovered when the vehicle was reversed off the tank transporter when delivered to Chertsey. More successful was the Signature Classification and Reduction (SCAR) programme, which resulted in Chertsey becoming world leaders in land equipment signature management. Other successful aspects of the CTDP were a bustle autoloader, an Automatic Target Detection and Tracking (ATDT) system and a panoramic thermal sight with an integrated CO_2 laser. A carousel autoloader was also constructed as part of a parallel research activity. The ODP investigated the endurance of three-man crews, command and control of a tank using indirect vision and the reliability of autoloaders.

The last significant MBT study undertaken by Chertsey was the Evolutionary National Tank concept, which generated an initial report in December 1986 with studies continuing into 1987. The resulting concept was for a vehicle with a three-man crew, a fully integrated fire-control system and a Battlefield Information System. It was planned to mount a 140mm main armament fed from a carousel autoloader, ammunition stowage being forty rounds with fifteen ready rounds in the carousel. Overall it was smaller and lighter than the Challenger, but with better mobility, firepower and protection. As well as the reduced crew number, size was also to be reduced through the use of a compact power pack. The engine was planned to be based on the CV8 and generate 1,000hp, giving a lower nominal engine power than the Challenger. However, the concept was being designed to be 10 per cent lighter than the Challenger and use the highly efficient TN55 gearbox to provide an effective power-to-weight ratio that was as good as or probably better than the Challenger. As well as a smaller engine and efficient compact gearbox the power pack had the engine mounted transversely to reduce size and hence used a 'U' shape, rather than traditional 'T' shape power pack configuration.

The programme to replace the remaining 600 tanks in the Chieftain fleet, following the partial replacement by Challenger 1s, was called the Chieftain Replacement Programme. It was undertaken after design authority for armour vehicles had been transferred from Chertsey to industry. The programme was therefore limited to a competition between existing platforms with varying degrees of modification to meet the British Army requirements, with the role of Chertsey to act as expert technical advisors. The full requirement for Chieftain replacement, Staff Requirement (Land) 4026, was issued in November 1987. The resulting competition was between the US Abrams, German Leopard 2 (Enhanced), French Leclerc and an improved Challenger, offered by Vickers Defence Systems. This had a largely unchanged hull but a new turret. An important requirement of the Chieftain replacement programme was to provide improved turret ergonomics and gun and fire-control equipment compared with the Challenger 1, the turret systems of which had largely been carried over from the Chieftain. In addition the MVEE Concepts Branch developed a 'benchmark' design to illustrate what could be achieved using mature technologies but starting from a clean sheet of paper. This design would have been significantly more survivable than any of the vehicles offered but would have required development from scratch. The competition was won by the improved Challenger – which entered service in 1998 as the Challenger 2. It had a later version of Chobham armour, improved turret ergonomics, the improved L30 120mm gun and an improved, state-of-the-art, gun and fire-control system. Although the overall hull design was largely unchanged, it incorporated 150 design changes, which were mainly aimed at improving reliability and maintainability. Challenger 2 was

Challenger 2.
(Copyright
W.Suttie)

'The Race.' The original of this picture, which shows three generations of Main Battle Tank developed at Chertsey, hung in the International Building for many years.

successfully deployed to the Balkans and used in action during the invasion of Iraq. However, in comparison with previous post-war UK MBTs it did not provide the world-beating capability leap that the Chieftain, for example, had given. One area where the Challenger 2 did make significant advances compared with the Challenger 1 and other contemporary vehicles was in the area of signature management. This was achieved by exploiting the output of the Chertsey SCAR programme, and Vickers Defence Systems directly funded the Chertsey experts to support their design effort. Proposals were made to increase the power of the engine from 1,200hp to 1,500hp, which would have been within the scope of the existing gearbox and suspension designs, but this was not taken forward.

One other area where Chertsey undertook some tank concept work during the final years of the establishment was for vehicles armed with an electromagnetic gun. These studies mainly demonstrated that, with the low maturity and limitations of the gun and associated power conditioning and storage systems, such a vehicle was impractical.

Medium and Light Tracked AFV Development

Although Chertsey is perhaps most well known for developing concepts and designs for Main Battle Tanks, it was responsible for a wide range of other armoured tracked and wheeled vehicles. One of the most noteworthy was the Combat Vehicle Reconnaissance (Tracked) – CVR(T) – family. Work had started during the Second World War for a new light tank – the A46 – to replace the US Stuart and Chaffee tanks and a contract was placed with Vickers to support the design work. It was intended as an air transportable vehicle with a target weight of between 14 and 16 tons. The possibility of transporting major subsystems such as the turret, or gun and tracks, in a separate aircraft to the hull, was considered to maintain aircraft range; this was long before the 'Fly Light – Fight Heavy' concept for vehicles was considered in the 1990s. Progress on the design was slow but a wooden mock-up was built, which resulted in a number of design changes including fitting a different engine, a 350hp unit based on the Meteor, called the Meteorite, and a revised transmission layout.

In 1946 there was renewed interest and the project was reinvigorated as the FV300 family of vehicles which included the FV301 light tank. The FV301 was designed to meet a requirement for a tracked reconnaissance vehicle to supplement wheeled armoured cars. It was designed to mount the 77mm gun, which was to be mounted well forward to minimise the space taken up in the turret. This resulted in an out-of-balance configuration and the use of equilibrator and a new concentric recoil system. The FV301 was intended to have 50mm frontal armour, a 500hp engine and weigh 21 tons. Flotation equipment and an appliqué dozer blade were also designed. The intended family of vehicles was:

FV301 – Light Tank;
FV302 – Command Post;
FV303 – 20pdr SP Gun;
FV304 – 25pdr SP Gun;
FV305 – 5.5in SP Gun;
FV306 – Light ARV;
FV307 – Radar Vehicle;
FV308 – Field Artillery Tractor;
FV309 – Ammunition Vehicle;
FV310 – Light APC;
FV311 – Armoured Load Carrier.

Of these FV301, FV302, FV303 and FV304 are known to have reached the prototype stage with the FV303 seen as the highest priority vehicle, required to replace Second World War SP guns. In addition to the above a design study was undertaken for a flamethrower version, but this was not taken forward due to cost considerations. Work to support the FV304 included the build of a mock-up of the crew compartment, which was trialled in July 1948 to assess the ability of the crew to load the weapon within the cramped confines. The mock-up included the proposed sixty-round stowage bin. In 1949 the decision was made to focus on the front-engine variants, in particular FV310 light APC, with rear-engine variants like the FV301 put in abeyance. The FV310 was to be heavier than the FV301 but have a slightly more powerful version of the Meteorite engine. It was to be protected with 17mm armour. Work on FV301 was stopped due to doubts in the utility of light tanks, but some aspects of the design, for example the torsion bar suspension, were carried over to later vehicle designs and then to the CVR(T) family. Another feature of the FV300 series, which became standard in future vehicles, was the combination of the engine and gearbox into a single unit for quicker fitting and removal. Work on the SP variants continued until 1953 when they stopped with the initiation of the FV3800 project for a series of SP guns based on Centurion power train and running gear. An FV300-series hull was, however, later used as test bed for the TN15 gearbox.

In 1960 the Armoured Vehicle Reconnaissance (AVR) programme was started as a replacement for the Saladin wheeled armoured car with requirements defined in GSR 1106. FVRDE drew up a number of wheeled and tracked concepts, which were presented to the Army General Staff in December 1961. A novel tracked concept was developed, which could mount either a 75mm or 105mm gun in a limited-traverse turret, with Swingfire Anti-Tank missiles in the rear. Another unusual feature of the concept was that the driver was positioned in the turret. Some automotive components were planned to be common with the FV432. The wheeled concepts exploited technologies from the TV1000 demonstrator. In parallel some studies were undertaken as part of a joint Australian, Canadian, UK and US light armoured vehicle project. However, the AVR concept was not taken forward as, at over 13 tons, it was considered too heavy. Work to meet the similar US requirement for an Armoured Reconnaissance Vehicle/Air Assault Vehicle eventually resulted in the M551 Sheridan. It was recognised that the British Army requirements could not be met by a single vehicle of low enough weight, and hence the concept of a family of vehicles was developed, which formed the basis of the Combat Vehicle Reconnaissance (Tracked) (CVR(T)) programme.

Work on the CVR(T) programme started with concept studies, which ran from 1963 to 1965 with requirements being defined in GSR 3301, issued in August 1964. As with AVR it was intended as a replacement for Saladin, but also the Saracen, and the design brief required it to have the same performance on roads as the wheeled vehicles it replaced. It was also required to have significantly greater off road mobility and access to marginal terrain. Some trials were carried out on a Tetrarch light tank with the turret removed to assess the mobility of low-ground-pressure tracked vehicles. Another key design driver was the requirement to be air-transportable and be air-droppable from a HAS 682 aircraft. To meet the demanding low-weight requirement it was decided that the vehicle would need to be built of aluminium armour. Aluminium had already been used on armoured vehicles, most notably the US M113 Armoured Personnel Carrier, but the CVR(T) was the first turreted AFV to be made completely of aluminium.

Some of the technologies and design aspects for the CVR(T) were demonstrated on a test rig called the TV15000. This vehicle was driven out of the workshops on Christmas Eve 1965, the workshops having been provided with the first drawings in June that year and given the challenge to have it finished within six months. This vehicle had an aluminium hull of the configuration adopted for the CVR(T). The engine was different to that adopted for the CVR(T) being a Rolls-Royce Vanden-Plas engine (a variant of the B60 engine). With a separate gearbox and steer unit, the resulting power pack would have been too large for CVR(T). The original engine was not running well during the roll-out and in the photographs of the event one member of the workshops can be seen on the hull operating one of the SU dashpots by hand. Different engines were used during the life of the TV15000, including the Jaguar engine finally selected for the CVR(T), which was fitted in 1966. It also used an early version of hydrogas suspension, but this was not taken forward for the CVR(T) as it was seen as being too high risk compared with the torsion bars already demonstrated on the FV300. Later it was fitted with a lightweight aluminium track and in this configuration it achieved a top speed of 77kph (48mph). Based on the concepts work, approval for the development of the CVR(T) was given in August 1965 and FVRDE proceeded with the build of two test rigs. The first was a static rig, which represented the front of the hull and was used to test the engine installation and cooling performance. The second was the Mobile Test Rig (MTR).

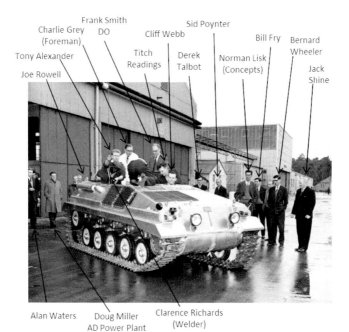

TV15000 Roll Out on Christmas Eve 1965, with some of the staff involved with the design and build. (Crown Copyright)

The TV15000 continued to be used as a research vehicle, for which it was run with and without its turret to assess the performance of vehicles with different power-to-weight ratios and to assess driver performance.

To meet the demanding weight requirements the CVR(T) used 7039 aluminium-zinc-magnesium alloy, which was lighter than the 5083 aluminium-manganese-magnesium alloy used on the M113 APC but much more difficult to weld. In addition to developing the armour specification, Chertsey undertook a significant amount of work to develop techniques for welding, forging, fixing stud inserts and corrosion resistance. Work was also undertaken to determine the optimum slope of the armour to defeat kinetic energy threats. The CVR(T) design also exploited research into aluminium components, such as wheels and suspension arms, to further reduce weight. As well as weight another design challenge was to limit the width to 2.1m (6ft 11in), a requirement specified for mobility in plantations and along narrow tracks. This width limitation was a particular issue for the front of the vehicle and packaging the power pack alongside the driver. The limited width of the engine compartment was one of the drivers for selecting the Jaguar XK six-cylinder engine. This was a militarised version of the car engine, running at 195bhp rather than 265bhp, but able to run on low-octane military grades of petrol. The design of the engine compartment also allowed for the potential to fit a General Motors diesel engine, but this was much heavier than the Jaguar engine.

In 1967 a development contract was placed with Alvis who delivered the first prototype on 23 January 1969. A total of thirty prototypes were built, prototypes 1 to 17 being Scorpions and the rest other variants. The vehicle was accepted for service in 1970 and a production contract placed with Alvis. Production vehicles were first fielded in 1972 with the Blues and Royals. The light weight and the use of tracks enabled the vehicle to operate over a wide range of terrains including soft soils and mud where many other vehicles would sink in – thus giving it the required high level of terrain accessibility.

The assessment of the CVR(T) included extensive cold-weather and mobility trials of a Scorpion in Canada in an exercise called 'Prairie Snow' carried out in 1971.

As discussed, an important feature of the CVR(T) was the family of variants to meet the British Army requirements, all with a common power pack and running gear, covering:

FV101 – Scorpion; Reconnaissance vehicle with the L23A1 76mm gun;
FV102 – Striker; Anti-Tank Guided Weapon launcher firing the Swingfire missile;
FV103 – Spartan; Armoured Personnel Carrier;
FV104 – Samaritan; Ambulance;

FV105 – Sultan; Headquarters;
FV106 – Samson; Recovery;
FV107 – Scimitar; Reconnaissance vehicle with 30mm gun.

A later development of the CVR(T) was the Stormer vehicle, an enlarged CVR(T) that was used to mount the Starstreak anti-aircraft missile system and the Shielder mine dispenser. A 'flatbed' load carrier called Streaker was also built but never went into production. In 1995, 136 Scorpion vehicles were modified by replacing the 76mm gun turret with surplus Fox turrets, which had the same 30mm gun as the Scimitar, this version being called the Sabre.

The CVR(T) saw action in the Falklands where it made a useful contribution to the success of the land battle and there are unconfirmed reports of the 30mm

I SEE IT – I DONT BELIEVE IT!

Cartoon inspired by the Prairie Snow winter trials of Scorpion.

CVR(T) Scorpion at the Armoured Trials and Development Unit.
(Copyright W. Suttie)

RARDEN cannon being used to shoot down an Argentine aircraft. It has been suggested that had its mobility and terrain accessibility been appreciated earlier then it could have made an even bigger impact on that campaign. It has also been used on operations in Kuwait, Bosnia, Iraq and Afghanistan. Testament to the original design is the fact that new CVR(T) vehicles made from an improved hull material were manufactured in 2011 for use in Afghanistan. The so called 'Scimitar 2' mated a Scimitar turret with a Spartan-based hull in a vehicle configured to have significantly enhanced crew survivability in the event of a mine or Improvised Explosive Device (IED) attack.

The establishment was also involved in the development of concepts for tracked armoured personnel carriers to take over the role of the Second World War Universal Carriers and 'Kangaroos', which were turretless tanks to carry infantry. An APC version of the FV300, designated FV310, was planned and APCs based on the Churchill (FV3904) and Conqueror were considered. In 1944 development had started of a new Universal Carrier called the CT20 or 'Oxford carrier'. This was much larger than the previous universal carriers, weighing 6 tons and powered by a Cadillac V8 engine of 110hp. Prototypes were built by the MG Motor Company at Abingdon in late 1944 and undertook user trials until July 1945. These highlighted defects with the Cadillac engine and the suspension. The CT20 was displayed as the future improved carrier at the July 1946 equipment exhibition at Chertsey. At that event it took part in a mobility demonstration alongside a German 8×8 armoured car and a Coventry armoured car.

In view of the shortcomings of the CT20, FVDD designed an improved version, called the CT25, with a Rolls-Royce engine and improved suspension. The improved automotives and running gear were designed to allow the extra weight of overhead protection to be carried. FVDD built a mock-up of the fighting compartment on an Alecto chassis along with a mock-up of the chassis for design approval. Testing went on at Chertsey throughout the late 1940s and trials included towing tests for a mortar baseplate (1947) and 25pdr gun (1949).

FV401
Cambridge
Carrier. (Crown
Copyright-MOD)

Model of the FV420 concept showing one half configured for the cargo role and the other half for the personnel carrier role. (Crown Copyright-MOD)

Around 400 were built and it was issued to BAOR and used in action in Korea[*] where Black Watch used them, with trailers, for ferrying ammunition across the difficult terrain. One vehicle was sent to Australia for trials as a replacement for the LP2A, which was a locally produced version of the Universal Carrier. Rolls-Royce also used some Oxford Carriers as test beds for developing their B Range of military engines. The CT20/25 design was superseded by the FV401, the Cambridge Carrier, a pilot model of which was built by Rolls-Royce in 1950. Compared with the Oxford Carrier this had an improved layout and better overhead protection. Six prototypes of the basic carrier were completed by June 1953 with prototypes 1 and 2 delivered to the infantry school for user trials. Five prototypes of the Observation Post vehicle variant (FV402) were delivered by the end of 1953. The FV401 undertook extended trials including mine-impact trials in 1956, but it did not enter production, despite a potential order of 482 from Australia.

In 1954 a requirement was formulated for an un-armoured tracked vehicle 'for use by the army to meet the tactical requirement for continuous cross-country movement under conditions of nuclear warfare'; this was intended as an alternative to conventional wheeled trucks with their limited mobility. Concept work was undertaken between June 1954 and July 1955 and resulted in a mock-up of what

---

[*] An Oxford Carrier is on display in the 'Victorious Fatherland Liberation Museum' in Pyongyang, North Korea.

was to be the FV420. The concept was based on FV401 running gear, which was strengthened and had an additional wheel station added. The engine was planned to be a Rolls-Royce B80 unit with steering by a Cletrac steering unit all based on the FV401, but the gear ratio in the final drive was reduced to reflect the lower speed and increased weight of the FV420.

The initial concepts covered a cargo/personnel carrier to transport 5 tons of cargo or twenty fully equipped soldiers, a command version, an armoured RE section vehicle and an armoured REME fitters' vehicle. The armoured variants were planned to have 14mm armour plate all round but no roof protection. The estimated unladen weight was to be 8 tons for the un-armoured version and 10¼ tons for the armoured version. A contract was placed with GKN Sankey for the build of four prototypes and ten trials vehicles, which were delivered in 1958. By this time the required family of vehicles was formalised as the FV421 Cargo Carrier with a payload of 5 tons, FV422 Personnel Carrier, FV423 Command Vehicle, FV424 Royal Engineer Vehicle, FV425 REME Vehicle and FV426 Missile Launcher. The FV426 was to be a launcher vehicle for the Orange William missile, an anti-tank missile being developed by the Weapon Division of Fairey Engineering Ltd as an alternative to the Malkara missile. Two prototype FV426s were planned to be delivered in April 1960, but the Orange William project was cancelled in 1959. The prototypes delivered by GKN Sankey included the cargo- and troop-carrying variants. FVRDE issued an interim trials report on the FV421 in January 1960 with a final report in August 1962.

The vehicle was designed to be amphibious and this was demonstrated in trials off Chesil beach in 1960. A prototype FV420 (OO CA 28) was later used by MEXE for trials into river-exiting to support winch development for FV434, exploiting the similarity between the vehicles. During these trials a prototype earth anchor was tested that eventually evolved into the design of the production

FV420. This vehicle is pictured during river exit trials in support of FV434 development, with additional winch and earth anchor equipment fitted. (Crown Copyright-MOD)

item fitted to the Combat Engineer Tractor. One prototype (OO CA 25) was later used for trials into the impact of mine blast on lightweight tracks.

The army then defined the requirement for a fully armoured troop carrier and so the FV420 design evolved into what became the FV432. The first prototype of the FV430 series of vehicles was the FV431 load carrier, which was built in 1960. Many design features of the FV432 were taken forward from the FV420 (on which it was based) and the Cambridge Carrier before that, including the torsion-bar suspension and running gear. The FV420 was used as the test bed for proving FV432 components including the development of the Cletrac transmission. Initially control of the brakes on FV432 was by hydraulics, but this gave rise to problems and so the hydraulics were replaced by a mechanical linkage system. At this time the 'Stockbridge run' described previously was still in use and the first vehicle to be thus fitted set out on this run. When overtaking a car on the A30 in Camberley a cotter pin on the left steering lever came out; fortunately the driver kept his nerve and did a sharp right turn, which took the vehicle across the grass at the entrance to Sandhurst, leaving twin track marks in the immaculate lawn before coming to rest in a hedge. Unfortunately this occurred just as the Sandhurst Commandant was about to drive out of the gates. A phone call from the brigadier in charge of trials at FVRDE was quickly made to give an apology and to assure the Commandant that it would never happen again (in the same place!).

The detailed design of FV432 was undertaken by GKN Sankey, who built four prototypes. These were followed by twenty vehicles for user trials, thirteen built by GKN and the other seven by the Royal Ordnance Factory. Unlike previous tracked armoured personnel carriers FV432 was designed for the Cold War battlefield and had a fully enclosed and armoured crew compartment with a Nuclear Biological and Chemical (NBC) overpressure protection system. Following formal user trials and acceptance GKN Sankey was awarded a production contract in 1962 and around 3,000 vehicles were built between 1963 and 1971.

It had been intended to call the FV432 'Trojan', but this suggestion was dropped after objections to the use of the name by the Trojan car company. The FV432 has continued in service long after the Trojan car company ceased making cars in 1974 and the name was later used for the Trojan engineer tank. The FV432 is still in service more than fifty years after the original design, the latest version, the Bulldog, being built for the Iraq campaign, with significant survivability enhancements including armour fits developed by ex-Chertsey staff in Dstl.

The FV432 was designed to be the basis of a family of vehicles which included:

FV431 – Armoured Load Carrier (Trident);
FV432 – Armoured Personnel Carrier (APC);

Prototype FV342.
The W14 on
the hull front
indicates it was
one of the twenty
pre-production
vehicles built for
user trials. (Crown
Copyright-MOD)

FV433 – Abbot 105mm SP Gun;

FV434 – Armoured Repair Vehicle;

FV435 – Wavell Communications Vehicle;

FV436 – Green Archer Radar;

FV437 – Pathfinder Vehicle;

FV438 – Swingfire Missile Launcher;

FV439 – Signals Vehicle.

All of these variants went into production apart from the FV431 and the FV437, which only reached the prototype stage. The role of the FV431 could be covered by Stalwart, which was due to enter service around the same time, although one prototype FV431 was retained as a trials vehicle. The FV437 was just over a ton lighter than the FV432 and was designed to swim. The design and equipment exploited experience with FV420, which had also been designed to swim. The FV437 was sent to Thailand for Exercise Mudlark, a series of mobility trials in the jungle, where it took part along with Stalwart and some US vehicles. A useful feature of FV437 was its winch, which performed well in the Mudlark trials both for recovering other vehicles and for self-recovery when bogged down. It was reported that without its winch none of the accompanying vehicles would have made it out of the jungle.

Turrets were fitted to some FV432 vehicles, including Fox turrets to those in the Berlin Brigade, but the basic FV432 remained a 'battlefield taxi' rather than a fighting vehicle. The next development of the Armoured Personnel Carrier was as an Infantry Fighting Vehicle (IFV) and some initial work on potential IFV concepts aimed at a replacement for the FV432 around 1977/78 began in early 1967. By the early 1970s more detailed design studies of the Mechanised Infantry

Fifty years on the FV432 is still in service. This version, the 'Bulldog', has additional equipment for use in Iraq. (Copyright W. Suttie)

FV431 prototype fitted with a crew pod for a crew human factors trial. (Crown Copyright-MOD)

FV437 on trials in Thailand. (Crown Copyright-MOD)

Combat Vehicle (MICV), as it was then called, were underway. The initial scoping studies carried out by MVEE considered a number of concepts, MICV Light at 14.6 tons, MICV Medium at 24.2 tons, and a MICV with additional armour at 28.9 tons. The MICV Light was designed to use the same engine as the Combat Engineer Tractor (CET) then under development. A number of variants were considered in the initial scoping study for the MICV Medium including a medium-weight tank with external gun and bridging and SP gun variants with an extra wheel station. It was recommended that the MICV Light could be used for command and ambulance variants that did not warrant the expense of a vehicle based on the MICV Medium; MICV Medium was projected to cost £55,000 and MICV Light £43,000.

Following the MVEE scoping studies proposals were submitted by GKN and Vickers for the Project Definition phase but were considered technically inadequate and hence in-house Project Definition Phase 1 feasibility studies were undertaken. A number of concepts were considered, the most advanced of which was a well-protected vehicle with Chobham armour and hydrogas suspension. The Chobham armour concept was rejected due to its higher weight (30 tons) and cost. In 1976 studies were undertaken into a concept that used a spaceframe construction that could be fitted with alternative armour packs. This was designed to enable the vehicle to be initially fielded with conventional armour but would allow this to be replaced by Chobham armour should the need arise. The concept also addressed the use of spall liners. A static demonstrator was built, but the scheme was never adopted. It is of note that when deployed in Kuwait, Bosnia, Iraq and Afghanistan the Warrior, the production vehicle that resulted from the MICV programme, was fitted with extra armour to increase levels of protection. Thirty-five years later, under the Warrior Sustainment Programme, the vehicle is being fitted with modular armour mounts to enable different appliqué armours to be more easily fitted.

The eventual preferred design option (MICV4A) was down selected and a competitive tender process for full project definition was undertaken. This resulted in GKN being awarded a contract for Prime Contractor in mid 1977; the contract covered Project Definition Phase 2, full development and the first production batch (Batch A). The MICV, or Mechanised Combat Vehicle 80 as it was then called, was a fully MOD funded design undertaken by GKN Sankey with guidance from MVEE Chertsey. The resulting design was owned by the MOD although GKN had exploitation rights. Further production batches were also competed with GKN winning the resulting contracts. A total of 789 were built for the British Army, entering service as the Warrior IFV.

Along with the CVR(T), Warrior was used in action in Bosnia, Kuwait, Iraq and Afghanistan. It has been improved extensively, particularly in terms of survivability with additional armour and mine-protection kits and Electronic Counter Measures

(ECM) fitted for operations. A new turret upgrade is being developed as the major component of the Warrior Capability Sustainment Programme, and the vehicle is due to remain in British Army service beyond 2035.

As with other such platforms a number of variants were developed and the resulting family of vehicles was:

FV510 – Infantry Section Vehicle;
FV511 – Infantry Command Vehicle;
FV512 – Recovery Vehicle;
FV513 – Repair Vehicle;
FV514 – Artillery Observation Post Vehicle;
FV515 – Battery Command Vehicle.

During the early stages of MICV development a comprehensive review of requirements for the future fleet of Armoured Fighting Vehicles was carried out under a project called 'AFVs for the 80s'. As discussed, Stage 2 of this project addressed the requirement for Main Battle Tanks, but Stage 1, which reported in 1969, addressed the requirements for medium-weight armoured vehicles with an emphasis on potential MICV-based variants. In addition the hull of the SP70, under development at that time, was considered for some roles, including as the basis for a bridge layer. Stage 3, which reported in January 1973, addressed a requirement for a self-propelled anti-tank (SPAT) system and an air-portable vehicle called ASPAT. The SPAT was to be a smaller and lower-cost vehicle to supplement tanks calculated to be 20 per cent cheaper than an MBT. The concepts focused on a vehicle of around 43 tons based on MICV components and mounting a 110mm gun. Versions with a three-man crew or two-man crew

Well-used Warriors in Iraq. (Crown Copyright-MOD)

plus autoloader were considered. Two weapon-aiming concepts were considered: semi-fixed, where the gun could elevate but azimuth aiming was achieved by turning the whole vehicle; and limited traverse, which was the same but with fine laying achieved by a limited (±2°) weapon traverse. The semi-fixed was recommended due to the complexities of gun and fire-control solutions for the limited traverse. However, the likely small numbers that the British Army would require, around 300, meant the vehicle was unlikely to be cost-effective and so was not taken further. The ASPAT was based on CVR(T) components and protection levels and was designed to weigh 12.2 tons. Again a range of two- and three-man crew concepts with a fixed or limited-traverse gun were considered, as well as 90mm and 100mm main armaments.

Later GKN Sankey proposed other variants of the Warrior including a reconnaissance vehicle, based on a shortened chassis, and a shorter, lower version of the Warrior called LOVATT as a solution for the Future Light Armoured Vehicle requirement.

As well as concept studies aimed at specific projects through the years, a number of more speculative concept studies were undertaken. One example was for a mine-resistant vehicle, which progressed as far as building rigs with representative sections of tracks and running gear that were used for mine tests. The concept included the use of a V-shaped crew compartment many years before such a layout was widely adopted for mine-resistant vehicle designs.

A more practical concept was an unmanned turret for the Warrior. This work, carried out by DERA in conjunction with industry, resulted in a turret design armed with a 40mm CTAi cannon. In 2000 a proposal was made for the build of a demonstrator turret based on the design, which had many advanced features focused on gun control and crew interface. Despite a willingness on the part of industry to contribute private venture capital to the project the MOD did not take it forward. Eleven years later approval was given for the Warrior Sustainment Programme, which will result in a new conventional manned turret for the

FV513 – Warrior Repair and Recovery Vehicle. (Copyright W. Suttie)

Mine-resistant track test rig – developed in support on the mine-resistant vehicle concept. (Crown Copyright)

Warrior with the same gun but lacking the survivability benefits and advanced features of the proposed demonstrator.

Wheeled AFV Concepts and Development

Throughout the Second World War Chertsey was actively involved with evaluation, technical advice and technology associated with wheeled armoured vehicles. After the war it became fully involved in the design and development of such vehicles starting with the Saladin in 1946. This was designed in response to an army requirement issued in January that year for a replacement for the Daimler MkII and AEC MkIII armoured cars. The original FVRDE concept had a crew of four and a 2pdr gun fitted with a Littlejohn adaptor. A contract for a detailed design was awarded to Alvis in 1947 and a mock-up was completed in 1948. It was then decided that the 2pdr gun was not powerful enough and that the L5A1 76mm, being developed at the Armament Design Establishment at Fort Halstead, should be fitted. This weapon was not ready until 1953, which delayed the build of the first of two prototypes of what was now designated FV601. Meanwhile Alvis was also awarded the contract for design parent of the FV603 Saracen. This was required to replace the half-track vehicles of US origin in service with the army, and its development was planned to follow on from that of the Saladin and use many of the same automotive components. Fielding the Saracen became more urgent than the Saladin when the requirement to support operations in Malaya arose. In order for Alvis to focus on that vehicle, the six pre-production Saladin vehicles were built by Crossley Motors. Saladin production started in 1958 and continued until 1972 by which time 1,177 vehicles had been made. Although the Saladin was replaced in British Army service by CVR(T) variants it

Saladin armoured car.
(Copyright W. Suttie)

continued to be used by other countries and was notably seen defending Kuwait City during the Iraqi invasion in 1990.

Alvis completed the first prototype Saracen in 1952 and it was rushed into service with production starting later the same year. This was slightly later than the original plan, which was to field the Saracen in Malaysia by August 1952, but there were some delays in meeting this date due to problems with the front wheel mountings and obtaining the required machine tools and materials. From 1963 onwards the Saracen was replaced in some roles by FV432, but it remained in British Army service until 1993 with the last vehicles being used in Hong Kong. Other members of the FV600 family were:

FV602 – A command vehicle which was cancelled in 1949;
FV604 – Saracen Command Vehicle;
FV610 – Saracen Command Vehicle with high roof;
FV611 – Saracen Ambulance.

FVRDE had also supported the development of the Ferret armoured car based on an army requirement drawn up in 1947. A mock-up was completed in 1948 and full design was started in 1949 with Daimler as the design parent. The first prototype was completed in 1950. The Mark I was an open-top vehicle and was followed by development of the Mark II, which had a turret. It was originally intended that the Ferret Mark II should have the same turret as the Saracen, but this was soon replaced as it was considered too small. The Ferret entered production in 1952 with the Mark II actually being first off the production line

Saracen. (Copyright
W. Suttie)

in October that year, followed by the first Mark I in December. A total of 4,409 were built and it was used by thirty-one different countries. A benefit of FVRDE being the Design Authority for all British Army vehicles was the ability to standardise components. The Ferret used the same engine as the Humber 1-ton vehicle and some suspension components common with the FV600 series. In 1963 FVRDE responded to a request to improve the automotive and swimming capabilities of the vehicle. Six prototypes of an improved Ferret vehicle were built by modifying standard vehicles; the major changes included fitting larger aluminium wheels, improved brakes and suspension, and a permanent flotation screen. Following user trials at Bovington further modifications were made and it went into production as the Ferret Mark IV or the 'Big Wheeled Ferret'. In 1967 FVRDE started work on the Ferret Mark V (FV712), which mounted a new turret with four BAC Swingfire anti-tank missiles. Although only thirty-two Mark Vs were manufactured, by Alvis, it was noteworthy in being the first example of the use of aluminium armour on a UK vehicle.

The Ferret Mark V was not the first example of FVRDE being involved in work to develop guided-missile launchers as the establishment had supported the introduction of the first guided anti-tank missile to enter British Army service; the Malkara. FVRDE worked closely with the Government Aircraft Factories of Australia who were developing the Malkara missile and also with Fairey Engineering who were developing the Orange William missile as a possible alternative. As well as being involved in the design of firing circuits, sighting systems and guidance wire dispensing systems, FVRDE built two launch trailers, which were designed to represent the configuration of a proposed

A Ferret Mark II on the FVRDE roster. This vehicle is being used in 'crossing trials' for a Centurion Ark. (Crown Copyright-MOD)

Centurion-based launcher vehicle – the FV4010. One trailer was used in trials in Australia in 1956 and the other for trials at Kirkcudbright in 1958. In the end the FV4010 was not taken forward, but FVRDE was involved in the design of the FV1620 Hornet missile launcher, which was based on the Humber 1-ton armoured truck. FVRDE also undertook concept studies into SP rocket launchers including one for 7in foil rockets. Concepts based on the FV433, Chieftain, CVR(T) and provisional MICV schemes were considered.

As stated previously, in 1961 FVRDE developed both wheeled and tracked concepts for the AVR to meet the requirements of GSR 1106. One wheeled concept was for a 6×6 vehicle armed with Swingfire missiles and a 76mm gun, which weighed around 13.6 tons and used skid steer as demonstrated on the TV1000. As with the tracked AVR concept it was not taken forward as it was considered too heavy. GSR 3301, issued in August 1964, called for a wheeled or tracked solution at around 6 tons. Two-wheeled concepts were proposed for what was called AVR(light), which carried over features from AVR; both had six-wheel skid steer and mounted a 76mm gun, but one was 6 tons and the other 8 tons. There remained doubts about the viability of skid steer and the tracked solution was selected as CVR(T). The army still had a requirement for a replacement for the Ferret and in June 1965 GSR 3358 for Combat Vehicle Reconnaissance (Wheeled) (CVR(W)) was issued. CVR(T) was the main development focus at that time and manpower and financial resources for this project were therefore limited. FVRDE carried out studies into concepts that were evolutions of the Saladin and the Ferret Mark IV design, and in September 1965 recommended two alternative Ferret options to the army. These were the Ferret Mark V, which was an all-steel vehicle with a one-man turret, and the Ferret Mark VI which was a more radical evolution with an aluminium hull and two-man turret. The Mark VI concept was accepted to meet the CVR(W) requirement and was developed as the 'Fox' armoured car. It used the same Jaguar XK engine as CVR(T) and had a new two-man turret, the design of which was based on the concept turret for the wheeled AVR Light and which was similar to that being developed for CVR(T). The additional hull stiffness due to the use of the thicker aluminium plates was exploited to remove the stiffening tube in the engine compartment to improve engine access. On 22 October 1965 a contract was placed with Daimler for a more detailed design and in 1966 full development started with David Beavan as the lead engineer, supported by Julian Walker and Norman Scutter. Further contracts were placed with Daimler for full design and prototype build. The first prototype was delivered in 1967 – a year before CVR(T). There was a degree of competition between the wheeled and tracked vehicle departments at FVRDE and so delivering the CVR(W) prototype first was seen as a victory. A further fourteen prototypes were built, with the last being delivered in April 1969. User trials were started in August 1968 and the vehicle was accepted for service in July 1970.

The production contract was not awarded to Daimler but was placed with ROF Leeds. This meant that when Ferret production at Daimler finished the last major link with the commercial automotive market was broken. Daimler had had a long involvement in armoured vehicles and had provided engines for the first Sims armoured car and for the first British tanks.

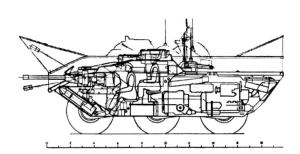

Wheeled Armoured Vehicle Reconnaissance Concept. (Crown Copyright)

Prototype Fox undertaking swimming kit trials. (Crown Copyright-MOD)

Vixen armoured car. (Crown Copyright-MOD)

In addition to the turreted version of the Fox a liaison vehicle with an additional crew space was developed to meet the role covered by the Ferret Mark I. The original concept was for a Fox hull with a higher roof line, but this was rejected, and hence instead of a 'Tall Fox' concept a 'Fat Fox' concept with a wider and lower hull was developed. The design concept was accepted in 1970 and a contract to build prototypes was placed with ROF (Leeds) in 1971. However, it never went into production having been cancelled as part of defence cuts in 1974.

High Level AFV Concept Studies Post 1982

Following the transfer of design authority to industry in 1982 Chertsey stopped undertaking detailed concept and design work. One important area of work that did continue was high-level concept work undertaken to support analysis and requirements definition. In order to assess the operational utility and performance of potential new equipment, high-level concepts were developed from which performance levels could be predicted. This predicted data was then fed into computer-based war games and other operational-analysis tools in order to assess how the equipment would perform in different scenarios. The modelling and analysis enabled different potential solutions and different levels of performance to be compared, for example different calibre cannon on an IFV, and hence requirements to be validated. Such studies supported a wide range of programmes including the Future Light Armoured Vehicle (FLAV) programme, the UK/US TRACER reconnaissance vehicle project and the Future Rapid Effects System (FRES). Once a requirement resulted in a design and development contract with industry, Chertsey staff then had a key role in examining potential concepts from industry and acting as an 'intelligent customer' on behalf of the MOD. This important work continues within Dstl with a number of ex-Chertsey staff still currently involved.

Other Vehicles and Equipment

In addition to concept and design work on tracked and wheeled armoured fighting vehicles, the establishment had varying degrees of responsibility for other types of vehicle, trailers and associated equipment that entered British Army service. The establishment generated technical, test and production specifications, carried out performance and endurance testing and in many cases worked with industry in support of development.

A good example was the FV1800 Austin Champ, which the Nuffield Organisation started to develop in 1947 as the Nuffield Gutty. Three prototypes

Thornycroft 5-ton 6x6 GS truck undergoing combat bridge compatibility trials.

were built to meet the requirements for the 'Car 4×4 5cwt'. Testing of these revealed serious shortcomings and the design was improved by a team at FVRDE under the leadership of Charles Sewell. The resulting redesign had excellent cross-country performance, better than its contemporary Land Rover, but was more complex and more expensive.

A 1971 booklet published by the establishment in conjunction with the Society of Motor Manufacturers and Traders Ltd, called 'British Military Vehicles 1971', lists 'vehicles sponsored by, or developed in co-operation with MVEE'. The list of equipment includes:

26 tracked vehicles and variants;
8 wheeled armoured vehicles and variants;
26 lorries and variants;
8 light wheeled vehicles;
35 trailers;
2 generators;
3 items of plant;
1 coach;
1 motor cycle.

Chertsey maintained a wide range of specifications covering vehicles, fabrication techniques, materials and sub-systems. An MVEE document issued in 1973 lists over 800 then current MVEE specifications. These covered a range of topics including speedometer cables, tyres, tilt testing of vehicles, Bicycle Mark V* (free wheel hub), leather straps general purpose, air-conditioning unit production specs, armour and vehicle production specifications. From the end of the Second World War each type of British Army vehicle was given a unique 'FV' number. Research to date has identified 350 different allocated FV numbers covering vehicles and trailers that in some cases were only proposals or concepts, others that reached prototype stage or went into production. All the vehicles listed would have had some association with Chertsey.

Although there was less focus on wheeled vehicle concepts at Chertsey, two projects are of note. The first was the TV1000, also called Rhinoceros or Rhino. This was designed and built in 1956/57 as a mobility test rig, and possibly to test technologies for the wheeled version of 'Contentious'. Its aim was to provide a wheeled platform with a cross-country performance as close as possible to that of tracked vehicles. It was a 6×6 vehicle with a 535hp Meteorite engine and at the time was the world's most powerful all-wheel-drive vehicle. It was skid steer and fitted with very large tyres, which had a central tyre inflation system allowing the tyre pressure to be reduced to increase the contact patch for running on soft ground. On one occasion it was driven from Chertsey to

Kirkcudbright to the likely amazement of other road users, showing that despite some concerns over skid steer it was a road-worthy vehicle. It was used for research until 1964 and at one stage was fitted with a Pneumatic Track system developed by Count Bonmartini.

The other, much later, wheeled demonstrator of note was the 6×6 High Mobility Demonstrator vehicle, a project led by Alan Arnott. After the high-mobility Stalwart had gone out of service, logistic vehicles in army use tended to be derivatives of commercial trucks with resulting off-road performance limitations. The 6×6 vehicle aimed to demonstrate that a very high-performance logistics vehicle could be built using commercial components. The resulting platform with its good power-to-weight ratio, high-performance driveline and suspension met its goals, but unfortunately was not developed further.

TV1000.
(Courtesy of Paul
Fenne)

6x6 High Mobility
Demonstrator.
(Crown
Copyright-MOD)

Northern Ireland Support, Explosive Ordnance Disposal and 'Wheelbarrow'

One final area where MVEE had a significant role in developing vital capabilities for the British Army was work in support of operations in Northern Ireland. Of particular note was Explosive Ordnance Disposal (EOD) and the development of the remote-controlled EOD vehicle called Wheelbarrow. The origins of Wheelbarrow came from two outline requirements drawn up in 1971: OR111 for the remote deployment of devices to disrupt Improvised Explosive Devices (IEDs), and OR116 for a man-portable shield provided with a remote handling tool. The object of the latter was to provide a device for an EOD operator to neutralise or render safe IEDs from behind protective cover.

Three types of remote-control vehicles were developed to meet the OR111:

- Roller skate, developed by RARDE Fort Halstead, a trolley running on two small bicycle wheels and a rear steering caster;
- DALEK, developed by the Atomic Weapons Research Establishment at Aldermaston and based on a wheelchair;
- Little Willie, developed by the Atomic Energy Research Establishment at Harwell which ran on three wheels.

The devices were all designed to carry a device called Pigstick, which used a water jet principle to disrupt IEDs. All these three devices had a major limitation in that they could operate only on relatively smooth surfaces.

The device to meet OR116 was developed at MVEE and consisted of a protective shield mounted on wheels with a manipulator arm that could be extended by up to 3.5m and be fitted with a range of tools.

By 1972 there was a growing problem of vehicles containing IEDs with substantial amounts of explosives. The first attempt at countering these was to develop a means of moving suspect vehicles to a safe location where they could be dealt with. The requirement was specified in OR122 issued on 17 March 1972. The day before Mr H. Bradfield, Assistant Director Vehicle Engineering (Logistics) (VE(L)) had chaired a meeting to discuss the requirement. As a result two lines of development were taken at MVEE to address the problem.

The first, called Packhorse, was proposed by Lieutenant Colonel (Retd) Miller of the Weapons Trials Branch and was inspired by his own modification of a lawn mower to automate grass cutting. His intention was to base a device on a gutted lawn mower, but following a visit to Robert H. Andrews Ltd, The Garden Machine Centre at Sunningdale, it was suggested that it would be better to base it on a small three-wheeled electric trolley called Packhorse. The resulting device was designed to be remotely driven to the suspect vehicle where it could attach a hook to the underside for towing it away. Responding to the requirement issued on 17 March the basic Packhorse was delivered to MVEE workshops on 20 March for modification. The workshops were then under the command of Mr P. Leaman (Superintendent) and his deputy Mr F. Harrison. There was insufficient time to develop detailed drawings and full instructions and so the workshops proceeded on the basis of sketches and verbal instructions. By 24 March it was ready for its first trial on the MVEE test track. It was not a success, but by 29 March a revised hook had been designed, manufactured and tested. A successful demonstration was carried out the following day for the Royal Army Ordnance Corps (RAOC), who requested that device be immediately dispatched to Northern Ireland. It was subsequently designated 'Wheelbarrow Mark I'.

The other solution was proposed by Mr D. White of VE(L) who suggested the use of a remotely controlled vehicle with air bags on a sledge to lift the car wheels clear of the ground so that it could be towed away irrespective of the constraints of car brakes and steering lock. Air bags were manufactured by Air-Log in Aldershot and delivered to Chertsey. The sledge was tested at Chertsey on 7 April 1972 when the device successfully lifted a car which was then towed away by a Land Rover. It was decided to use two Packhorse chassis to remotely position the sledge under a suspect vehicle and a control system was developed by Mr W. Pattinson, from the Fighting Equipment and Electrical Branch (FEL). The resulting device, called Wheelbarrow II, was tested operationally but found to be cumbersome and not suited to rough roads or use on hills; hence it was not further developed. The control system was, however, used for further developments of Wheelbarrow I.

The first operational use of Wheelbarrow 1 was on 26 June 1972 when it was used to move a Ford Cortina that had been left at a petrol station. With the Wheelbarrow attached the car was towed by a Humber 1-ton APC to the middle of the road where the explosive device was set off safely by firing Carl Gustafs at the vehicle. The Wheelbarrow was destroyed but the unit's commanding officer reported: 'One Motorised Grapnel died heroically saving a possible major fire and a large explosion on 26 June 1972.'

Six more Wheelbarrow Is were manufactured and a Mark II, which had improved controls based on the system developed by Mr Pattison, was built. The army requested improved mobility and so within four days a four-wheel-drive version of Packhorse was built. This was fitted with a hook, jib and controls by MVEE workshops and was ready for trials on 8 August 1972. The device demonstrated the ability to cross rough ground and mount kerbs and, designated Wheelbarrow I Mark III, it was dispatched on 13 August. It was an immediate success with four more being ordered. With the success of Wheelbarrow I Mark III and work stopping on Wheelbarrow II there was a rationalisation of names and the Wheelbarrow I Mark III became the Wheelbarrow Mark III, also called 'Goliath' by the user.

Following two incidents in November 1972 when explosive devices could not be reached by Wheelbarrow a request was made for a step-climbing ability. The need for a tracked version had already been recognised, but the challenge was finding suitable tracks. The solution came from a Mr Fry who worked in the rig bay at the MVEE workshops in an area alongside that where Wheelbarrows were being manufactured. He suggested using Chieftain toothed fan belts. Actual Chieftain fan belts were too short at 60in and so 80in versions were ordered, these were delivered on 23 December 1972. A Wheelbarrow Mark III was modified with the addition of a raised front idler, a rear idler and an additional small wheel between the existing large wheels. These supported a rhomboid track configuration. Tests showed that the motors were not powerful enough for the new configuration and this led to changing the electrical system from 12V to 24V. In addition modifications were made to the equipment jib to maintain stability when climbing and additional strips were stapled to the track to improve traction. Permission was obtained to use the Barrow Hills Officers' mess as a test location in order to assess performance on stairs and carpets. The first two tracked Wheelbarrows, designated Wheelbarrow Mark IV, were shipped to Northern Ireland on 2 February 1973, where the user called it Brownie. An improved version with longer tracks was ordered on 17 March 1973 and this became Wheelbarrow Mark V.

In addition to the ongoing improvements to the mobility of the Wheelbarrow there were rapid improvements to the controls and equipment fits. A range of cameras, disruptors and manipulators were developed which required ongoing development of the jib. The full set of attachments in the Complete Equipment Schedule for the Wheelbarrow Mark V were:

Wheelbarrow Mark VII.
(Crown Copyright)

- Car hook (two piece);
- Deck release to enable a TORPEX CANDLE to be laid under a car;
- Window breaking gun;
- Incendiary release on jib;
- BEGINE emplacement device;
- PIGSTICK clamp and sensor;
- Scissors;
- Nail gun;
- Shot gun mounting;
- Small general purpose grapnel (carpet grabber);
- Towing pylon.

In addition to developing new chassis and equipment fits, the MVEE workshops were kept busy repairing damaged units. For example, one Mark V unit was sent to Northern Ireland on 4 May 1973, and was damaged in Belfast on 7 May while approaching a 40lb bomb. It was returned to Chertsey on 14 May where it was repaired and returned to Northern Ireland on 21 May.

By June 1973 a total of twenty-two Wheelbarrows had been built for use by EOD units and it was agreed that they should all be brought to the Mark V configuration. The allocation of the units was fourteen to Northern Ireland, three for training and five held in reserve and available at twenty-four hours' notice to replace damaged units. With the move to standardise on the Wheelbarrow Mark V, industry was brought in and on 12 May 1973 a contract was placed with Hunting Engineering to generate 'production drawings'.

Shortly after this production and support for the Wheelbarrow was transferred to industry but Chertsey continued to undertake research to improve the capability and ongoing prototype manufacture and demonstration. In September 1983 Chertsey issued RARDE Specification 827 with requirements for the Mark VIII. There was a midlife update programme for the Mark VIII initiated in 1993 and following further improvements to the Mark VIII the Mark IX, built by a UK subsidiary of Northrop Grumman, was introduced in 2010.

The rapid development of the Wheelbarrow from the original three-wheeled Mark I in March 1972 to the very mobile and capable Mark V in March 1973, plus the associated developments in controls and special equipment is testimony to the calibre and dedication of the Chertsey staff and workshops. On 13 July 1973 Lieutenant General Sir Frank King KCB MBE wrote to Mr D. Cardwell, Director of MVEE:

> l would like to thank you and your staff for the contribution to the campaign in Northern Ireland made by Wheelbarrow. Seven equipments have been blown up. This is a small price to pay for the hundreds of thousands of pounds worth

of property saved from terrorist bombs and the reduced risk to my ATOs. Please pass on my sincere thanks to those members of your staff for their excellent and dedicated work. It is much appreciated by us all.

MVEE also provided support to other equipment requirements including specialist lorries for transporting EOD teams and their equipment and modifications to the FV1611 Humber 'Pig'. Around 1,700 of these vehicles had been built in the 1950s as a stopgap armoured personnel carrier and it went out of service in the late 1960s. The characteristics of the vehicle, being a wheeled vehicle shaped like a small lorry, made it very suitable for use during the Troubles in Northern Ireland, providing protected transport for personnel and equipment. Around 500 were rapidly brought back into service and MVEE supported the development of a number of specialist versions and associated automotive upgrades to carry the additional weight. Variants developed included:

- Flying Pig: a standard vehicle with extending riot screens;
- Holy Pig: with rooftop hatch surrounded by Perspex screen – so called after the Popemobile;
- Kremlin Pig: with wire screening for protection against rocket propelled grenades;
- Squirt Pig: fitted with a water cannon beside the driver for riot control;
- Foaming Pig: fitted with a foam generator to mitigate the blast from bombs;
- Felix Pig: modified for EOD duties.

12

SURVIVABILITY RESEARCH AND DEVELOPMENT AT CHERTSEY

Armour and Materials R&D

From the first tank up to and including the design of the Chieftain, armour protection was largely provided by armoured steel. The primary threat was from solid shot Kinetic Energy (KE) rounds, which could best be defeated by a large mass of steel in the path of the round. Although armour configurations with air gaps were developed prior to the Second World War (e.g. on the A13 Mark III) research into different configurations of armour gained impetus with the advent of shaped charge (SC) weapons. These gave the potential to penetrate thick sections of homogeneous armour steel using lightweight man-portable weapons. Defeating the SC threat using weight-efficient solutions became a major driver for armour R&D at Chertsey.

Research into alternative materials to steel had been ongoing since the establishment had been set up, although at the 1947 RAC Conference it was noted that 'nothing so far gives as good protection as steel. At present the scientists see little likelihood of producing a substance that will prove superior to steel.' Despite this, assessment work on different materials continued and eventually resulted in advanced aluminium, composite and ceramic armour solutions.

FVRDE carried out early experiments on high-performance high-hardness steel plates with air gaps. These demonstrated some improvement in performance against KE and High Explosive Squash Head (HESH) rounds compared with solid armour of the same weight. As an example, an up-armouring scheme was considered for the Centurion and a comparison made between a 44mm appliqué plate on the hull glacis and an array with a stand-off plate of equivalent mass. The trials against 120mm HESH rounds demonstrated a significant improvement in survivability using the spaced array, and against 20pdr Armoured Piercing Discarding Sabot (APDS) some improvement was achieved over 75 per cent of the target area, but there was no improvement against 90mm High Explosive

Centurion spaced-armour appliqué test rig. Note the hole from a HEAT-round attack right of centre in the lower appliqué plate. (Crown Copyright-MOD)

Anti-Tank (HEAT) rounds, which generated SC jets. Another scheme consisting of 14mm plates spaced 4.5in off of the hull and turret front was also built and tested against the French SS10 anti-tank missile.

Another example of up-armouring using spaced plates was a scheme demonstrated on a Conqueror tank, potentially as a system for the proposed FV215 heavy self-propelled anti-tank vehicle. This scheme included the addition of armour plates to the hull glacis to increase the armour thickness to 150mm and appliqué turret armour with 14mm spaced plates. The weight of the additional armour was around 1 ton. The up-armoured vehicle was used in trials to assess the performance of US 'DART' 178mm shaped charge warhead and resulting damage on the vehicle. However, because the armour system performed so well in initial trials it was subsequently removed in order to ensure some penetration occurred with resulting damage for assessment.

The benefits of spaced plates against KE threats increased with very large gaps between the plates and this approach was proposed for the Contentious concept. To help minimise the size of the Contentious the resulting gap was used as a fuel tank, exploiting the potential of the fuel to further enhance protection. Despite best efforts there remained problems with the hydraulic shock effect causing structural damage and so this protection approach was never adopted.

In addition to research into the performance of different configurations of armour steel plates, there was supporting research into the welding of armour materials and the configuration of welded joints. Joints can be an area of weakness and the challenge of the research was to develop joints that were robust but did not require expensive machining to manufacture. A 1954 report entitled 'The Strength of Welded Joints in Heavy Armour' records how a number of rigs representing different welded hull front configurations for a heavy tank were manufactured from 82mm plate and tested. One of the weapons used in the tests was an ex-German Second World War 128mm gun firing AP ammunition.

Up-armoured Conqueror concept. (Crown Copyright-MOD)

Weld Configuration test rig following an attack by a 5.25in AP round. (Crown Copyright-MOD)

In trials of steel armour arrays against SC jets the performance largely remained a function of the total mass of material in the path length, with no significant benefits from a layered configuration with air gaps. Therefore in 1963 a new research programme was initiated by Dr G.N. Harvey, the Assistant Director Armour Research, which aimed to provide enhanced levels of protection against SC rounds within acceptable weight limits. A year later the research by Harvey, supported by trials carried out by J.P. Downey, started to bear fruit and resulted in what became universally known as Chobham armour, although in the early days of development it was called Burlington armour. Trials demonstrated that Chobham armour could defeat shaped charge jets with armour packs half the weight of homogeneous armour steel of the same performance. By 1968 the armour technology was well developed and at the point where it was mature enough to be incorporated into concept designs and subsequently into the design and build of the FV4211. The technology was also shared with the USA and Germany who incorporated it into their M1 Abrams and Leopard 2 tanks respectively. The existence of Chobham armour remained secret until an MOD formal press release issued on 17 June 1976. This states about Chobham armour:

'It is no exaggeration to say it represents the single most significant development in the design of tanks since World War II.'

Although it is the development of Chobham armour that Chertsey was most famous for, equally important work was carried out into aluminium armour and supporting research into fabricating with armour-grade aluminium. Research covered welding, forging and extrusion techniques, joint design, corrosion prevention, stress modelling and mounting studs. This work was vital to the CVR(T) and Warrior programmes. As well as research into aluminium armour for light and medium vehicles it was also considered for MBTs with the Test Vehicle Aluminium (TVA) having the world's first aluminium MBT hull. Another demonstration MBT hull was built from steel and aluminium in support of the MBT80 programme. It used the different materials to optimise structural performance and protection while minimising weight, utilising novel 'transition joints' between the two materials.

In another departure from the use of conventional metallic armour, research was undertaken into the use of composites for armoured vehicles. The first practical step was a demonstration Warrior rear door, which provided the same protection as the conventional door but at reduced weight. This was followed by the build of a full demonstrator, the Advanced Composite Armoured Vehicle Platform (ACAVP). Up until then other nations, such as the US, had built large sections of armoured vehicle structures in composites, but ACAVP was the world's first complete composite armoured vehicle hull. It was based on Warrior running gear and mounted a Fox turret. The high-grade composite used was designed to give protection against KE threats at a lower weight than an equivalent aluminium hull and reduce behind-armour damage if over matched. The structure was moulded in two parts comprising the upper and lower hull. Some areas of the structure were comprised of the thickest composite cross sections ever manufactured at that time for any application. ACAVP was dubbed the 'Plastic Tank' and along with the technical leader of the project, Dr Mark French, made an appearance on the television programme *The Big Breakfast*. In a follow-on project a hull for a wheeled internal security vehicle was manufactured and mounted on a non-running chassis. Although a tracked composite vehicle has not been built as a result of ACAVP, the skills and knowledge developed were used in the design of the crew compartment of the Foxhound light mine-resistant vehicle.

The armour team was active in a wide range of other armour technologies including the development of some of the earliest versions of Explosive Reactive Armour, titanium armour, spall liners and high-performance ceramic armours.

One of the final activities by the armour team before the closure of Chertsey was research into electric armour. This is a very high voltage system for disrupting a shape charge jet as it penetrates between two electrodes using a system known as Walker plates. Much of the basic research for this technology was undertaken by

Advanced Composite
Armoured Combat Vehicle.
(Crown Copyright-MOD)

a small team of four based at Fort Halstead and led by Professor John Brown. The armour team undertook the world's first full demonstration of a vehicle fitted with electric armour. The host vehicle with an electric armour side pack was a Warrior and the demonstration was carried out at the army ranges at Lulworth. Following the firing of a representative threat against the vehicle it was driven away none the worse for wear.

Throughout its existence the establishment carried out work to enhance the ability of vehicles to resist mine attack, but work in this area was reinvigorated in response to experience in the Falklands and Bosnia where there were casualties due to mine events. Activities included the development of appliqué armour systems to resist floor deformation or perforation, improved joint configurations to prevent rupture and the assessment of mine-resistant seats. The work addressed both armour vehicles and support vehicles. Chertsey placed emphasis not only on trials to characterise mine effects and solutions but also the development of a theoretical understanding of mine events and design tools. This combination of practical knowledge and understanding supported the rapid development of solutions for a wide range of different platforms deployed on operations. The knowledge and capabilities developed at Chertsey were retained by Dstl and have supported recent procurement programmes and vehicle upgrades for operations in Afghanistan.

In addition to research in support of front-line military vehicles, the establishment also carried out work in support of internal security requirements including the protection of VIP vehicles and police vehicles. This included the development and testing of lightweight armour systems and underfloor protection.

As well as conventional ballistic and mine-protection tests sometimes other types of trials and assessments were carried out. A good example was a test to check that emergency services could gain access to the occupants of a protected vehicle if it was flipped onto its roof. This involved dropping a vehicle roof down from the drop-test gantry.

Electric Armour on a Warrior hull being subjected to a RPG attack. (Crown Copyright-MOD)

Testing under-floor protection at Kirkcudbright. (Photo courtesy of Paul Fenne)

Drop test of a vehicle to check vehicle access after rolling. (Photo courtesy of Paul Fenne)

The Chertsey armoured coach. (Photo courtesy of Paul Fenne)

A 'one-off' prototype designed at Chertsey was an armoured coach. This had an extra non-driven axle added to carry the weight, which at 20 tons, was higher than hoped. It was painted in fictitious operator colours and for a while was used operationally by the Metropolitan Police before ending its days in a quiet corner of Porton Down.

Instructions for another security-related trial came from a very high level when Prime Minister Margaret Thatcher, on seeing CCTV footage of the Poll Tax riots, was concerned about attempts to set on fire the minibuses used by the police. A surplus police vehicle was prepared for the trial to assess its vulnerability and whether the fuel system, which was modified to resist an under-vehicle fire, did in fact work. The fuel tank was filled to the brim with petrol and an attack simulated by setting fire to a tray under the vehicle filled with 20 litres of petrol. After a while the tray fire boiled the petrol in the tank and the vapour escaping through the filler ignited like a massive blow lamp. Gulps of liquid petrol also escaped, adding to the fire underneath. The fire grew for several minutes and the cameras had to be taken further away because of the heat. Eventually the establishment fire service was called to extinguish the blaze. After the trial it was discovered that almost 120 litres of fuel in the tank had burned away in just a few minutes but the tank did not explode. The trial had not gone unnoticed and Heathrow airport controllers, having seen the smoke plume, contacted the Test Track Control concerned that there was a major fire and flights would have to be diverted.

Signature Management

A research programme on signature management, sometimes called Stealth, was initiated by Alan Arnott in 1983. It was part of the Component Technology

Demonstrator Programme run in support of the Future Tank Programme. Some work on signature management for land platforms had already been undertaken in the UK at RARDE and RSRE Malvern, but the scientists there lacked the necessary understanding of the military vehicle environment to generate viable solutions. This was illustrated by a device 'designed' to reduce the thermal signature of a tank gun barrel; it was fitted to a vehicle for firing trials and was observed to 'peel like a banana skin' with the first shot fired. Work had also been carried out in other countries, notably France and the US, but the UK 'Signature Classification and Reduction' (SCAR) programme soon established Chertsey as the world leader in this area. The initial driver for the SCAR programme was a requirement to defeat smart top-attack weapons with radar or thermal seekers, but the research soon expanded to address signature management to counter a wide range of threat surveillance and target acquisition systems. The SCAR project developed signature-prediction computer models, for use as design tools, and signature-reduction technologies. A very important part of the programme was the build of demonstrators to show the user and industry that 'stealthy' land platforms were viable.

After a number of ad-hoc modifications to vehicles the team built the Signature Integration Demonstrator (SID) based on a Chieftain.

Although some demonstrators had already been built in other countries, this was the world's first fully functional stealthy tank, retaining the full fighting capability of a Chieftain. SID successfully reduced the radar, thermal and acoustic signatures of the vehicle, although drivers reported it was harder to drive as they could not hear the engine! As an example of the practical aspects of the design there was an increase in the number and volume of stowage bins along the hull sides and around the turret; this was in recognition of the fact that to maintain a

An early example of Signature Management Experimentation: a Saracen with a 'Stealth Coating' and wheel-hub covers.

low radar signature the user would no longer be able to 'hang' additional kit on the outside. Two SID vehicles were built. They were funded by a weapon system development programme and were intended to be used as representative future targets for testing the sensor and targeting system. They were so successful that in trials the sensor system then under development could not find them, resulting in rework and delays to that programme. When the Chertsey site closed, one of the SID vehicles was dismantled, but following the removal of sensitive technologies the Chertsey signature team persuaded management to donate the other to the tank museum where it remains today as a reminder of the groundbreaking work of the 'SCAR' team. When first built the SID vehicles were classified as secret; on one occasion the Secretary of State for Defence Procurement visited the site and a SID and a standard Chieftain were displayed side by side so the differences could be easily explained to the non-technical minister. The official photographer was somewhat put out when told that his photographs of the minister stood next to an experimental tank could not be published as it was secret.

SID was followed up by a low-signature truck – based on the Bedford 8-tonner, a generator and a HQ vehicle based on the FV439. The generator was used as the basis for the design of the field electric power supply (FEPS) generator, the world's first stealthy generator, currently in service with the British Army.

Trials of classified vehicles by the signature team often presented a challenge. On one occasion when a disused airfield was being used there was alarm when a lost glider pilot decided to land there. One of the more unusual trials was one to assess the impact of mud on the performance of radar absorbing materials. Sample plates of material were fixed at various locations on the hull and turret of a prototype Challenger and the driver tasked with driving around the muddiest parts of Long Valley to ensure the plates were suitably soiled.

SID parked outside the heavy tank hangars at Chertsey. The '1485' refers to the weapon project that it was built to support. (Crown Copyright-MOD)

13

MOBILITY RESEARCH AT CHERTSEY

Chertsey carried out research into all aspects of vehicle mobility and was world leading in many areas, including suspension and developing mobility theory. The work continued until 1987 when the decision was made to stop power-pack and mobility-related research within the MOD research programme; thus ending areas of research and development that had their origins with the very first tanks of the First World War.

Power Packs

As discussed, by the end of the Second World War the poor reliability of British tanks during the early years had been addressed by use of a version of the Rolls-Royce V12 Merlin engine called the Meteor. In the Comet, the last new tank to see action in the Second World War, the engine ran at 600hp. This was increased to 650hp for the Centurion Mark III and, by replacing the carburettors with fuel injectors, it was pushed to 810hp for the Conqueror tank. In addition a 'cut down' V8 version called the Meteorite was developed. This was used in the Thornycroft Antar tank transporter, the TV1000 and prototypes of the FV300 series.

Another important range of engines that came from the same team at the Rolls-Royce Clan Foundry at Belper was the B-Series of engines. W.A. Robotham started work on these after the responsibility for the Meteor had been transferred to Rover and he returned from a secondment to the Ministry of Supply. The design of this series of engines was based on three goals: to provide the maximum power within the minimum volume; to use common components to facilitate efficient servicing and spares; and to operate at high efficiency with low-grade fuels. This family of engines was adopted by Chertsey and used in a number of platforms designed by the establishment. The basic range of engines was:

- B40 4-cylinder 2,838cc engine mainly used on the Austin Champ
- B60 6-cylinder 4,256cc engine used on the Ferret and Humber 1-ton truck
- B80 8-cylinder 5,675cc and B81 6,516cc used on Saladin, Saracen, Stalwart, etc.

Even in the 1950s the establishment recognised the need for engines of up to 1,000hp and so investigated the use of gas turbine engines. A contract was placed with C.N. Parsons and Company for a 1,000hp gas turbine. The resulting engine fell well short of the required 1,000hp, but it was installed in a Conqueror hull in 1954 and in doing so FVRDE built the world's first gas turbine powered tank. A 901hp gas turbine was then built, but this form of power was subsequently rejected by Chertsey due to the high fuel consumption. Some twenty years later the US developed a gas turbine, the AGT-1500, for use in the M1 Abrams tank and attempted to persuade the establishment to adopt it for MBT80. It was rejected because in the view of the experts at Chertsey gas turbines were still too thirsty. This view was confirmed in the First Gulf War where in the heavy going of the desert Challenger 1 tanks had a far superior range and endurance compared to that of the US M1 Abrams tank, which required refuelling every five hours; called the 'five hour suck'. A further issue was that although a basic gas turbine engine is compact a full pack with the required air filtration and ducting is larger than a conventional diesel power pack. It is of note that in 1973 Norman Scutter and Peter Nottley, who at that time worked in the power plant department, visited the US to view progress on the AGT-1500. At that time a prototype was running in a mobile test rig, which had completed 850 miles. In addition to concerns about fuel consumption they questioned the reliability of the engine, issues with the control system and the performance of the air cleaners. At the time of their visit the 1973 fuel crisis was at its height and following discussions with their US counterparts they noted that many experts in the USA also thought a diesel was preferable due its lower fuel consumption.

When design work started on 'Medium Gun Tank No. 2' it was recognised that a new design of engine was required as at that time none existed that would generate the required 700hp and fit within the volume constraints. Initially two contracts were placed to develop a suitable engine, one with the Rover Agency Factory and the other with Leyland. Both contractors started looking at V8 concepts, but after they had both generated initial concept designs Rover made the decision to withdraw from the military-engine market. Meanwhile Leyland concluded that a V12 engine would be required to generate the required power. The solution was then impacted by a requirement from a 1957 NATO agreement that all fighting vehicles had to be capable of running on a range of fuels from light diesel to petrol. In 1952 Chertsey had started to investigate this requirement and had identified one engine configuration that showed

promising multi-fuel performance – an opposed-piston two-stroke. Engines
of this configuration had been developed by the Rootes group in the form of
a 105hp engine, the TS3, for a new range of Commer trucks. The trucks had
a modern 'cab forward' design and required an engine low enough to mount
under the driver; hence the interest in that engine configuration due to its 'flat'
configuration. Development of the engine had been started by a core team of
only seven people under Chief Engineer Eric Coy at the Humber plant at Stoke
Aldermoor. In 1954 Rootes' diesel development production was moved to the
Tilling-Stevens plant in Maidstone. The 'TS' in the engine's name derives from
Tilling-Stevens, a company acquired by Rootes in 1950, and the '3' referred to
the number of cylinders. Once design issues related to the pistons, piston rings
and chain drives had been addressed, the engine was viable and Rootes worked
with Lister on marketing it for vehicle and marine use. As well as being fitted to
Commer and Karrier trucks one engine was fitted to a Polish Star 21 truck. By
1957 Chertsey had been in contact with Rootes, who provided two vehicles
with the TS3 engine. These had a special in-line pump and were fitted with a
sight glass and taps in the cab to demonstrate the effects of fuel change-over.

FVRDE successfully ran this engine in a multi-fuel configuration for several
thousand miles. Based on these results in January 1958 Rootes was contracted
to build two single-cylinder engines, one for Leyland and one for FVRDE, as
proof-of-concept engines upon which Leyland could base their design. Thus
Leyland Motors was given the job of developing the engine, the L60, based on
the TS3 configuration. Although it was a compact pack with the potential to
run on different fuels, it was beset with reliability problems. An ongoing
programme aimed to both increase the power of the engine and improve
reliability, but issues with the piston design were never fully resolved and the
engine always had the reputation of being the one major weakness of the
Chieftain. Ironically the requirement for a multi-fuel capability was never really
needed. L60 development:

Year	Activity
1958	May: L60 Specification agreed, August: development contract placed
1959	First prototype engine ran. Cooling and lubrication issues highlighted
1962	Chieftain user trials in BAOR with Mk2 engine – user raised issues of poor reliability and lack of power
1964	Mk4 engine commenced running, but cylinder scuffing an issue on type testing
1965	Production of the Mk4 engine started
1966	Symposium held to identify potential alternatives to L60; none found

1966/67	Rissole 1 and Rissole 2. Trials of design changes to reduce fuel consumption and increase fan belt life
1967	Scotch Mist programme started, aimed to increase power to 650bhp and achieve 3,000 miles. Resulted in new liner materials and modifications to sump, fan belts and air filters
1968	Fleetfoot programme started, aimed to increase power to 750bhp. Resulted in more efficient fans, improved airflow into engine and changes to pistons and rings. Achieved 720bhp
1969	Mk5a engine introduced with changes from Scotch Mist programme
1970	Mk6a engine introduced with new low-loss air filter and other modifications to oil pipes and tank
1971	Dryfoot trial. Trials in Yuma desert to support overseas sales. Three engines achieved 2,049, 1,708 and 1,617 miles
1971	High Noon programme started, aimed to achieve 4,000 miles at 720bhp
1971	Mk7a engine introduced with changes from Fleetfoot programme
1972	Dark Morn programme started, aimed to ensure that the production version of the Mk7 engine achieved the same reliability as achieved by the Fleetfoot engines
1973	December, Mk8a engine introduced, changes to liner, piston crowns and scavenge blower
1974	New liner introduced. Mk8 engine achieved 2,800 miles in user trial
1975	Bright Morn trials. Trials of reworked engines incorporating Dark Morn improvements
1976	Sundance Trial. Yuma desert trials of two vehicles to confirm performance and reliability
1977	Mk9a engine introduced with further changes to liners, piston crowns and rings
1977	Mk10a engine introduced, Mk9 engine fitted with revised blower for overseas sales
1979	Mk11a/n and 12a/n engines introduced with revisions to 'O' ring fit
1979	Exercise Tunnel Light to monitor the reliability of Mk11a engines at BAOR and BATUS
1980	Mk13 engine introduced

In 1962, in an excursion from conventional engine design, Chertsey started work with Rolls-Royce Motors to develop a Wankel diesel engine, which promised a more compact power source than conventional engines. By 1968 an experimental rotary diesel was successfully running and in 1970 a larger 350hp engine was built, but the concept was never fully developed.

By the 1970s the 4030 Phase 2 order for Iran initiated a study into a new engine for the Chieftain. The engine selected was the Rolls-Royce CV12 TCE 800hp, one of a family of V engines being developed by Rolls-Royce Motors at that time. The CV12 was based on two V6 units joined together and this was a lower power version than that being developed for 4030 Phases 2 and 3. A trial installation was made in a standard Chieftain in order to gain experience of running the engine and test the impact of the increased power on the gearbox and running gear. The original trials plan for the re-engined vehicle required 3,000 miles with a mix of road and cross-country. The 3,000 miles were achieved with no major incidents and the trial was extended to 4,000 miles. The vehicle undertook 2,013 miles road running, 1,987 miles cross-country and 152½ hours idling. The trials report stated that 'performance checks during the trial showed it to be as good as the L60 engine version in all respects and measurably better in most'.

The FV4030/2 and FV4030/3 were required to have significantly more power and within eighteen months Rolls-Royce Motors had developed a 1,200hp version of the CV12. This was linked to the TN37 gearbox, which was also in development. Such rapid development of the power pack meant that there were some initial reliability issues and a common sight at Chertsey at that time was a FV4030 crossing the bridge to the test track first thing in the morning, to be followed about an hour later by a recovery vehicle sent to retrieve it. As basic reliability issues were sorted attention focused on the engine control unit (ECU), which required optimisation. At that time FV4030 was likened to appointing a Pope with either black smoke or white smoke coming from the exhaust outlets either side of the hull. One driver could even manage white smoke from one cylinder bank and black from the other. When there were failures the fact that the FV4030 power packs could be quickly changed was a key benefit of the design. It was rumoured that the sale of Khalids to the Jordanians was sealed when a prototype vehicle broke down during a demonstration at Longcross, so the Jordanian delegation were taken to lunch and by the time they returned the vehicle was running again. The reliability issues were progressively addressed as testing continued. The extensive testing was not without incident and on one occasion a vehicle returning from the test track to the main site went out of control when descending from the connecting bridge and ran into a stores building. Julian Walker, who was running the FV4030 project at that time, was amazed when within a few hours of the accident he was presented with a comprehensive list of items in the store that had been written off. Clearly a stores officer had seen an opportunity to try to write off a number of 'unaccounted for' items. Through the development trials reliability greatly improved and, as discussed, the resulting vehicle performed well, with a high operational availability, during the First Gulf War.

In 1993 Chertsey undertook analysis of a 1,500hp version of the CV12, which was well within the capability of that engine, as an upgrade for the Challenger 2.

The analysis also looked at the use of wider tracks to reduce ground pressure and improve terrain accessibility. Neither proposal was taken forward.

In support of the compact power-pack design for the Evolutionary National Tank, studies were carried out into a 1,000hp version of the CV8 engine used on the Warrior. To help generate the increased power a two-stage turbocharger was planned. The engine was to be mated to the TN55 gearbox but was never built although the design was assumed for a number of vehicle concepts.

Transmissions

The UK had a strong heritage in the development of gearboxes and steering units that can be traced back to the early designs by Major W.G. Wilson for First World War heavy tanks. He continued to develop improved designs of gearboxes and steering units between the wars including work on epicyclic gearboxes. He also developed a double-box system for the A6 which had two interlocked gearboxes working in unison to provide differential speeds at the tracks. He later developed a revolutionary combined unit that linked the gearbox to the steering unit using epicyclic gears. This unit enabled the driver to make three different radii of turn for any gear employed. The unit did not go into production and in the early 1930s all in-service track layers, including light tanks, Medium Mark II and Dragon still had simple clutch and brake steering. The Mechanisation Board was aware of the limitations of this steering system and had started to look at the possibility of using epicyclic chains. In 1936 H.E. Merritt started work on a braked differential gearbox for a light tank and in 1937 was appointed as Assistant Superintendent at DD(M) at Woolwich. There he undertook studies into steering requirements and carried out experiments at MEE to understand the sprocket torques for tracked-vehicle steering units. Based on this work he designed a double-differential gearbox for the A16, which became the first UK tank to be fitted with such a system. DD(M) called it the Merritt-Maybach system – Maybach from the use of a Maybach-type vacuum pre-select shift system. The unit was a 'regenerative' system, which enabled power to be transferred between tracks on steering and hence allowed vehicle speed to be maintained when manoeuvring.

Meanwhile Wilson was developing a geared epicyclic box intended for the A20 tank, but Merritt then developed a concept for a triple-differential steering unit and in November 1939 build of a prototype started. This was installed in the prototype A20 in May 1940. The first version used hydraulics to actuate gear changes, which proved to be problematical, and so a redesign using mechanical gear change was undertaken. At this time Merritt moved to become a technical director of David Brown Tractors Ltd where he helped them develop the capability to manufacture gearboxes to his designs. The resulting

Merritt-Brown gearbox was more compact than other contemporary designs and, most importantly, was easier to manufacture. The first application for this type of the gearbox, the H4, was in the Churchill tank, which was the first in-service tank able to undertake a neutral turn by running the tracks in opposite directions. The gearbox design was further developed as the Z5 series, which was first used in the Centaur, then the Cromwell and Comet and finally evolved into the gearboxes used in the Centurion and Conqueror, although by this time it was outdated. Merritt maintained links with DTD and lectured at the School of Tank Technology set up at Chertsey.

The first significant all-new post-war gearbox developed by Chertsey was the TN10, the configuration for which was developed by G.V. Cleare. It consisted of the Merritt triple-differential steering mechanism linked to a Wilson-type epicyclic gearbox. The detailed design and build of TN10 transmission was undertaken by Self-Changing Gears, a company founded by Major Wilson and John Siddeley to develop Wilson's pre-selector gearbox. The basic TN10 concept was used as the basis for the TN12 gearbox used in the Chieftain and the TN15 used in the Scorpion. The TN15 presented a challenge as CVR(T) was being designed to be lightweight and compact but have a high power-to-weight ratio. Initially a Cletrac gearbox had been considered – this was the type used in the Oxford Carrier and further developed for the FV432. However, there were doubts whether such a unit could cope with the high speeds and manoeuvrability requirements for CVR(T). There was also a requirement that the gearbox had to be designed to work with any of the engine options being considered at the time – the Jaguar 4.2-litre petrol engine, the GM 4-53T diesel engine and the Perkins T6-354 diesel engine. A hydrostatic gearbox was also considered but was not mature enough at that time. Therefore the establishment developed a concept for a combined transmission and steering unit using the Merritt system. The design was passed to Self-Changing Gears and in February 1966 a contract was placed for the production of more detailed designs along with cost and performance estimates. The value of this contract was £1,200. Following further design studies a contract was placed in October 1967 for the build of thirty units. The first unit began testing at Self-Changing Gears early in March 1968 and the second unit supplied to MVEE in July 1968 for testing in the mobile test rig. In December 1968 prototype transmission No. 5 was delivered to Alvis for fitting to the first prototype vehicle. There were some issues that had to be addressed during the development, in particular with the gear selector controller and some of the friction plates. Also some design changes were made to improve performance when swimming, but overall the development was considered a great success.

The Cletrac steering unit fitted to FV432 had the benefit of being a relatively simple device and based on well proven designs. The production vehicles were different to the prototypes in that they did not have separate braking and steering brakes. Braking was reliant on use of the steering brakes alone and thus required both steering brakes to be pulled on together. The reason for the changes between the prototypes and production vehicles is not recorded, but it is suggested that an army major running FV432 troop trials decided that the M113 would be a better match for the needs of the British Army. One of the reasons given was that the M113 did not have the 'unnecessary expense and complication' of separate steering and main brakes; hence, to please the army, the main brakes were removed. A feature of the design was that once the vehicle had stopped, buttons on the end of the steering levers could be engaged to lock the levers in place and act as a handbrake. The fact that the buttons were to be engaged *once the vehicle had stopped* was important as discovered on one occasion by an apprentice who was allowed to drive an FV432 back from the test track to the main site. When descending the bridge over Chobham Lane he applied the brakes and accidentally pressed the locking button on one side; when he released the levers the brake on that side remained on and so the vehicle steered in that direction and over a parked car. The fact that the prototypes had independent main brakes made them more suitable for ongoing mobility research although because they had different tracks and other components to production vehicles maintenance was more demanding.

Work on more advanced hydrostatic drive transmissions started in 1967 with an experimental gearbox called TN16X. This led to the TN17 gearbox used in the Warrior and the TN37 developed for the FV4030 programme. The requirement for a gearbox for FV4030/3 had to be met against very demanding timescales. Although hydrostatic gearboxes had been developed before the Second World War, the TN37 pushed the technology to its limits in terms of power transmitted and internal oil pressures. It is said that the first gearbox delivered by David Brown Ltd to Chertsey seized when run up in the workshops. The next three all

FV432 prototype P4 suspended on a Trifilar Pendulum. This measured the rotational moment of inertia of the vehicle to support research into tracked-vehicle steering. (Crown Copyright-MOD)

destroyed the steering brake pads the first time the driver tried to steer, but within a few weeks the problems had been addressed resulting in what became a reliable gearbox. Further work led to the development of the TN54 gearbox, which was an improved version of the TN37 with a lower reverse gear. It was adopted for the recovery and engineer variants of the Challenger and later for the Challenger 2.

Parallel research had addressed issues of automatic gearboxes and improved efficiency in support of the FMBT programme. This resulted in a successful project run by John McKnight to automate a Chieftain TN12 gearbox with a very early example of electronic control. The controller used was an analogue device designed and built by Maurice Hearne from Hawker Siddeley. Meanwhile it had been recognised that a gearbox for FMBT would need to cope with higher powers than the TN12 and would require multi-plate clutches to cope with the torque and energy dissipation during gear changes. There was concern about losses in such a transmission and this led to a project to automate the very efficient layshaft transmission of the type used in the Centurion. At the time there were five Comet tanks at Chertsey, one of which had been fitted with a Meteor Mark IV engine and a Z51R Centurion gearbox, and hence was an ideal host for a demonstrator. The Chertsey team, headed by Simon Davis as the project leader, was supported by GEC Mechanical Engineering Laboratory at Whetstone who developed the controller solution. Tony Woodruff was initially designated as the GEC lead engineer on the project because he had a tracked-vehicle driving licence having been involved in the maintenance of contractors' plant. He was invited to Chertsey to scope the work and gain more understanding of how high-performance tracked vehicles behaved. He brought a small spring balance with which he intended to assess the gear-lever forces. He did not bother to use this after asking Don Crutchley, who was one of the drivers, how much force was required to make a gearshift. Don, who practised weightlifting in his spare time, had replied: 'I don't know, but it takes both hands.' A demonstration of a Comet manoeuvring had been laid on with Topper Brown, a very experienced driver, driving while Don Crutchley commanded. Topper brought the vehicle out of the hangar in first gear at walking pace, and turned left towards the onlookers. Tony Woodruff watched this manoeuvring with interest, comparing the way this vehicle moved smoothly in contrast to the more jerky manoeuvring of a tracked bulldozer. Topper then turned right, snapped the throttle open, went up through the 'box, and up to top speed in a few vehicle lengths. Each gearshift was accompanied by great bursts of flame from the exhaust fishtails. Tony Woodruff was observed stood with his mouth wide open with shock for some time. Despite the realisation that automating a tank gearbox would be a challenge the GEC team proved to be very competent and it was agreed with them that a microprocessor controller would be used. At the time microprocessors were very new and unproven for such an application, but the decision proved to be the right one and the work resulted in a successful and groundbreaking system. The system was offered to customers who still used the Centurion tank, including Sweden, who came to the UK to see a demonstration on the Longcross test track. Although not taken further, the work did feed into the design of the TN55 gearbox.

Based on experience with automatic gearboxes and the TN37, Chertsey started work on a high-efficiency low-volume transmission called the TN55. Development began in 1987 as part of work on the compact power pack proposed for the Evolutionary National Tank, in which it was to be matched to a 1,000hp CV8 engine. The transmission developed the Merritt triple-differential layout to a quadruple system to improve high-speed steering performance. Efficiency was significantly improved by the elimination of slipping multi-plate clutches to effect gear changes and by utilising a mechanical steering system in place of less efficient hydrostatic steer units. The dry sump layshaft gear configuration was controlled using fast-acting actuators to select ratios by engaging dog clutches providing eight speed ratios, the lowest being a crawler gear with a ratio of 15:1 and the highest being approximately 1:1. A challenge was to ensure that the dogs engaged and disengaged within a short time but would stay engaged during power transfer. In order to determine just how much time could be taken to effect a 'dog swap' gear change a Challenger with a modified transmission was trialled on the Chertsey test track. The oil feed to the steer unit was modified to include a dump valve, operated by a solenoid, which could be opened at the discretion of a trials officer for discrete periods of time. The effect of dumping the oil was to render the vehicle without a steer capability. A series of cones was placed in a curve and the driver, who had no prior knowledge of the objectives of the trial, was asked to steer as close to the cones as possible. During this manoeuvre the steering was interrupted, initially for 0.1 seconds, with no noticeable detriment to the control of the vehicle. The test was repeated with progressively longer steer interruptions until, at about 0.7 seconds, the driver reported that he might have hit a large stone, which had caused a minor deflection in steering but no loss of control. The results of this trial therefore gave a first order indication of the maximum time that could be allocated for a gear change to be completed.

The Chertsey team was supported by a team from GEC who carried out work on the power hydraulics and the actuating mechanism. A team at the Royal Military College of Science, at Shrivenham, consisting of Mike Bennett, Peter Moss and Stuart McGuigan, carried out modelling and design to develop gear engagement dogs. Supporting research looked at electrorheological fluids and magnetic clutches. The work was stopped with the closure of the Automotive Branch and the end of funding for mobility research. The only tangible final output of the project was a wooden model of the power pack, which ably demonstrated how much smaller it would have been compared with contemporary power packs.

Project Research Vehicle 1. Based on a 4030 hull this vehicle was used for trials of a number of research power-packs. (Crown Copyright-MOD)

Another transmission project carried out was a shunted mechanical transmission based on the standard Chieftain TN12 gearbox. The idea of this project was to turn the stepped transmission into a continuously variable transmission by using a variable hydrostatic pump and motor arrangement to 'bridge' the steps between the fixed ratios. In theory this had the advantage that the inefficient variable hydraulic elements only had to handle a proportion of the power, and did not require such a large speed range compared with a full hydrostatic transmission. This project was also stopped before it could come to a successful conclusion, but the principle was shown to be sound as it was later used by the US in the HMPT 500 gearbox used in the multiple-launch rocket system (MLRS).

Suspension

Following extensive use of Christie suspension on Cruiser tanks, Horstmann-type was used on the Centurion, Conqueror and Chieftain, selected because it was easier to maintain and provided better resistance to mine attack. Torsion-bar suspension was developed for the FV300 series of vehicles and used on the Cambridge Carrier and FV420 before entering service on the FV432, CVR(T) and Warrior. A significant advance was made at Chertsey with the development of hydro-pneumatic suspension. Work started in the early 1960s and the first version was designed for a light vehicle in support of the CVR(T) project. An initial set of units were built in-house and fitted to the TV15000 demonstrator. As discussed, the technology was not considered mature enough at that time for use on CVR(T) and so a version sized for a 30-ton vehicle and aimed for use on the MICV was developed. With the decision to adopt a cheaper, lighter and less well-protected concept for the MICV, these were not adopted.

By 1973 R&D for hydrogas suspension, as it was then called, was focused on a version for a 60-ton vehicle in support of the Future Main Battle Tank programme. Extensive rig testing of prototype units had been completed by December 1975 and in May 1976 a Chieftain-based test vehicle (SPR5) was fitted with twelve units. This vehicle undertook extensive trials and by September had completed 3,680km of which 2,048 were cross-country. The trials identified a number of durability and performance issues, which were then addressed. By this time the suspension R&D activities were directed to support the FV4030 project. Suspension aspects for this project went through a number of phases, first the standard Chieftain suspension was modified to have dampers fitted to the rear stations. Next improved bogie suspension with longer travel was developed. An early version of hydrogas was then assessed before improved hydrogas units with higher damping rates were finally selected. Units representing the final build standard were then tested on a prototype FV4030/3 hull, V3A2, which mounted an open observation turret. The resulting system was successful and went into production for the Challenger tank, giving that vehicle a very high level of cross-country performance, well in advance of contemporary vehicles. This excellent suspension solution also provides a very stable platform for firing on the move.

In the early 1970s research into active suspensions started and a research vehicle, called the Suspension Research Vehicle (SRV), was built. This utilised a CVR(T) hull with the standard suspension replaced with hydrogas units. An actuator system based on two-stage Citroën gas springs was used to control hull pitch and heave. Some limited benefits in ride were demonstrated, but there were issues with the controller. Next a semi-active system developed by Lucas was fitted to the SRV, and again ride benefits were demonstrated, but the improvements did not justify the complexity of the system. Then in 1980 MVEE started work with Lotus on an active system leading to the build of a modified Scorpion. This had

Active suspension
research vehicle.

active actuators at each corner wheel station and low-rate torsion bars at the other wheel stations. It also had a digital controller, which aided performance optimisation. A vehicle with an improved passive suspension was also built for use as a baseline for assessing the benefits of the active suspension. Following controller optimisation the vehicle demonstrated significant ride improvements over the baseline vehicle, resulting in a more stable platform that was easier to operate and less tiring for the crew. The final stage of work on the Lotus Scorpion was to fit an active track tensioner; this was done to reduce the risk of throwing a track but it also provided further improvements in ride.

The passive suspension baseline studies resulted in a test vehicle called the 'Sprung Idler Test Vehicle' (SITV). Based on a Striker hull it was run in reverse and so had a rear engine and sprocket. The vehicle had hydrogas suspension on the front wheel station, standard-rate torsion bars on the centre three stations and a stiffened torsion bar on the rear wheel station. The dampers were a Horstmann rotary-vane type. The idler was of a sprung-compensated type with a compensating linkage to the front road wheel. The benefits of the sprung idler system included reduced shock loads, maintenance of track tension and reduced dive during braking. Trials and optimisation of the vehicle continued until 1988 when reduced-rate torsion bars were fitted and an assessment of removing the dampers was carried out. Trials demonstrated that the SITV could traverse a random suspension course 67 per cent faster than a standard CVR(T) for the same level of hull disturbance.

The SRV was to be used as the test bed for the next phase of research, which was the use of a terrain profile sensing system to give a predictive capability for the active suspension. A mechanical system was fitted to support the generation of control solutions, but in 1989 all research in this area was stopped before significant progress could be made.

Sprung Idler test vehicle. (Crown Copyright-MOD)

Wheeled Vehicle Enhanced Mobility

During the 1950s there was a significant programme of research into novel solutions to improve the mobility of wheeled vehicles on marginal terrain. The goal was to achieve terrain accessibility close to that of tracked vehicles. A number of concepts for wheels with retractable spuds were developed and rigs built to test the ideas. A special towed test rig, which imparted wheel slip, was built to measure the tractive effort generated by different wheel configurations. Mechanical and hydraulic methods of retracting the spuds as the wheels turned were developed as it was discovered that retracting them as they left the ground reduced soil disturbance for following vehicles. Supporting work looked at resilient wheels that did not require tyres. Concepts for metal/rubber sandwich wheels and rubber bobbins were built and tested.

Mobility Modelling and Prediction

As well as research into technologies to improve mobility Chertsey was a leading institution in the development of the theoretical understanding of factors that impact on mobility. During the Second World War E. Micklethwaite was attached to the School of Tank Technology at Chobham. There he carried out studies into the interactions between tracks and soft soils and developed the application of Coulomb's equation for the sheer strength of soils to the problem. This made it possible to predict the maximum tractive effort that a tracked vehicle could develop on different soils. Another driver for mobility is sinkage and a means of predicting sinkage for comparing different wheeled and tracked vehicle configurations was required. The standard metric widely used for many years was Nominal Ground Pressure (NGP), the weight of the vehicle divided by the total area of the tyre contact patches or tracks in contact with the ground. Even before the Second World War, DTD at Woolwich had realised that NGP had limitations for tracked vehicles and it was the peaks in pressure, not the average pressure, that drove sinkage. No method of taking these variations into account existed until D. Rowland, then working at Chertsey, derived the concept of Mean Maximum Pressure (MMP), based on the average of peaks under the tracks, and the means of calculating it. MMP is now the standard method of assessing this aspect of tracked vehicle mobility. Work to understand factors that affected mobility and terrain accessibility continued at Chertsey and special mobile rigs were constructed to measure soil properties. These included a Howard compactor that dropped weights to measure soil compaction and an 'Evans Vane' device that measured the torque required to twist a pair of vanes through 90°. A rig built later to study performance aspects of wheels and tracks was the 'Mobile Tester' that could test

Mobility test rig in tyre test configuration. (Crown Copyright-MOD)

Prototype 8x8 vehicle (the Mercedes-Benz EXF demonstrator, a 31-ton vehicle loaned to DERA for the trials) highlighting the challenge of multi-pass mobility. (Crown Copyright-MOD)

the tractive effort and other performance aspects of different tyres and tracks. Chertsey worked closely with colleagues at Christchurch who also needed to understand soil performance and its impact on engineering equipments.

Work on mobility theory and modelling continued and in 1993 a report updating MMP theory for wheeled vehicles was issued. One of the last major pieces of work carried out by the establishment on mobility and terrain accessibility was 'trafficability' tests on soft ground with an emphasis on multi-pass performance. This work, in recognition of the fact that vehicles often operated in convoys, assessed the extent to which the passing of vehicles degraded the ground and inhibited the passage of following vehicles.

Closely linked to mobility studies of wheeled vehicles was ongoing work on the performance of tyres. This was a continuation of that which had started at MWEE in the early 1930s.

Novel Mobility Technologies

Chertsey never avoided innovation, and this was also the case in the field of mobility. A range of different mobility solutions and mobility aids were investigated. Some proved impractical and others worked, but clearly the improvements in mobility did not always justify the increase in complexity or impact on other aspects of vehicle performance.

In the latter category were technologies like the 'Screw Drive' Land Rover. This used elongated screw structures along each side, which could be lowered for crossing very muddy areas. Although the system worked it was a complex system and the bulk, weight and reduced ground clearance could not be justified.

Another area of investigation was the use of hovercraft. The establishment was actively researching this area when a meeting was held at FVRDE on 4 December 1962, chaired by the Director of Royal Engineering Equipment. In attendance were representatives from other research establishments and the Inter-Service Hovercraft Trials unit. Presentations included:

- Air Cushion Vehicles (ACVs) for the army by Major A.J.D. Hughes, which concluded that load carrying was the most likely application;
- Land Rover using variable aircushion by Mr F.J.H. Tutt of FVRDE;
- Trials of the Cardington Bubble by Lieutenant Colonel I.R. Hollyer of the Royal School of Military Engineering. This equipment consisted of a canvas air-supported 'bubble' on the inside of which could be suspended a load;
- The incorporation of ACVs into amphibious bridging equipment by Colonel R.L. France.

FVRDE had started trials of a Land Rover-based hovercraft designed and built by Vickers Special Products at South Marsden in 1962. This vehicle proved to be impractical for traversing conventional terrain with trials videos showing the problems crossing rolling terrain and steering on a side slope, including comparisons with a conventional Land Rover.

Screw Drive Land Rover. (Crown Copyright-MOD)

14

FIGHTING AND SUBSYSTEM RESEARCH AT CHERTSEY

Gun and Fire Control

The Cold War scenario placed a high demand on being able to destroy massed enemy armour quickly and at range. Tank guns were developed at RARDE at Fort Halstead, but Chertsey was responsible for weapon mounting and the systems for accurate control and aiming, called the 'Gun and Fire Control Equipment' (G&FC). This was another area where the establishment carried out world-leading work and achieved a number of 'firsts', including:

- fume extractor;
- muzzle boresight (for Centurion 1953);
- ranging machine gun (Centurion Mk6/2 1954);
- laser rangefinder in MBT (ruby TLS in Chieftain 1974);
- muzzle reference system (Chieftain 1974);
- development of a free sight system (FCR/WSD 1978/79);
- digital fire control system (IFCS in Chieftain, ISD 1979);
- solid state electric gun control (1981);
- panoramic thermal imager with integrated CO_2 laser (PANTILI) (1987);
- Integrated automatic target detection & tracking system (1988).

DTD first looked at gun-stabilisation systems in 1941 when a hydraulic elevation stabiliser of the type fitted to US Lee/Grant tanks was tested on a cruiser tank at Lulworth, but this approach was not taken forward. In 1943 work started on an electromechanical system developed in co-operation with Metropolitan Vickers and tested on a Centaur. This exercise gave confidence in the solution and led to the development of a system for the Centurion, the prototype of which was tested in 1946. The equipment was installed in a development turret mounted on the prototype hull P2 and used in trials at Kirkcudbright. By October 1947 six Centurion Mark IIs were at Lulworth for user trials, following which the system was accepted for use on production vehicles in 1948. The Centurion was thus the first tank to have electromechanical stabilisation for the main weapon in both azimuth and elevation, a system which gave a significant chance of hitting a target when moving. The use of electrical weapon stabilisation contributed to Centurion being a more survivable vehicle than contemporary vehicles with hydraulic stabilisation systems. From the Centurion onwards Chertsey maintained programmes of state-of-the-art R&D into G&FC systems to ensure British Army tanks could exploit the available firepower through the ability to detect and hit targets.

The Centurion was followed by the Conqueror, which, as discussed, introduced the concept of the 'Hunter-Killer' mode where the commander designated targets for automated handover to the gunner to engage them. The Conqueror exploited development work that had been ongoing in support of FV201 and which included systems to automatically align the main gun with the commander's sight, allow the gunner to search arcs independently of the commander and to automatically set the weapon elevation based on target range data.

The Centurion gun and fire control was updated when it was fitted with a ranging machine gun (RMG). This was ballistically matched to the main gun out to normal engagement ranges and a burst of three rounds could be fired to determine target range prior to firing the main armament. A July 1961 report[*] outlines a comparison of the RMG with traditional visual rangefinding and coincidence rangefinders favoured by some other nations at the time. It concluded that while both RMG and Coincidence rangefinding gave a 20–30 per cent improvement in first-round hit probability with APDS ammunition when compared to visual range-finding, the RMG was 20 per cent better than coincidence methods when using High Explosive Squash Head (HESH) ammunition. The Centurion also saw the introduction of the thermal sleeve to reduce barrel bend.

The Chieftain tank was brought into service with a high-performance G&FC system utilising a ranging machine gun. Significant upgrades were carried out through the service life of the vehicle, in particular the Improved Fire Control System (IFCS) which further improved performance when firing on the move and introduced laser rangefinding.

Work on Optical Pulsed Light Rangefinding had started at the Royal Radar Establishment in the early 1950s under the name OPTAR. A report on the basic feasibility was published in 1954 and the technology was considered for

---

[*] ARDE Report (B) 7/61: Direct fire control with the ranging machine gun: an analysis of the errors involved.

the Contentious. Work on laser rangefinding specifically for Armoured Fighting Vehicles started at Chertsey in the early 1960s and by 1963 the world's first mobile laser rangefinder was operational and being used for trials. It was a Q-Switched Ruby Laser, which took up the back of a small van. John Prince, who was a member of the team, recalled in a letter to *Engineering and Technology* magazine a worrying incident on Chobham Common in Autumn 1962. He had set up a laser aimed at a 3m square green panel on the common in an experiment to measure the energy density at a range of 1km. Meanwhile a colleague with a driver had been dispatched to the target location in order to attempt to photograph the laser spot on the target. John and another colleague firing the laser suddenly noticed that the undergrowth around the target had burst into flame and their two colleagues at the other end were frantically trying to put it out. The local fire brigade were called and quickly had the fire under control. Concerns about having to explain how the laser had unexpectedly set the common on fire were dispelled when it was discovered that the fire had started when the driver had thrown down his cigarette when asked to hold a camera.

During the 1970s the Fire Control Rig (FCR) was built and used to support the MBT80 project. The FCR used one of ten FV4211 turret castings that had been manufactured and it was mounted on a Chieftain hull using a spacer ring. The casting was one of two rescued from the scrapheap at ROF Leeds for use by Chertsey, the other being used for an armour test rig. It is believed another casting was provided to GEC Marconi at Leicester who mounted it on a hydraulic rig for testing gun-control equipment for out-of-balance turrets. The MBT80 gun and fire-control system was being designed to provide at least a 33 per cent reduction in engagement time when compared to Chieftain

The Hull Motion Simulator (HMS), a key test rig for the development of advanced gun and fire-control systems. A contract for the development of the HMS was placed in 1973 and it was commissioned in June 1979 and housed in the rotunda. (Crown Copyright-MOD)

Weapon System
Demonstrator. (Crown
Copyright-MOD)

with IFCS.[*] FCR had independently stabilised (free) sights; on the Chieftain and Challenger 1 the sights were mechanically linked to the gun and the FCR was the first such system ever built. The 'Free Sight' system used a solution of 'coincidence firing' where, once the aim point had been determined, the gun was brought on target and only fired when coincident with that aim point. This solution, which meant that only the sight mirrors had to be stabilised to a very high level of accuracy, was later brought into service with the Challenger 2. The FCR also had solid-state gun-control equipment which ran at 56V (±28V) and used a digital data bus to link the main subsystems. When MBT80 was cancelled the FCR was retained and research continued under the Fire Control Technical Programme (FCTP). The turret was then reworked in 1981 and fitted to a FV4030 automotive hull (SPR11), which was modified to take the turret. It was used in this form from 1981 to 1983 to test a number of different sighting solutions. The FCTP ran until March 1986 when the turret was then renovated and in 1987 it was fitted to a Challenger 1 prototype hull for ongoing research under the title of the Weapon System Demonstrator (WSD), the replacement hull having the benefit of being stiffer than that previously used.

Meanwhile to support studies into the integration of a 140mm gun as part of the Future Tank Main Armament project, a rig was designed and built at Chertsey to investigate the problems associated with mounting the main armament significantly out of balance in the elevation axis. An L11 gun was mounted out of balance in a modified Chieftain turret to support research into weapon control, both when static and moving, and to understand the factors that impacted on

---

[*] MVEE Report 79014, June 1979. The Electrical System and Electronic Equipment for MBT80.

errors and how to compensate for them. This work enabled techniques and control algorithms to be developed that could not only stabilise an out-of-balance gun in elevation but provide the same, or even better, first-round hit probability compared with in-service vehicles with balanced weapons.

Meanwhile research using the FCR/WSD continued and a system comprising a panoramic thermal imager, an integrated laser rangefinder and Automatic Target Detection and Tracking (ATDT) was integrated. The sight was called the Panoramic Thermal Imager Laser Integrated, or PANTILI, and was the world's first panoramic thermal sight with de-rotation optics. It was used in its final configuration in trials reported in 1993, which compared the use of fixed and free thermal sights and manual and automatic tracking.

Research into advanced gun and fire-control solutions continued through the periods when the establishment was part of DRA and DERA. Research topics included automatic muzzle reference systems, robust stabilisation algorithms and the use of advanced algorithms to track rounds and hence predict fall of shot when they were still in flight. A final trial of a Challenger 2-based demonstrator achieved what was close to the theoretical highest probability of first-round hit capability for moving platforms against moving targets.

Vision and Sighting Systems

The high-performance gun and fire-control systems needed to be matched by high-performance sighting systems and the specification and test of optical sights was an ongoing activity at Chertsey. In the 1950s work was carried out to develop Infrared (IR) systems using IR searchlights and IR sights. The challenge was to ensure that the searchlights did not emit a significant amount of visible light but did still generate enough IR output for the sights to be effective. By 1953 systems with a range of 750yd had been demonstrated. A significant capability improvement for British tanks came with the introduction of Thermal Imaging sights. The Royal Signals Research Establishment was developing this technology and a major breakthrough was made with the 'TED' detector, named after its inventor, Tom Elliott. The TED detector was incorporated into a family of thermal imagers under a programme called the TICM (Thermal Imager Common Module). Work on integrating thermal sights had started at Chertsey in 1976 and resulted in the TICM based Thermal Observation and Gunnery Sight (TOGS) being fielded in 1982. TOGS was fitted to the Chieftain and Challenger 1 and these were the first tanks to have an integrated thermal sight, introducing a full night-fighting capability.

As camera and display technologies improved Chertsey carried out research into remote vision. The location flexibility of cameras can help avoid blind spots and support external gun concepts. The 'Vidi-Vici' project, which was carried out as part of the Future Tank Operational Demonstrator Programme, was a comprehensive investigation of operational aspects of remote vision. Three CVR(T) vehicles were fitted with mock-up turrets equipped with a range of stabilised and fixed cameras. They were used for a number of trials and demonstration activities investigating display configurations and performance aspects. The findings were published in March 1987 in the 'Commanders Choice' report. Although camera and display technology at that time was assessed to be inadequate, the work set the standard for future activities and the assessment of improving technologies.

The vision work at Chertsey culminated with the WASAD programme (Wide Area Surveillance and Automatic Detection), led by Bob White. This was an advanced panoramic vision system that could operate in the thermal or visual bands and utilised an advanced crew interface and automatic target detection. Innovative image-processing techniques were developed so that the system could display and analyse a full 360° image when the vehicle was on the move.

WASAD was integrated onto the Challenger 2-based Gun and Fire Control demonstrator, which also incorporated aspects of the advanced crew interface and voice recognition for target allocation. This vehicle had a threat acquisition and engagement capability that has not yet been bettered to date in any in-service MBT system.

Electronic Architectures

Chertsey also carried out world-leading research into electrical systems and the integration and exploitation of electronics. MBT80 was being designed as the first tank to fully exploit microprocessor technologies for its subsystems and aimed to use standardised electronic systems. It was also being designed to have advanced power and data distribution systems.

Research into the approach proposed for MBT80 continued under an activity called SAVE (Systematic Approach to Vehicle Electronics). This programme defined electronic system components and requirements and generated a number of standards and specifications. An important aspect of SAVE was the use of electronic systems that were nuclear hardened. SAVE was supported by a racking system called the 'Modular Assembled Vehicle Installation System' (MAVIS). This was defined in the 'Electronic Equipment Packaging Code of Practice for Military Vehicles' generated for MVEE by Thorn EMI.

As the scope and potential of electronic and data systems developed and crew/system interactions became an area of concern, a project called the Vehicle Electronics Research Defence Initiative (VERDI) was initiated. An important

VERDI 2 demonstrator. (Crown Copyright-MOD)

goal of VERDI was to assess how improved integration and automation of vehicle systems could improve crew performance and enable a reduction in crew numbers. VERDI was a joint programme with industry and culminated in the build and test of the VERDI 2 demonstrator. This vehicle had:

- A two-man crew;
- Multi-function crew stations where either crewman could do any task;
- Full remote vision;
- An advanced electronic data bus;
- An unmanned surveillance robot that could be operated from the vehicle;
- External unmanned weapon systems;
- Multiple sensors;
- Automatic target alerts.

A series of trials were carried out using VERDI 2 covering crew workload, performance and driving with remote vision. There was also a major back-to-back trial comparing the performance of VERDI against CVR(T) over a twenty-four-hour period with the respective two- and three-man crews carrying a representative battlefield mission. The outputs from VERDI informed the next phase of research in this area and helped inform programmes such as the UK/US TRACER reconnaissance vehicle.

VERDI highlighted the benefits of an integrated approach to electronics on land platforms and the use of open interfaces. Chertsey therefore started the Vehicle Systems Integration (VSI) programme, led by Colin Newell, which

A VERDI 2 Crew Station.
(Crown Copyright-MOD)

developed standards and guidelines. An important aspect of the programme was the close involvement of industry to ensure that any standards adopted were affordable and viable, and hence would be acceptable for use by industry. An early in-service example of the exploitation of the VSI approach was the Terrier Engineer Vehicle. The VSI standards and guidelines have now been incorporated into the Generic Vehicle Architecture Defence Standard which is mandated for all new UK military vehicles.

Crew Stations

Closely related to the Electronic Architectures research and supporting VERDI was the Crew Stations research programme. The challenges of operating complex armoured vehicles were well known and the situation was often made worse by ongoing vehicle upgrades and additional subsystems. As well as improving vehicle capability, better crew stations were seen as key to crew reduction, crew endurance and better workload sharing. The research also addressed the need for crews to cope with the increase in information made available through Battle Management Systems and the 'Network Enabled Capability' (NEC). The extensive research activity addressed displays, human machine interface (HMI) devices and overall crew concepts. An important thrust of the work was the early use of synthetic environments to enable the crew to assess HMI devices and crew-station concepts in a realistic laboratory environment before trials on vehicles. The work on synthetic environments with associated vehicle response models, terrain models and visualisation solutions also gave rise to research in support of the development of simulation-based training systems.

Research into displays and HMI resulted in standards and guidelines for controls, icons and display layouts, sizes and colour. These guided the development of the Battle Management Systems implemented on UK vehicles as part of the Bowman programme. This work was also fed into the Generic Vehicle Architecture Defence Standards and continues to inform vehicle HMI design, including for recent vehicles such as the Foxhound.

The crew-station concepts work focused on the use of multi-function displays, crew stations and related aspects of crew workload and task sharing. Following the design and assessment of the VERDI crew station an enhanced concept called the Advanced Land Platform System Crew Station (ALPS) was developed. This had three multi-function displays and a fourth display on a yoke with controls. The yoke was designed to swing up when the crew member was operating head out, ensuring he could still access controls and information. A mock-up of the crew station was built and linked to a synthetic environment for laboratory trials and later elements were implemented in a mobile rig and then the Challenger tank was used to host the WASAD demonstrator.

ALPS Crew Station Rig.
(Crown Copyright-MOD)

Robotics

Around 1980, MVEE initiated a comprehensive research programme on robotic systems. Work on remote-control vehicles had already been undertaken by MVEE, most notably with the Wheelbarrow. In addition MVEE had developed radio-controlled vehicle solutions including a special version of the Wheelbarrow for mine clearance in the Falklands and radio-controlled versions of the Eager Beaver forklift truck and a County tractor. The potential uses and attributes for robotic vehicles were reviewed in a study carried out by Director Science Land, which reported in July 1981 with a paper called 'A Review of the Factors Affecting the Design and Exploitation of Military Robots, with Recommendations for Future Activity'. Based on this study and initial research at MVEE a proposal was submitted to the Basic Research Advisory Committee (BRAC) for resources to be allocated to a programme of work; this resulted in the Mobile Autonomous Intelligent Device (MAID) research programme. It started with basic research to investigate the technologies available to support autonomous intelligent vehicles and explored the idea that the advances in microcomputers, software and sensors, along with the emerging concepts of artificial intelligence and robotics, might make viable relatively cheap autonomous platforms suitable for military tasks. Progress on the MAID programme was presented at a major Unmanned Land Vehicle conference at MVEE on 23 November 1984. The MAID research had focused on mobility, sensors, navigation and operator awareness and by the conference significant progress had been made in the first two areas.

A number of concepts were considered for the provision of good mobility before selecting the 'Bellyless Vehicle' for the demonstration phase. This had two very wide tracks that were almost touching along the centre line of the vehicle. This configuration provided a very low centre of gravity and avoided ground-clearance issues.

Short- and medium-range sensors were developed. The short-range device developed at MVEE used a laser and Charge Coupled Device (CCD) array to generate a range map out to 5m ahead of the vehicle. The medium-range sensor consisted of a pulsed laser rangefinder and a coaxial scanner, which enabled the ranges to objects out to 50m to be measured. The scanner for this was developed for MVEE by colleagues at the RSRE Malvern.

The technologies developed were brought together on an experimental demonstrator called the Unmanned Research Vehicle (URV). It weighed 700kg without payload and was 2m long.

Work also started on what was called the Integrated Driving Control Experiment (IDCE). The aim of IDCE was to develop a common set of controls and sensors that could be used to operate a range of different remote-control platforms.

MARDI demonstrator. (Crown Copyright-MOD)

Having developed and demonstrated a number of underpinning technologies for robotic vehicles, the next phase of research was started in September 1988; called the Mobile Advanced Robotics Defence Initiative (MARDI). It was undertaken as a collaborative partnership between industry and the MOD with the objective 'to enhance the UK capability in the technology of unmanned vehicles and provide timely demonstration of concepts suitable for military applications'. The partnership involved twelve UK defence contractors and two universities. As part of the project a prototype CVR(T) Streaker was converted for remote operation. It weighed 6 tons, and carried a surveillance system with two daylight cameras, a thermal imager and a laser rangefinder. It mounted a turret with a Hughes 7.62mm chain gun, a LAW80 spotting rifle and a SlMFlRE laser umpire's gun. The vehicle also carried a gas turbine smoke generator to demonstrate the ability to lay a smoke screen to protect manned platforms. Remote operation was carried out by a crew of two (plus a safety operator) from a military shelter carried on a 4-ton truck. In 1992 the vehicle was successfully operated at ranges of up to 6km and at speeds of up to 50kph over cross–country terrain. However, it famously went out of control at a VIP demonstration when, having lost communications, the emergency stop failed and the vehicle only came to rest when it encountered a large ditch.

HARP Robotic
Surveillance Vehicle.
(Crown Copyright-MOD)

DRIFT demonstrator.
(Crown Copyright-MOD)

A small remote-control vehicle called HARP was also built. This was a small sensor-carrying vehicle that was demonstrated as part of the VERDI programme. Carried in the back of the Warrior-based VERDI vehicle, it could be remotely driven to observation points and so provide enhanced surveillance capabilities. The electric-drive vehicle was powered by a small diesel engine as a backup to the batteries and demonstrated enhanced endurance over battery-only-powered robotic vehicles.

Another application identified for remotely controlled vehicles was for route-proving. A demonstrator called DRIFT (Driving Remotely In Following Truck) was built based on two DROPS (Demountable Rack Offload and Pickup

System) trucks. The lead DROPS truck was remotely driven by an operator in the following vehicle. The vehicles were attached via a constant tension cable to transfer the necessary control signals and video (from a camera mounted on the front vehicle). The angle of the cable relative to the two trucks helped provide the steering inputs to the following vehicle. The lead vehicle was fitted with a scatterable mine-clearance device to indicate the route-proving capability. The quality of the MVEE drivers was demonstrated by the fact that the driver testing the system developed the technique of sitting sideways when in the following vehicle in order to decouple himself from the motion inputs of that vehicle and hence concentrate on steering the lead vehicle.

Under MARDI research was also carried out into tele-operation over RF links and this work formed the basis for the remote-control system fitted to the Terrier engineer vehicle. One element of the research was the use of very low frame rate video, to reduce bandwidth, with updates every five to ten seconds. The technique devised was called RUDA (Reduced Update Driving Aid) and it utilised a graphical overlay that represented how far, and in what direction, the vehicle had moved since the last frame of video had been captured, transmitted and displayed.

Work was also carried out on fully autonomous vehicles and resulting technologies were demonstrated on ROVA (Road Vehicle Autonomous), which could drive fully autonomously in simple environments. The base vehicle was a 3.5-ton Dodge van equipped with an automatic gearbox and modified for computer control by the addition of servo actuators for the steering, accelerator and brakes. Television cameras for vehicle guidance could be positioned to view the scene through front and side windows and an advanced image-processing system was developed based on image-flow techniques. The image-processing techniques and skills developed were further exploited under a project called SECURE. This was a joint programme with Jaguar to generate a smart automatic cruise control system. A radar system was used to detect objects in front of the car, but the image-processing system was able to track the relative motion of other vehicles and detect lane changes, and hence could cue the system to avoid unnecessary braking.

Combat Identification

A new area of research started after the Gulf War, that to develop a 'Combat Identification' solution to prevent the vehicle-on-vehicle 'friendly fire' incidents of the kind that had occurred during that conflict. The actual number of incidents in that conflict was not high, but due to the very small number of casualties caused by enemy action they represented a relatively high proportion of UK casualties. Key to the work was developing a solution that would be adopted by other NATO nations – especially the US. The work was started by Peter Penney and Julian Starkey at Chertsey with support from staff at Malvern. They worked with France, Germany and the USA in a four Nation Technical Working Group to identify a suitable technology. In 1997 William Suttie took over as international chairman of the Technical Working Group then tasked with developing a NATO standard for an interoperable device. He was supported by Steve Press as the UK 'Waveform Subgroup' representative. They worked with THALES Missile Electronics in Basingstoke and colleagues in the MOD procurement organisation at Bristol to develop the UK version of what was then called the Battlefield Target Identification Device (BTID). The culmination of this work happened in September 2005 with a successful international interoperability exercise hosted by the UK on Salisbury Plain. Somewhat tongue in cheek, the trial, called Exercise Urgent Quest, was described as the biggest concentration of foreign armour and forces on UK soil since the build-up to D-Day. Although nothing like the size of D-Day, the scope was not dissimilar to the pioneering armoured formation exercises on Salisbury Plain in 1927. One difference was that the 2005 trial used the laser-based Direct Fire Weapon Effects Simulator (DFWES) to simulate engagements and so, unlike the 1927 exercises, was not constrained by a reliance on umpires. In total the 'coalition force' taking part comprised seventy vehicles and over 400 troops. Vehicle types included UK Challenger, CVR(T) and Warrior vehicles, US M1 Abrams and Bradley, Swedish CV90, French VAB and VBL and the Italian Dardo IFV. Additional troops from Australia and Canada took part along with helicopters and fixed-wing aircraft from the UK, US and Norway to address air-to-ground issues. The UK provided the 'opposition force' made up of members of the Black Watch.

Urgent Quest line-up showing US Bradley, Swedish CV90 and UK Challenger and CVR(T) vehicles. (Copyright W. Suttie)

15

SPECIAL DEVICES

Special Devices was a section within the Vehicle Engineering department that had its origins in the development of the 'Funnies' – the specialist armoured vehicles developed for use by the 79th Armoured Division. After the end of the Second World War the 79th Armoured Division was disbanded and the responsibility for specialist vehicles taken on by the Specialist Armour Establishment (SAE) of the Royal Armoured Corps.

The 'Duplex Drive' swimming Shermans had been used on D-Day and there was interest in swimming versions of the Centurion with two different requirements covering the crossing of inland waterways and launch at sea for a beach landing. Therefore in the 1950s Chertsey started a programme of work to address these requirements, but the Centurion, being much bigger and heavier than the Sherman, presented a significant challenge. A key member of the team carrying out the work was Johnnie Whatmaugh who had invented the 'camera bellows' screen used on the DD Shermans. A number of concepts were considered including inflatable and rigid versions of the screen concept, a fully sealed version that could be towed, pannier floats and a flexible mat ferry.

Inflatable ring concept for a swimming Centurion being tested in the wading pit. In the background is a Centurion ARV ready to extract the vehicle if required. (Crown Copyright-MOD)

Following an assessment of the alternatives, variations of the flotation screen were trialled for what had been designated FV4008. The development was not without difficulties and one FVRDE incident report records how a variant of FV4008, using a non-rigid flotation screen, sank during water speed trials on Gaerloch on 24 May 1957. The report records that the vehicle started to fill up with water and reached the point at which 'as the driver was now up to his shoulders in water the commander ordered him to apply the brakes, put the vehicle in gear and leave his seat'. Despite such setbacks a solution was developed but was never put into production.

As well as his work on the swimming Centurion Johnnie Whatmaugh also helped develop the systems for the Saladin and Ferret.

The Chieftain, being an even heavier vehicle, required a different approach to crossing water obstacles. The solution developed was a deep wading system that sealed the vehicle and had a large snorkel tube through which the engine

FV4008 Swimming Centurion using a screen over rigid panels. (Crown Copyright-MOD)

The Chieftain Deep Wading solution installed on a prototype vehicle. (Crown Copyright-MOD)

breathing and cooling air was drawn. Unlike similar Soviet snorkel systems Chertsey developed a remote driving solution, which enabled the driver to operate the vehicle from the relative safety of the top of the tube – a solution locally referred to as 'The monkey up the stick'. Although successful the system was never put into production. The installation included cages fitted to the exhaust outlets with plastic balls that, due to their buoyancy, were forced up to block the outlet pipes and prevent water entering. The ideal-sized balls were found in a toy shop but they were manufactured in China. In view of the origin of these strategic defence items a stockpile was procured and for many years a large container of coloured balls sat in the corner of the Special Devices hangar.

Despite the fact that a water-crossing solution was not taken forward for heavier vehicles, there remained an ongoing interest in swimming armoured vehicles and work was undertaken to understand the hydrodynamic requirements and track design for water propulsion in support of systems for lighter vehicles. The research included testing of scale models in a test tank at the National Physical Laboratory.

The FV432, Fox and CVR(T) were all designed with floatation screens that enabled them to swim. Systems were tested extensively. As an example the FV432 system started with trials in the wading pit on the Longcross test track, including tethered running trials to ensure engine and transmission cooling was sufficient. These were followed by trials at Horsea Lake, which included an assessment of different types of track, sea trials at Instow Bay and river crossing trials at Waser. The final trial was a prolonged seagoing trial, which involved the vehicle crossing from Stokes Bay near Portsmouth to a beach on the Isle of Wight near to Osborne House and back. The distance covered each way was around 9 miles and waves of up to 3ft high were encountered.

A challenge when designing screens was to ensure that they could survive the dynamic effects when entering and leaving the water at the required entry angles, which were specified as 14° minimum and 24° desirable. Washboards were developed for FV432 and CVR(T) to supplement the basic screens.

Other work addressed the requirement for higher water speeds and improved manoeuvrability. The CVR(T) flotation screen had proved to be particularly robust and reliable and so that vehicle was the ideal candidate for improved swimming capabilities. A set of propulsion units were developed for fitting to the front sprockets, which comprised a 90° bevel drive to a propeller facing backwards. These worked very well but were not popular operationally as they were unwieldy to fit. To aid rapid removal if used operationally a remote disconnect for the units was developed, although never fully optimised.

Despite having a wide range of prototype and production swimming solutions, by the 1980s most army armoured vehicles had had their screens removed.

The establishment also undertook studies into providing an amphibious capability for other vehicles. In the late 1960s FVRDE tested an amphibious

Photograph showing that at the time of this trial further development of the FV432 wading screen was required. (Crown Copyright-MOD)

Propeller device fitted to CVR(T). (Photo Courtesy of Paul Fenne)

lightweight Land Rover (20BT91). This was modified to support large flotation units fitted to the sides, front and rear and was propelled in the water by a Dowty hydrojet. Trials were carried out on Horsea Lake near Portsmouth where performance in the water was said to be good. The vehicle was then sent to the Amphibious Trials Unit at Instow before being sold in 1971.

Another novel idea for an amphibious Land Rover was the use of very large balloon tyres. The 1975 MVEE Journal includes a lament to the 'Waterbug', which describes the project opening with:

> The soldiers come the soldiers go
> To swim their Land Rover we must show
> How to do it and with what
> They have no interest, they care not

The poem goes on to describe how blocks of foam and air bags were considered until balloon tyres were suggested:

> From Cardington the tyres came
> That Bedford skill and Zeppelin fame

By all accounts the vehicle did successfully swim, but the demonstrator was abandoned after it was found the system put too much stress on the steering and the track rod broke. Thus:

> Trussed up now this sorry boat
> Defying laws to stay afloat
> A fitting epitaph to hot air fame
> Alright for words but not this game

Work was also undertaken on waterproofing a wide range of vehicle types for wading, including wheeled vehicles of various sizes. Much of this work was

HMS *Waterbug*. (Crown Copyright-MOD)

undertaken in conjunction with the REME Fording Trials Branch at Instow in Devon.

A system consisting of angled rockets along each side of a vehicle to provide lift for crossing small gaps had been tested in the Second World War. In 1948 the army requested that the work continued and be extended to evaluate the same approach for self-extraction of bogged vehicles. FVRDE successfully demonstrated the system for self-extraction on a Universal Carrier and a DD

Testing a deep wading kit for a Land Rover. Paul Fenne, a member of Special Devices, is driving in the first picture and a passenger in the second, which indicates that the vehicle was able to undertake several passes through the wading pit. (Photo courtesy of Paul Fenne)

Dipole measuring equipment for Flail Tank Station Keeping on a Churchill. (Crown Copyright-MOD)

Sherman. Studies into rockets for the more demanding task of gap crossing continued with mixed results. In one infamous trial with the rockets fitted down each side of an FV432 they only fired on one side, resulting in the vehicle flipping over.

Work on mine ploughs continued after the Second World War and in the 1950s research was carried out into vibrating rollers to improve performance. One requirement that FVRDE looked at was the need for two flail tanks to operate together to generate a lane wide enough for vehicles to follow. This required the second vehicle to follow the first accurately with just a 12in overlap between the cleared paths. A 1954 report described the developed solution, which consisted of a long dipole electromagnetic generator on the lead tank and directional measuring equipment on the following vehicle. The signals from the measuring equipment were used to provide guidance to the driver of the following vehicle to control relative distance and offset. As the British Army became more focused on defensive warfare in north-west Europe, work on mine clearance became lower priority. However, in the 1980s work was revitalised with studies into track-width and full-width mine ploughs. This resulted in equipment developed by Pearsons, which was successfully used operationally in the Gulf War and other operations. Another special-to-role equipment that was the responsibility of Special Devices was the dozer blade kit developed for the Chieftain.

The section also had responsibility for heavy recovery tanks such as the Centurion and Chieftain Armoured Recovery Vehicles and base vehicle aspects of bridge layers – for which it worked closely with colleagues at Christchurch. It was also responsible for the Centurion Beach Armoured Recovery Vehicle (BARV).

Another specialist technical area addressed by Special Devices was Nuclear, Biological and Chemical (NBC) protection, where it was responsible for the

Chieftain with a track width mine plough at Chertsey. (Crown Copyright-MOD)

Chieftain Armoured
Repair and Recovery
Vehicle. (Crown
Copyright-MOD)

Centurion
BARV. (Crown
Copyright-MOD)

provision of 'Collective Protection' systems for vehicles. As discussed, work on such systems had been carried out as long ago as 1931 at Porton Down with the one fitted to the Vickers Medium III. Chertsey took over responsibility for this area in 1944.

Collective protection requires an NBC pack that provides filtered clean air at a rate that ensures the crew compartment is pressurised slightly to prevent contaminated air entering the vehicle. Such systems were first applied as production fits to the FV432 and Chieftain.

A notable member of the NBC team in Special Devices was Birmingham-born Alan Glassbrook, who had a very direct attitude to getting things done. He told a story that during the war he was working in an aircraft parts factory when problems arose with stamping Spitfire undercarriage cowls and getting

Early days of
NBC Collective
Protection:
pressure/
smoke test of an
Abbot SP Gun
to determine
the air leakage
paths. (Crown
Copyright-MOD)

Spartan in the
Light Vehicle
Hangar at
Chertsey
with an NBC
filtration pack
open. (Crown
Copyright-MOD)

the stamped products quickly out of the press. He claimed that to address the problem, one Saturday when nobody was around, he winched the press up and hung it upside down from the roof girders so the cowls fell out under gravity.

A challenge with NBC protection was that army personal frequently complained that due to leakage they could not get the vehicles to pressurise even with the NBC pack fans running full speed. Al Glassbrook's approach was simple, he would get out his cheque book and offer £100 for anybody who could find him a Chieftain he could not pressurise. Nobody took him up on his offer, which was as well for he could always find the problems and sort them. As with many other areas Chertsey was seen as world leaders in this area with collective protection and UK-designed filtration pack technologies being adopted by the US for their vehicles many years after use on British vehicles. In addition to filtration packs the team worked with Porton Down on detectors and carried out early work on 'Ion Combination Effect' detection devices and use of thermal imagers and lasers for chemical agent detection.

One other area that Special Devices covered was fire-fighting systems covering the engine bay fire detection and suppression systems. The section also carried out early research on explosion suppression systems.

APPENDIX A

GENEALOGY OF CHERTSEY

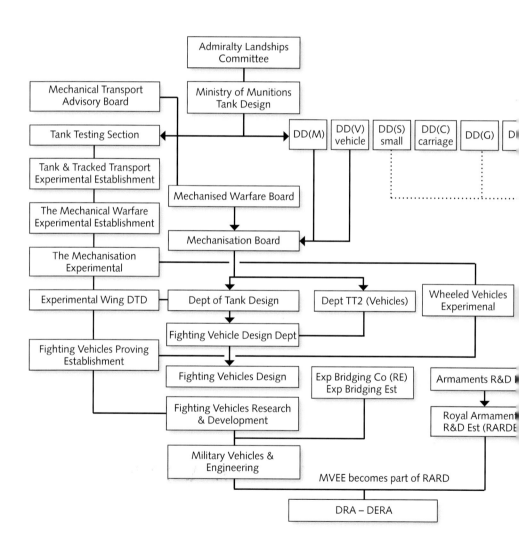

APPENDIX B

LINEAGE OF DIRECTOR MVEE

Director of Tank Design, Ministry of Supply
    1940–45   A.A.M. Durrent CBE
    1945–46   A.E. Masters CB CBE

Director Fighting Vehicle Design Department, Ministry of Supply
    1946–48   A.E. Masters CB CBE

Chief Engineer, Fighting Vehicle Design Establishment, Ministry of Supply
    1948–52   A.E. Masters CB CBE

Chief Engineer, Fighting Vehicles Research and Design Establishment, Ministry of Supply
    1952–56   A.E. Masters CB CBE

Director, Fighting Vehicles Research and Design Establishment, Ministry of Supply
    1956–60   A.E. Masters CB CBE

Director, Fighting Vehicles Research and Design Establishment, War Office
    1960–64   C. Dunbar

Director, Fighting Vehicles Research and Design Establishment, Ministry of Defence
    1964–67   C. Dunbar CB
    1967–72   D. Cardwell

Director, Military Vehicles and Engineering Establishment, Ministry of Defence
    1972–76   D. Cardwell CB
    1976–78   I.H. Johnston
    1978–85   J. Ellis CB

APPENDIX C

LONGCROSS TEST TRACK FACILITIES

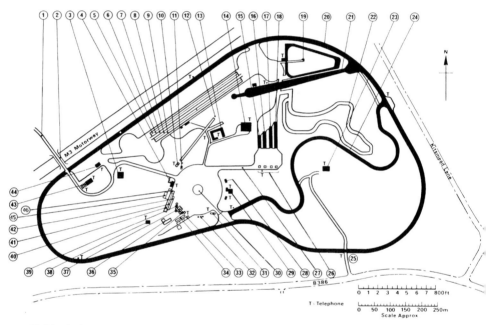

Test track plan.

The above plan of the test track is taken from a 1992 Test Track Facility Brochure. The main test track facilities at the Longcross site are described below and the numbers refer to those given on the plan.

MAIN TRACK (HIGH SPEED TRACK) [20]:
- 2-mile asphalt circuit over 10m wide
- Banked on main bends
- Nominal speed limit 70mph
- During normal running operated on a one-way basis

SNAKE COURSE [24]:
- Designed as severe-handling course for larger vehicles
- 1,038m diversion off the main track with asphalt surface
- Gradients of up to 15.9 per cent
- Series of tight bends including adverse cambers

SLIP PAD [30]:
- Large circular pad approximately 155m in diameter and marked with circles at 3m apart out to 30m and then at 45m, 60m and 70m radius
- The pad was slightly domed, being 300mm higher in the centre than the edges
- Used for brake tests (surface could be wetted), turning circle tests, stability and vision tests (measuring the field of view through episcopes and sights)

ROUGH ROAD DEMONSTRATION COURSE [22]:
- 1,021m gravel track
- Designed for use by smaller vehicles, but not used for extensive testing as longer routes over similar terrain were available at the Bagshot test track
- Included inclines up to 15.9 per cent
- Used for testing suspensions and damage to tyres and vehicles due to flying flints

STRAIGHT AND LEVEL [21]:
- 305m-long tarmac course level to within plus/minus 3.2mm
- Used for braking, rolling resistance and steering drift tests

SUSPENSION COURSES:
A number of parallel tracks with suspension courses 450m long and with a parallel camera track [7], consisting of:
- Pave: Random granite blocks of uniform size of 150mm x 225mm with random potholes [9]
- Boulder course: A sand-covered course with random blocks approximately 600mm across and random iron 'mushroom' inserts [8]
- Sets: Tracks with uniform and randomly spaced concrete sleepers 100mm wide and either 25mm or 50mm proud of the running surface [5&6]

OFFSET TOWING COURSE [19]:
- Track with bump strips, random blocks, kerb ends and cobbles set in concrete base
- Used for accelerated testing of towed equipment while towing vehicle drove on a smooth surface

Chieftain on the Boulder Course. (Copyright W. Suttie)

Suspension courses showing, from front to rear, a pave, boulder, tarmac/camera track and set courses. The vehicle is a Leyland FV1119 Recovery Vehicle. (Copyright W. Suttie)

TEST SLOPES:
Used for speed tests in different gears, stop-start tests and engine lubrication tests. Available slopes:
- 1 in 10 (10 per cent) [27]
- 1 in 4 (25 per cent) [18]
- 1 in 3 (33.3 per cent) [17]
- 1 in 2 (50 per cent) [16]
- 1 in 1.73 (57.8 per cent) [15]

Test slopes.

RAIN TEST FACILITY [34]:

- 30m long and 6m wide for testing of static or moving vehicles
- Rain fall from 10mm per hour to 6.7m per hour possible

Antar Tank transported on the tilt platform. (Crown Copyright-MOD)

TILT PLATFORM [31]:
- Used for measuring the side tilt at which equipment would roll over
- Tilted at 6°/minute to a maximum of 50°
- Safe working load 90 tons
- Suitable for vehicles with a wheelbase of up to 14.47m and a track of up to 3.86m

Articulation gauges. (Copyright W. Suttie)

ARTICULATION GAUGES [32] [35] [37]:
Used for measuring the relative movement that could be achieved between wheels without losing contact with the ground, covering:
- Simple gauge: relative movement between wheels on different axles with axles level
- Complex gauge: wheels on adjacent axles raised or lowered in opposite directions on each side
- Single wheel: one wheel raised while all others remain at the same level
- Belly clearance

Belly clearance gauge. (Crown Copyright-MOD)

LOADING GAUGES [40] [41] [42]:
- Representing loading ramps into a Land Craft Tank (LCT), Landing Craft Ship (LCS) and aircraft
- Also used to check functionality of vehicles on a forward or reverse slope, e.g. checking turret rotation and engine oil starvation

STEP OBSTACLES [63]:
- Used to measure achievable vertical step heights
- With addition of sleepers could accommodate steps of 279mm, 406mm, 533mm, 660mm, 787mm or 914mm (11in to 3ft)

WADING POOL [33]:
- Used for swimming or deep wading trials
- Entry ramps 25 per cent (1 in 4) and 45 per cent (1 in 2.2) configured to represent landing craft ramps
- Base 47.2m long
- Maximum depth of water 4.7m (15ft)

Wading Pool: Conqueror ARV about to cross a Centurion Ark. (Crown Copyright-MOD)

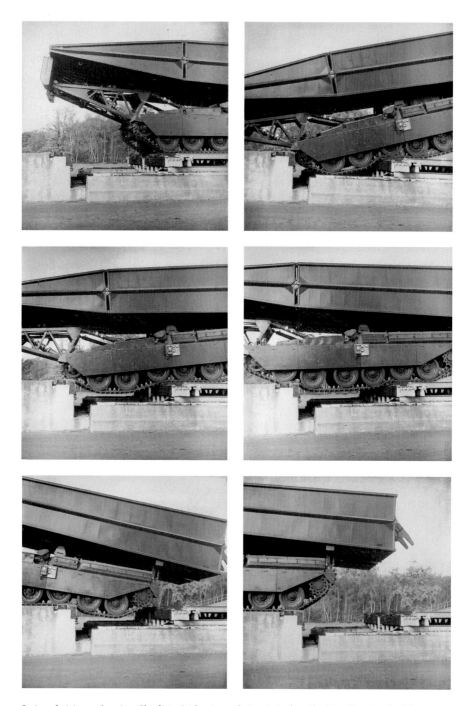

Series of pictures showing Chieftain Bridge Layer being tested on the Gap Crossing Facility. (Crown Copyright-MOD)

DYNAMOMETER [38]:
- 2 dynamometers capable of absorbing 800hp

WINCH TEST FACILITY [10]:
- Facility for testing vehicle winches
- 134m cable run area
- Winch house capable of a direct pull of up to 35 tons on the winch under test

DROP TEST GANTRY [46]:
- Capable of freefall tests of equipment of up to 10 tons
- Working height 8m

GAP CROSSING [36]:
- Adjustable rig for measuring maximum gap that a vehicle can negotiate

BIBLIOGRAPHY

The following documents were used in compiling this history of the tank factory:

Open Source

RAC Tank Museum Publications:
An Illustrated Record of the Development of the British Armoured Fighting Vehicles
1915–1918; 1919–1939; 1940–1946 and 1946–1970
British Tanks 1939–1945 The Second World War

Armour in Profile Series; Profile Publications Ltd:
No. 1: Tank Mark IV
No. 4: T3 Christie
No. 5: Cromwell Mark 4
No. 16: Carden Loyd Mk VI
No. 23: Centurion 5

Branch Lines Around Ascot, Vic Mitchell and Keith Smith (Middleton Press)
Cold War Hot Science: Applied Research in British Defence Laboratories 1945–1990,
    Robert Bud and Philip Gummett (eds) (Harwood Academic Publishers, 1990)
The Guinness Book of Tanks Facts and Feats, K. Macksey (Guinness Superlatives
    Ltd, 1972)
British Tanks and Fighting Vehicles 1914–1945, B.T. White (Ian Allen, 1971)
Scorpion Reconnaissance Tank AFV Profile 34, R.M. Ogorkiewicz

Rolls-Royce Enthusiasts Club website
Parliamentary Statement: Future Tank Policy, 14 July 1980
Military Modelling March 1971: Article on the Medium D series
Tanks: 1914–1918, Lt Col Sir Albert Stern KBE CMG

MOD Reports, Publications and Papers

In addition to information from over fifty MOD technical reports published by FVRDE, MVEE, DRA, DERA, RARDE and other establishments, information from the following documents has been used:

The Steering of Tracklayers, H.E.Merritt. A paper read before the School of Tank Technology, 16 March 1944

Tracks for Fighting Vehicles, School of Tank Technology notes dated July 1944

NATO Armaments Group: Lessons Learnt During the Anglo-German FMBT Project 1971–1977. Dated 21 September 1981

Journal of Defence Science Vol. 1 No. 3: The Prospects for Unmanned Ground Vehicle on the Battlefield.

Journal of Defence Science Vol. 5-4 October 2000. Various mobility articles.

MVEE Journal articles

The Tank Factory: Seventy Years of Government Tank Design, Col H.W.B. Mackintosh

British Military Vehicles 1971 (Jointly Published by MVEE and The Society of Motor Manufacturers and Traders Ltd)

INDEX